PRIME CUTS

PRIME CUTS

THE COMPLETE GUIDE TO CHOOSING, UNDERSTANDING, AND COOKING MEAT

JESS PRYLES

murdoch books
Sydney | London

CONTENTS

CUTS & RECIPES

CUTS & RECIPES

CUTS & RECIPES

INTRODUCTION

This is the book I wish had existed when I wanted to learn more about choosing and cooking meat – an ultimate meat guide for newbies and meat-enthusiasts alike.

I didn't grow up knowing how to buy or cook meat. Like many people, I'd choose something from the grocery store without really understanding the cut, quality or best way to cook it. That changed when I discovered real Texas BBQ. It sparked a fascination with how fire, smoke and time could transform tough cuts into something tender and deeply flavorful. Driven to learn everything I could, I moved from Australia to Texas, immersing myself in the heart of live-fire cooking.

What started as curiosity turned into a full-scale pursuit. I read, traveled, cooked and asked endless questions from pitmasters, butchers and professors alike. Eventually, I earned a Graduate Certificate in Meat Science from Iowa State University so I could understand both raw and cooked meat at the cellular level and apply that knowledge in both indoor and outdoor kitchens. I've spent years refining techniques that work just as well for a backyard brisket as they do for a perfectly seared steak.

Since then, I've judged world-class BBQ competitions, hosted TV shows and developed products trusted by both home cooks and professionals. But I've never forgotten what it felt like to be unsure at the meat counter or second-guess myself as a cook. This book is my way of sharing clear, practical guidance that bridges science and practical applications – so you can buy with confidence, master the cook and truly enjoy the process of making exceptional meat at home.

PONCHO

HOW TO USE THIS BOOK

Most people want to cook better meat but aren't sure where to start – this is the book that finally makes everything click. It shows you the cuts, the prep and the methods that matter, explained in a way that's approachable enough for beginners yet detailed enough for the meat-obsessed.

It also helps you approach the meat counter with confidence so you can cook just about any cut you might find at your butcher or grocery store. It's written for both newcomers and seasoned meat lovers, with a focus on skills you can use right away.

Every recipe in these pages has been chosen and developed to earn its place – no padding, no throwaway condiment recipes. Whether you cook your way through it cover to cover, or treat it as a go-to reference, you'll find clear, reliable guidance.

The book isn't structured like a butcher's chart, referencing every possible cut in order. Instead, some cuts appear where they make the most sense. For example, you'll find *teres major* in the rare steaks rather than the chuck section. The aim isn't to catalog meat exhaustively, so I've focused on the most common and widely available cuts you're most likely to find, buy and cook.

My goal is simple: answer your meat questions, share insights you might not have considered and leave you confident, empowered and excited to buy, cook and enjoy meat. It's the distilled knowledge of over 15 years of cooking, learning and studying meat science – designed to give you just about everything you've ever wanted to know about meat.

• PRO TIP •

One of the best ways you can get the most value out of this book is to buy whatever's on sale. You can rest assured you'll find a recipe for it here, along with advice for storing it until you're ready to cook it.

BEFORE YOU GET COOKING

SALT

There is no such thing as a standard teaspoon of salt. It's a fundamental ingredient when it comes to meat, so this is a really important note to consider before you tackle any of my recipes. I cook with Morton kosher salt. If you are not using the same salt as me, your version may turn out saltier or underseasoned.

The reason is density. Different salts have different crystal shapes and sizes – flaky, chunky, coarse or fine – and that changes how much sodium fits into a teaspoon. A teaspoon of flaky salt contains less sodium than a teaspoon of dense rock salt. It is, quite literally, less salty. The most accurate way to measure salt is by weight, not by volume. That's why, if you can't get hold of the same brand I use, it's essential you know the weight equivalent for your preferred salt.

SALT CONVERSION CHART

Approximate weight of 1 teaspoon

Morton kosher:	5 g
Diamond Crystal kosher:	2.8 g
Table salt:	5 g
Maldon flakes:	2.3 g
Pickling salt:	6 g

The one area where you have to follow the salt exactly is where it's used for curing or brining purposes (like the bacon calculator on page 67).

LAWS AND REGULATIONS

There are a few regulatory standards and laws referenced in the book. At the time of writing, they were current and correct, but please bear in mind that some policies and regulations may have been updated and changed.

GRILL VS. BBQ

In many parts of the world (especially in Australia, where I grew up), all outdoor cooking is loosely referred to as barbecuing. But it's time to get more specific. In this book, any high-heat cooking over charcoal or propane is referred to as 'grilling' (or 'using a grill'), while smoking slowly at low temperatures is called 'BBQ' (or 'barbecue,' or even 'barbeque' if that's how you roll). And while I have the opportunity to stand on my soapbox, I'd like to point out that a 'pellet grill' is an extremely misleading name, and that it should have been called a 'pellet smoker.' End of rant.

SPELLING AND TERMINOLOGY

Yes, I was born and raised in Australia, and still have a predominantly Australian accent (actually, it's more of a hybrid), but I've lived in the US for 11 years. Since this book is available all over the world, we had to pick a standard of spelling, and my day-to-day language won out. So, you'll see 'cilantro (coriander)' and 'flavor' instead of 'flavour,' but I'm confident you'll still be able to understand me just fine.

TEX-MEX FLAVORS

You'll also notice that a lot of my recipes favor Tex-Mex, Southwest and Mexican ingredients. See above for the part about living in Texas for the last few years ...

NEUTRAL OIL

Several recipes call for a 'neutral oil.' That just means an oil without a strong flavor. Extra virgin olive oil, for example, has a unique and robust flavor. I know a lot of folks are trying to move away from using seed oils (I personally use them in my cooking), but I thought it would be more helpful to let you choose the oil that's right for you.

MSG

Some recipes in this book contain monosodium glutamate (MSG). All I'm gonna say is this: decades of scientific research have failed to prove that ingestion of MSG causes any issues like headaches and numbness. Additionally, major international health agencies like the World Health Organization consider MSG safe when consumed in normal amounts. The reality is this: MSG is delicious. It makes food taste better. If you don't wanna use it, it's optional. But if you like eating as much as I do, you'll leave it in.

BUTTER

Every recipe in this book uses salted butter. Honestly, I don't bother keeping unsalted butter in the house. Even when baking sweet treats, a little salt always balances things out.

GRILL TEMPERATURES

You'll see me refer to different grill temperatures throughout the book. Here's the cheat sheet:

Low: 250°F (120°C)

Low-medium: 300°F (150°C)

Medium: 350F–400°F (175–200°C)

Medium-high: 400–450°F (200–235°C)

High: 500–600°F (260–315°C)

Blazing: Anything over 600°F (315°C)

I don't actually use the last temperature in this book, but at least you have a reference – that's hot!

WILD GAME

You may notice an absence of wild game in the recipe and reference sections (well, except for a venison backstrap – I couldn't resist). This book focuses on meats that are part of the standard commercial meat supply. Wild game and less common meats like rabbit are not easily accessible to most home cooks, so they didn't feel like the right fit here. (My first cookbook, however, does include an entire section devoted to game.)

CHOOSE IT

Most people think cooking meat starts in the kitchen, but the journey begins long before the pan hits the heat. It starts with the choices you make at the store or butcher counter. The cut you pick, the quality you reach for, even the small details on the label – they all shape the final result. And while meat can be one of the most intimidating ingredients to shop for, it doesn't have to be. If you've ever stood at the meat case wondering what the hell you're looking at, this is where it all starts to make sense.

BUTCHERY BASICS

Understanding how a carcass breaks down helps explain why the exact cut you're looking for isn't always available at the store or butcher shop.

Butchery might look like pure craft, but it's shaped by meat science. As we've learned more about muscle structure and tenderness, that knowledge has changed the way we cut. Meat science can tell us which muscles are more tender (and therefore more valuable), and butchery helps us cut them accordingly.

A carcass follows a basic roadmap: first broken into large sections called primals, then subprimals, and finally the familiar cuts like steaks and roasts. You'll see many of those primals referenced throughout the recipe section. It's important to note that different countries cut meat differently, especially when it comes to the final steaks and roasts. Global trade has pushed some standardization, but you'll still see distinct regional styles. For example, a French butcher doesn't break down a carcass the way an Australian butcher would.

Butchery is a series of choices - and every cut affects what is left. Think of it like slicing a cake: once you've cut it into wedges, you can't turn those same pieces into neat little squares. The same muscle can't be two different cuts at once.

Here are some examples of cuts where you have to choose - cut it one way, and you can't have the other:

- If you cut **boneless filet mignon**, then you can't have **T-bone steaks.**
- If you cut **flanken beef ribs**, then you can't have **whole BBQ ribs.**
- If you cut **top blade steaks**, then you can't have **flat iron steaks.**
- If you cut **bone-in pork chops**, then you can't have **baby back ribs.**

WHOLE CARCASS VS. BOX BEEF

Traditionally, butchers got whole hanging sides or carcasses, broke them down in-house, and sold the resulting cuts. Each carcass only yielded so much: two tenderloins, two briskets, two tri tips, etc. Once a specific cut was sold, there wasn't more to replace it - customers chose from what was left.

Things shifted in the 1960s with the evolution of boxed beef. Instead of sending out whole sides, packing plants started breaking beef into primals. By the '80s and '90s, butchers and supermarkets could order boxes filled with a single cut without needing to purchase the rest of the carcass.

This really opened meat up to global trade. Different regions prize different cuts, so processors could export 'low-value' cuts in one market to 'high-value' markets elsewhere. For example, chicken feet often go to China, pork jowl to Italy and beef liver to Egypt. To this day, many retailers only bring in a handful of cuts they know will sell, which is why some meat counters feel so limited.

Single-cut ordering remains a double-edged sword. It streamlined supply and made popular cuts easier to access, but it also narrowed selection in many stores and reduced the demand for skilled butchers. In recent years, social media and global events like the World Butchers' Challenge and Butcher Wars have helped reignite respect for traditional craft butchery.

This brief history of meat processing explains why you can't always find the cut you want. Stores that order by cut usually offer a limited but consistent range, while whole-carcass butchers may have a broader variety but not always the volume. No matter where you shop, if you can't find what you're looking for, it's always worth asking the butcher or meat cutter.

QUALITY AND GRADING

Many factors determine meat quality. When we talk about 'meat quality,' we're referring specifically to **palatability and eating performance**, not nutrition or preferences about how animals are raised. So while terms like 'pasture-raised' or 'traceability' may influence your buying decisions, they don't directly impact flavor, texture or tenderness.

For a consumer, the most visible and accessible indicator of meat quality is grade. In the US, grading is a voluntary program that requires hiring an independent USDA inspector to assess each carcass and assign a quality grade. You've probably heard of the big three: Select, Choice and Prime (there are others, but those are the main ones). These grades help consumers navigate their options, and they help the industry scale their pricing appropriately.

Many other countries have grading systems, including Australia, New Zealand, Canada, Japan, South Korea, Mexico, Argentina and the European Union. In places like Japan and Australia, it's common to use meat imaging cameras (like the MIJ system) to automate grading and reduce human error. But while the systems may share some goals, there's no global standard - each country uses different measures, terminology and scoring methods. And to make things more confusing, some brands create their own unofficial labels, like 'gold' or 'black' grade beef.

You'll mostly see quality grades applied to beef because it's the most variable meat in terms of marbling, tenderness and flavor. Grading helps set expectations and determine value. Pork and chicken are far more uniform, which is why they're not graded the same way (and why I'm mainly focusing on beef here).

When it comes to eating quality, traits like tenderness, color and ossification (bone development) are measured. But the most important one, and the easiest for you to identify on your own, is marbling.

MARBLING

Marbling refers to the thin streaks of intramuscular fat - those white lines you see within the muscle itself that look like tiny lightning bolts. It's influenced by genetics, age and feed, and it's the last fat to develop in the animal. Marbling matters for two big reasons: it adds flavor, and because fat is softer than muscle, it helps reduce bite resistance, improving tenderness.

As a general rule, no matter where in the world you are, the more marbling you see, the better the eating experience.

MEAT LABEL DECODING

The labels on meat packages are filled with buzzwords – some legit, most just clever marketing. Here's a handy guide to help you cut through the noise:

AIR CHILLED

Most chicken in the US and Australia is processed by being dunked in chilled water to rapidly cool the carcass – a critical step for food safety and shelf life. Antimicrobials like chlorine are often added to the water, which can affect the meat's texture and flavor. In contrast, air-chilled chicken is cooled by rapidly moving very cold air without water immersion.

RAISED WITHOUT ANTIBIOTICS (ALSO WRITTEN AS 'NO ANTIBIOTICS')

To carry this claim, animals cannot be given antibiotics at any point in their lives. However, there is a broader ethical issue to consider: this also prevents animals from receiving antibiotics even if they genuinely need them. Federal regulations already require that all meat be free from antibiotic residues by the time it reaches the shelf. If an animal is treated, its body metabolizes and excretes the drug, and a mandatory withdrawal period must pass before it can be processed for food.

HUMANELY RAISED/ CERTIFIED HUMANE

This claim (along with others like 'RSPCA Approved' and 'Animal Welfare Approved') refers to the welfare conditions under which the animal was raised, as well as how it was handled prior to and during slaughter. 'Certified' means those conditions were verified by an independent third party, based on their specific set of standards.

ENHANCED (ALSO WRITTEN AS 'INJECTED' OR 'CONTAINS A SOLUTION')

This refers to meat that has had water added. Sometimes, that water contains flavorings like salt and spices. It's usually found in pork and poultry – two meats notorious for drying out and lower marbling. Though enhanced meats have a bad reputation for being 'filled with water' to make them weigh more, they were actually developed to improve the consumer experience by making it less likely for the meat to dry out, especially when cooked at higher temperatures.

FLASH FROZEN

This is rapid freezing by exposure to extremely cold temperatures – much colder than a standard freezer. The speed of the process forms smaller ice crystals than conventional freezing, which causes less damage to muscle fibers and helps reduce moisture loss during defrosting.

GRASS-FED

This claim can be misleading. All cattle eat grass at some point, so technically, all beef is grass-fed. What really matters is how the animal was finished. For example, beef labeled 'grass-fed' may still be grain-finished, meaning it spent its final months on grain to increase marbling. The exception to this is the claim '100% grass-fed.'

GRASS-FINISHED

Often used alongside 'grass-fed,' this means the animal was raised on a diet of grass or forage for its entire life, with no grain feeding at any stage.

HGP FREE

Stands for 'hormonal growth promotant' free. This claim is redundant in some regions, like the UK and the EU, where the use of HGPs is banned entirely.

MINIMALLY PROCESSED

This means the meat has been processed in ways that don't significantly change its natural form. Simple steps like cleaning, cutting, grinding or freezing are allowed, as they don't alter the meat's inherent character. Often seen on labels as part of the 'natural' definition.

NATURAL

This term means far less than you might think. It's regulated, but with very limited scope. It simply indicates the product contains no artificial flavors, colorings, chemical preservatives or other synthetic ingredients, but it says nothing about how the animal was raised or what it was fed.

NO ADDED HORMONES

This label means the animal wasn't administered any growth-promoting hormones, but it comes with a caveat! It's relevant for beef in the US and Australia, where hormone use is allowed under regulation, but when it shows up on chicken or pork, it's pure marketing fluff. Hormone use is already banned in those species, so the claim is legally meaningless but still used to sway consumers. In the EU and the UK, hormone use is banned across all livestock, making the label unnecessary altogether. You won't see the phrase 'no hormones' since all animals naturally produce hormones.

NO NITRATES OR NITRITES ADDED

Usually found on processed and cured meats, this means no synthetic sodium nitrate or sodium nitrites were used. However, manufacturers can still use naturally occurring nitrates or nitrites from plant-based sources like celery or beets, which serve the same preservative function.

ORGANIC

This means the product has been certified organic by an approved verification program. The claim cannot be used without proper certification. Certification verifies that the animals were raised according to defined organic production standards, which vary by program but generally cover feed, medication use and farming practices.

PASTURE-RAISED

In this case, the animal had access to pasture for a significant part of their life. However, supplemental feed (such as grains) is allowed and usually provided to meet nutritional needs that pasture alone may not supply.

REGENERATIVELY RAISED

An agricultural approach that emphasizes soil and ecosystem health, with a focus on topsoil regeneration to increase biodiversity. The term is not regulated, so definitions and practices can vary between producers.

RETAINED WATER

This refers to moisture absorbed by meat during processing steps like chilling or rinsing. In many countries, including the US, Australia and the European Union, it must be declared on the label if it exceeds a certain percentage. Unlike 'enhanced' meats, the addition is unintentional.

MEAT NAMES UNPACKED

One of the most daunting things about buying meat can be the titles and names of the various cuts. Often, there are several different names for the same cut, many times determined by region or country. Sometimes, the difference only lies in the cut being bone-in or boneless.

WHAT'S IN A NAME?

Most steak names are considered to be 'common cut names' and are therefore unregulated. So, sometimes butchers or restaurants will create names to make their product seem more exciting and exotic. It's mostly a marketing play. Unfortunately, this can often end up being super confusing for meat lovers!

MEAT CUT SPECIFICATION GUIDES

Two of the few formal reference guides for meat cuts are the NAMP Meat Buyer's Guide (US) and Ausmeat (Australia). They provide a meat roadmap through the carcass, breaking it down by primals, subprimals and some retail cuts. These guides assign numbers to cuts to create a consistent standard, but they're mostly used by processors, packers and large retailers. Many smaller butcher shops don't even know the codes exist. Additionally, many of the cuts in the books only go as far as whole muscles, rather than the steaks that are cut from them.

THE BUTCHER VARIABLE

It's also important to remember that butchery is a profession without a centralized standard of training. There's no universal school or course you can take for it, so people learn different styles, usually from the butchers who trained them. This can mean your local butcher may not have even heard of the latest trending steak if they aren't trained in where to cut it from. It can also lead to contentious debates about where a particular steak is actually cut from. For example, some folks consider a Delmonico steak to be a chuck eye, while others classify it as a ribeye.

There are some standards of identity which are regulated (by the USDA in the US), such as what can go into ground beef, hot dogs, ham and bacon. But it might surprise you to learn that there's no standard of identity (and therefore no regulation) for the name 'filet mignon.'

CUTS THAT AREN'T REALLY CUTS AT ALL

I've tried to be exhaustive in covering the major meat cuts, but some meat names warrant a closer look. In many cases, what sounds like a specific cut is actually a looser term that can refer to several different things depending on where you are or how it's being prepared. Some originated as dishes or cooking methods and were later applied to certain cuts, while others are old butcher's terms.

MINUTE STEAK

Any super-thinly sliced steak, usually from the tougher cuts, that benefits from thinner slicing. Designed to cook 'in about a minute.'

LONDON BROIL

A cooking method for steak that's been marinated, then cooked and sliced to serve. Some meat markets will label meat as London broil, but the actual muscle is unspecified, so it could be anything from a top round to a flank steak.

DECKLE

A non-standard butcher's term with inconsistent meaning. For some it refers to the brisket point (*pectoralis superficialis*); for others, the fatty cap over the rib primal (*trapezius, rhomboideus* and associated fat). Some also use 'deckle' more broadly for any cap-style muscle.

CHIPPED STEAK

Paper-thin slices of beef, usually from the round and often shaved on a deli slicer. Best known as the meat used for Philly cheesesteaks.

CUTLET

Sometimes used to mean a bone-in chop (Australia, NZ, UK, Europe), but also used to refer to a thin, crumbed boneless piece of meat (US).

CUBE STEAK

This is not a cut of steak – just any steak that has been run through a mechanical tenderizer, often leaving small 'cube' shapes on the surface.

MILANESA

This term refers to the dish, not the cut. It typically uses tougher cuts, like round steaks, which are tenderized or pounded thin. The meat is then used to make 'milanesa' – a crumbed and deep-fried dish popular in Argentina, Mexico and Uruguay, with Italian origins.

FRENCHED

This is purely a presentation term. It means scraping away the meat and fat from the end of a bone for appearance (think a rack of lamb or tomahawk steak). It doesn't change the cut itself, just how it's trimmed.

COUNTRY-STYLE RIBS

Pork cut into pieces resembling ribs. Sometimes taken from the sirloin/caudal end of the pork loin, other times from the pork butt. Occasionally, they are bone-in or have a small piece of rib attached, but it's more common to find them boneless.

CARPACCIO

An Italian dish made using raw meat, usually beef, that's sliced incredibly thin. It's usually made with filet mignon, eye of round or similarly tubular cuts.

ROPA VIEJA

Meaning 'old clothes,' it's a Cuban dish with shredded stewed beef. Any number of cuts can be used, most commonly brisket, chuck and flank.

TARTARE

A French dish made with raw meat, hand-minced with a knife and mixed with ingredients like capers, shallots and mustard. (You can try my recipe on page 162.)

SALTIMBOCCA

Another Italian dish that refers to the cooking style of wrapping with prosciutto and sage leaves. It can be made with a variety of veal, chicken or pork cuts.

STEAKS BY ANOTHER NAME

Butchers, marketers and chefs have rebranded muscles to make them sound more appealing, or to turn underused cuts into something new and desirable. I've compiled some of the more obscure ones here, along with details of the corresponding common cut. As you peruse this list, bear in mind that anyone, at any time, can start naming steaks anything they like. So take them all with a grain of salt (they're going to taste better that way, too). Most folks won't ever need this list, but meat nerds like myself will appreciate the detail.

NAME	ACTUAL CUT/MUSCLE
Ambassador steak	Strip loin (NY strip/AU sirloin)
Apartment steak	Tri tip (bottom sirloin)
Baja steak	*Teres major* (petite tender)
Baseball steak	Center cut top sirloin (rump)
Beauty steak	Chuck eye steak or ribeye (used for both)
Book steak	*Infraspinatus* (flat iron)
Butcher's steak	Hanger steak (diaphragm)
Butler steak	*Infraspinatus* (flat iron)
California steak	*Tensor fasciae latae* (tri tip)
Club steak	Bone-in strip loin (first cut of short loin/AU sirloin)
Coulotte	Top sirloin cap (picanha/rump cap)
Cowboy steak	Bone-in ribeye, frenched, with a short amount of rib bone left intact
Delmonico	Chuck eye steak or ribeye (used for both)
English steak	Chuck clod steak
Kansas City strip	Strip loin, bone-in (AU sirloin)
Manhattan steak	Strip loin medallion (steak cut in half and tied to resemble a filet) (AU sirloin)
Market steak	Chuck eye steak or ribeye (used for both)
Merlot steak	Heel of round
Nevada steak	Chuck, specifically *subscapularis* (sometimes *serratus ventralis* is used)
Newport steak	Tri tip (smaller portioned cut)
Onglet	Hanger steak
Patio steak	*Infraspinatus* (top blade/oyster blade)
Petite sirloin	Ball tip (bottom sirloin/round junction)
Ranch steak	Shoulder center (chuck clod)
Santa Fe steak	Top round cap
Saratoga steak	Originally ribeye filet/eye (*longissimus dorsi*), now more commonly strip steak
Shell steak	Strip loin, bone-in or boneless (AU sirloin)
Sierra steak	*Splenius* (from the chuck underblade)
Spencer steak	Boneless ribeye or the eye of the ribeye (*longissimus dorsi*)
Spider/oyster steak	A small muscle attached to the aitchbone/hip bone
Triangle steak	Tri tip (bottom sirloin)
Vegas strip steak	Chuck, specifically *subscapularis* (sometimes *serratus ventralis* is used)
Vein steak	Strip steak from the hip end, including a portion of *gluteus medius* (AU sirloin)
Velvet steak	Heel of round
Western steak	Bottom round
Zabuton	Chuck short rib (*serratus ventralis*)

HOW TO CHOOSE THE BEST CUT FOR THE JOB

These days, it's pretty easy to just head to the store and find what you need all pre-cut and ready to go. Stir-fry meat. Fajita meat. Stew meat. But, if you've ever been curious to choose and cut your own, here are some suggestions on which cuts to use.

BURGERS/GROUND BEEF

Chuck, brisket or sirloin/rump for a leaner option.

FAJITAS

Outside skirt, inside skirt, bavette/flap/bottom sirloin, flank.

JERKY

Eye of round, top round/topside and possibly sirloin/rump or flank. The key is to choose something lean.

ROASTS (DRY HEAT)

Prime rib, tenderloin, rump/sirloin cap, tri tip, chuck clod/bolar.

SCHNITZEL/MILANESA/ CHICKEN-FRIED STEAK

Top round/topside, pork loin, bottom round/silverside, sirloin/rump, sirloin tip/knuckle.

STIR-FRY

Flank, bavette, sirloin/rump, chuck, top round/topside (only if tenderizing).

STEWS

Top round/topside, bottom round/silverside, sirloin tip/knuckle, chuck clod/bolar, brisket, pork butt.

GRASS-FED OR GRAIN-FED BEEF?

This is one of the questions I get asked the most: what's the difference between grass- and grain-finished beef?

As you learned in the meat label decoding section (pages 16–17), all cattle are grass-fed at some point in their lives. From there, they'll either remain on pasture until slaughter (grass-finished) or be transitioned onto a grain-based diet (usually in a feedlot/feed yard) for a faster finish. Historically, much of the beef industry has favored grain finishing because it produces larger animals with more consistent marbling.

It's important to understand that grass-fed doesn't automatically mean high eating quality. While grass finishing can produce beautifully marbled, flavorful beef in regions with rich, consistent pasture (e.g. Ireland, Tasmania or New Zealand), that's not always the case everywhere. In areas with poor or seasonal forage, cattle may be leaner and produce tougher meat. So, while choosing grass-fed may align with certain health or ethical preferences, it doesn't always guarantee a better eating experience.

Both feeding approaches produce good beef – it just depends on what you value most.

• GRASS-FINISHED •

High in iron, zinc and B12

More omega-3 fatty acids

Contains higher amounts of conjugated linoleic acid (or CLA), which is linked to decreases in blood pressure

Lower in monounsaturated fats

Fat can have a yellowish appearance from the beta-carotene found in grass

Sharper, gamier and earthier flavor

• GRAIN-FINISHED •

High in iron, zinc and B12

Lower carbon footprint

Contains higher amounts of oleic acid, a heart-healthy fat

Cattle 'finish' to get to market faster

Usually fed a blend of corn, oats and barley, but can also include upcycled byproducts not suitable for human consumption, like spent brewers' grain

Subtle, smooth and buttery flavor

BEST-BEFORE DATES

You've probably seen the videos: someone in a grocery store holding up a pack of meat that's 'past its sell-by date,' shaking their head in horror and racking up views by scaremongering. But here's the truth: **fresh meat doesn't actually expire on a set date.**

Any 'best before' or 'use by' dates you see on meat packaging are mostly about stock rotation and quality control, not food safety. Meat isn't a mass-produced widget with a predictable shelf life; it's a biological product. And its 'expiration' depends on a whole range of factors.

The type of cut has an influence: for example, ground meat will spoil faster than a whole muscle. Packaging matters, too: vacuum-sealed meat lasts longer than something exposed to air in a foam tray. Temperature fluctuations can cause major longevity issues, even if the meat technically stays 'cold.' And of course, where and how the meat is stored – whether in a commercial cold chain or a home fridge – makes a big difference. FYI, home refrigerators are notorious for being inconsistent and warmer than they ought to be. So, while printed dates offer a helpful guideline, they're not a definitive clock.

That's why two packs of meat with the same date can look and smell completely different. One might still be perfectly good, while the other should've been tossed days ago. Your best tool is your sense of smell – a deeply unpleasant sour or sulfurous smell that really singes your nostrils is the best sign that something isn't right. A dull grayish-green color is also an indicator, but a dark color alone doesn't mean spoilage. Previously vacuum-packed meats can naturally deepen in hue with time and oxygen exposure.

Spoilage bacteria are responsible for breaking down meat and causing 'off' smells, sliminess and discoloration. These microbes are different from the pathogenic bacteria that cause foodborne illness, but their presence signals that the meat has begun to degrade. If a cut smells sour, funky or otherwise 'off,' it's best not to use it. Ultimately, you should trust (and protect) your gut – when in doubt, toss it.

WHAT IS WAGYU?

One of the buzziest words in the last couple of decades, Wagyu has exploded onto the worldwide scene, driven by dedicated breeding programs and the global appetite for rich, luxurious steaks.

Wagyu is a breed of cattle, which literally translates to 'Japanese cow.' There are actually four types of Wagyu cattle, with the two most common being Japanese Black and Japanese Brown (also known as Akaushi), though the other two are less commonly seen in meat production.

Maybe you've heard about them being fed beer while being massaged? While it might be true of some of the original Japanese rearing techniques, those practices are not used in most Wagyu production today. The real magic is in their genetics, which are predisposed to incredibly intense marbling. The fat itself is special, too – rich in monounsaturated fatty acids, which give it a lower melting point than other beef. This buttery richness provides a sumptuous experience that has contributed to Wagyu's popularity. However, it should be noted that the ultra-rich fat content can actually be overwhelming for some palates.

Genetics are hugely important in the world of Wagyu. Breed lines are carefully traced and tracked, and if you're buying the premium stuff, your beef may even come with a certificate telling you about the lineage. Progeny (offspring) of sires are monitored down the line, and prize bulls are named and numbered, with pedigree taken seriously. And though the breed began in Japan, Australia is fast becoming one of the top Wagyu producers in the world, having developed exceptional Wagyu genetics from years of rigorous selection.

If you've ever tried Wagyu and walked away wondering what all the fuss was about, you're not alone – not all Wagyu is created equal. The term 'Wagyu' refers only to a breed type, but the quality, genetics and marbling levels can vary dramatically depending on lineage and crossbreeding. If you're going to seek out Wagyu, it's worth understanding what the classifications actually mean.

Australia and Japan also have sophisticated grading and labeling standards for Wagyu, giving consumers a clearer sense of breed purity and marbling levels, so they know exactly what they're paying for. In the US, 'American Wagyu' only needs to have a minimum of 50% Wagyu genetics, which can often result in steaks that look comparable to Prime grade. That's where the confusion sets in – people hear the hype, try a crossbred steak, and wonder what the big deal is. True fullblood Wagyu is a totally different experience, but it's significantly more expensive. So, while crossbred Wagyu offers a more accessible option, it's not the same thing, and understanding the difference matters!

• FULLBLOOD WAGYU •

This is 100% genetically Wagyu beef, the unadulterated, genetically pure meat with the highest marbling levels.

• PUREBRED WAGYU •

This is 93.75% genetically Wagyu beef, referred to within the industry as F4.

• CROSSBRED WAGYU •

Anything under the 93.75% mark falls under crossbred. To be labeled as Wagyu, it needs to contain a minimum of 50% Wagyu genetics, which is called F1. If you are buying Wagyu that's not much more expensive than a regular steak, it's most likely a 50/50 Wagyu Angus cross.

And finally, a word about **ground** Wagyu meat. Many might consider a Wagyu burger to be an indulgent use of the product, but they're not grinding up Wagyu ribeyes to make a burger blend! Wagyu cattle have less desirable cuts and trim pieces, just like any other beef animal. So, is it worth it? In its own way, yes. While manual grinding will always mechanically tenderize any meat, the Wagyu fat remains unique and can provide a different mouthfeel and richness, even in a burger.

PREP IT

There's a lot you can do before the cooking even starts that will still shape the final result in big ways. Meat prep like brining, marinating and even using the right tools can change how meat tastes, feels and cooks, long before any heat is involved.

TENDERNESS

A tender bite is what many people look for in good meat. That's why the tenderloin commands such a high price – tenderness is consistently one of the most sought-after qualities.

Tenderness is actually quantifiable thanks to an instrument called the Warner-Bratzler shear force machine. This machine uses a blade to slice through samples of meat and assign a numerical value of tenderness based on the resistance it feels. It even has interchangeable blade designs to mimic different biting or chewing actions, allowing researchers to better compare the results to the consumer eating experience.

Here are some of the ways meat can be tenderized.

MECHANICAL TENDERIZATION

This is an official way to describe the physical disruption of the muscle structure. Mechanical tenderization includes pounding with a meat mallet, grinding and piercing (also known as blade tenderizing).

VELVETING

A form of tenderization used in Chinese cooking, velveting involves applying a slurry of baking soda, egg white, cornstarch (cornflour) and oil to the meat. The alkaline pH increases the negative charge on the muscle proteins, creating electrostatic repulsion that keeps the fibers from contracting tightly during cooking. This reduced contraction helps the meat retain moisture and results in a softer texture.

ACIDIC MARINADES

This is another form of chemical tenderization, but it works in the opposite pH direction. When acids like vinegar, citrus juice, beer, buttermilk and yogurt are added to the meat, the low pH changes the charge on the proteins, disrupting their bonds. This causes the outer layers to denature, giving a softer surface texture.

ENZYMATIC TENDERIZATION

Also known as proteolytic tenderizers, enzymes like papain (found in papaya), bromelain (found in pineapple) and actinidin (in kiwifruit) break peptide bonds, achieving a more tender result. It also weakens the connective tissue network for added tenderness. It's these same enzymes that are in shakers of 'meat tenderizer' you can buy at the store. Enzymatic tenderizers work really quickly at ambient temperatures, but there's an increased chance the meat will turn 'mushy' in texture with overuse.

SLICING

While not a true act of tenderization, the thickness at which you slice meat can drastically increase the 'ease of chew' by shortening the fiber length. For example, while a thick slice of seared pork butt would be a real jaw workout, a super-thin slice is great on the grill (and you can see for yourself with the recipe on page 62). The same principle applies in deli meats, where items like roast beef made from tougher cuts seem more tender when shaved thin.

AGING

This is perhaps the most important of all tenderizers, which is why it got its own dedicated section on page 45. Notably, it's the only tenderization process that occurs naturally within the meat itself – no outside intervention required!

And finally, don't forget that the cooking process itself is an act of tenderization, too. Turning a firm, tough brisket into a soft, gelatinous slice is great proof of that.

TOP TEN MOST TENDER BEEF MUSCLES

Researchers at the University of Nebraska-Lincoln's Meat Science Department have conducted extensive studies on beef tenderness. Based on Warner-Bratzler shear force data, they've identified the ten most tender muscles in the carcass.

1. ***Psoas major*** – filet mignon
2. ***Infraspinatus*** – flat iron steak/oyster blade/top blade
3. ***Spinalis dorsi*** – ribeye cap
4. ***Serratus ventralis*** – denver steak, boneless short rib
5. ***Multifidus dorsi*** – small muscle found in some ribeye and chuck eye steaks
6. ***Subscapularis*** – part of the chuck, sometimes called chuck blade
7. ***Teres major*** – petite tender/shoulder tender
8. ***Rectus femoris*** – sirloin tip/outside round/bottom round/silverside
9. ***Tensor fascia latae*** – tri tip
10. ***Biceps brachii*** – arm roast (rarely sold whole and often used as stew meat)

At the time of writing this book, my favorite steak is the picanha, which ranks down at #31. It's not always about tenderness but the overall enjoyability of the bite!

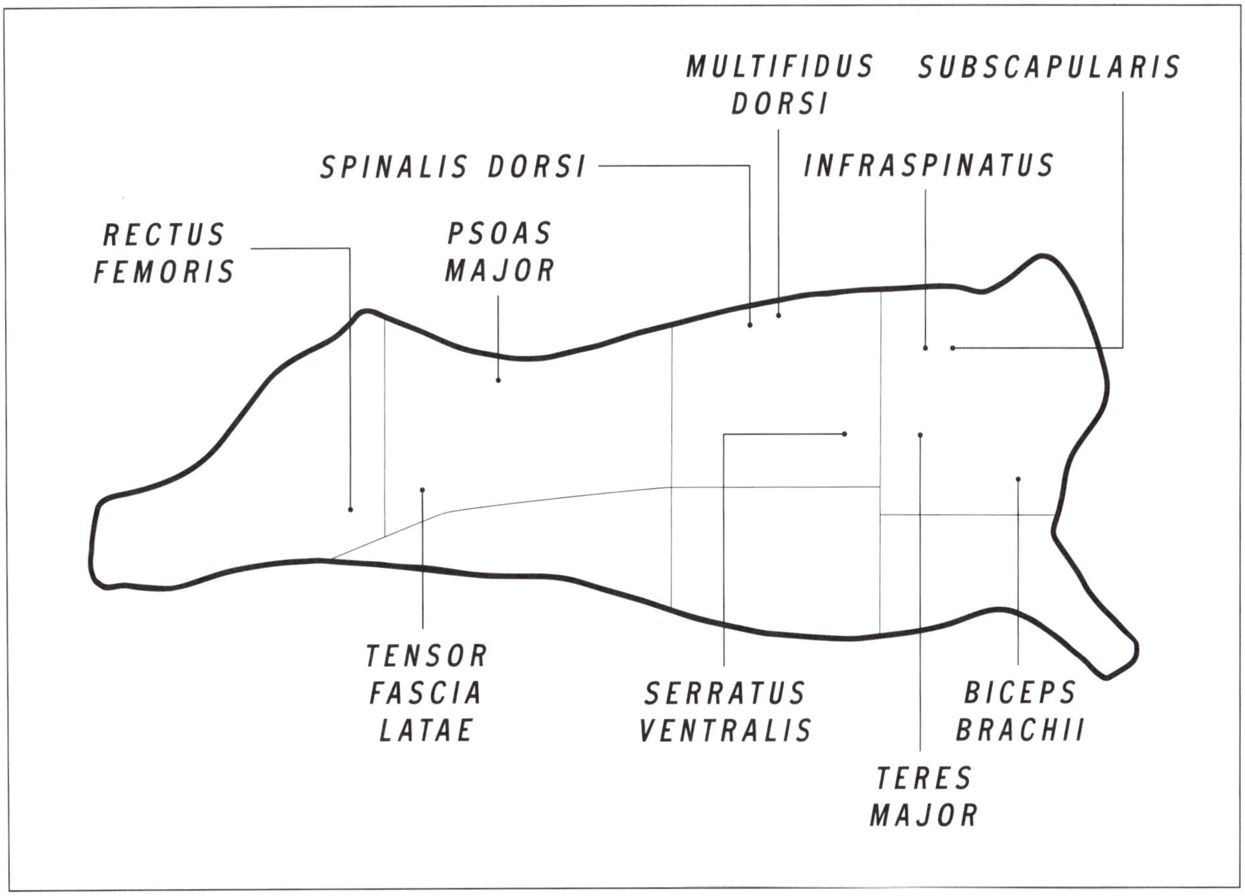

MEAT TOOLS

1 SCIMITAR

The preferred knife for cutting steaks and doing less detailed work than the boning knife.

2 BONING KNIFE

My fave is a 6-inch (15-cm) semi-flex blade, perfect for most butchery, trimming, frenching and bone removal – an absolute workhorse of a knife.

3 THERMOMETER

The most precise way to check for meat doneness and verify safe cooking temperatures.

4 TENDERIZER

Also known as a meat mallet. The smooth side is best for flattening and evening, and the textured side is for more aggressive manual tenderizing.

5 SKIN PIERCER

Ideal for pork belly or skin-on chicken, it's used to pierce the surface with tiny holes to allow fat to render out and skin to crisp.

6 BONE SCRAPER

Meat that has been cut with a band saw (like some steaks and pork sections) can have small bone fragments. Dragging this tool across the surface can clean up any bone dust or fat smearing.

7 STEAK WEIGHT

Sometimes called a bacon press, this is a flat, heavy tool usually made of cast iron. It's used to keep meat flat and encourage full contact with the cooking surface for an even sear.

8 BURGER PRESS

Similar to a steak weight – but round and lighter. You grip the handle to smash meat onto a hot griddle or skillet, creating ultra-thin 'smashburger' patties.

8
6
5
7

BRINING

Salt and meat have a complex and fascinating relationship. Salt is both an essential nutrient and a self-regulating ingredient that has three primary functions in meat:

- it intensifies food flavors
- it alters the bacterial populations in the meat (antibacterial qualities)
- it increases shelf life (a brine strength as low as 4% can inhibit bacterial growth).

Brining uses salt to keep meat juicy. Meat loses a significant amount of water as it cooks. That's why well-done steak can seem so dry, while a long braise in liquid stays moist. Leaner, lighter meats like pork and poultry tend to benefit most from brining. It's not as common for beef because it can dilute the flavor and give tender cuts a slightly spongy texture, though there are certain cuts like corned beef and pastrami where the brine is integral to the recipe.

HOW BRINING WORKS

At its most basic, a brine is a solution of water and salt that can be introduced to the meat through soaking or injection. The aim of brining is to increase the water content at the start to offset what will be lost during cooking and, most importantly, end up with a juicier result. Put simply, you brine to add and retain water.

On a molecular level, meat proteins carry a net charge and act like magnets. The chloride in salt shifts the isoelectric point of the proteins, increasing their charge so they repel each other and create more space to hold more water. That is how brining works to combat dryness.

EQUILIBRIUM BRINING

When you soak meat in a brine, salt and water start moving into the meat while some of the meat's own water moves out. Over time, they 'trade' until both the brine and the meat have the same salt concentration. That balance point is called 'equilibrium.' Stronger brines get there faster, but they can make the meat too salty if left too long. Weaker brines take more time, but they're more forgiving and can let you brine overnight without overseasoning the meat.

INJECTION BRINING

Injection brining works the same way as soaking, with salt and water moving into the muscle and replacing some of the liquid that would otherwise be lost during cooking. The difference is speed and evenness: because the brine is delivered directly inside the muscle via needle, diffusion happens from the inside out as well as the outside in, significantly cutting down brining time and giving more consistent results.

DRY BRINING

Unlike a traditional water-based brine, dry brining uses salt applied directly to the surface of the meat. The goal is the same; it's just a different method of getting there. Since salt works by osmosis, it will naturally pull some moisture out of the meat to the surface. Over time, the salt dissolves into that liquid to form a natural brine, which is then reabsorbed deeper into the muscle.

Whereas adding water can dilute flavor, dry brining concentrates it slightly. The ultra-dry surface is also the perfect candidate for the Maillard reaction (see page 34), which means better browning. It's especially effective for crispy-skin poultry and individual steaks, but less practical if you prefer to season with spice blends, since those flavors tend to dull as they sit in the fridge.

To dry brine, use about 2.5 g of salt per pound of meat and apply it evenly over the surface. Place the meat on a rack set over a tray (to catch drips), leave it uncovered in the fridge for 12–24 hours, then pat dry before cooking – no need to rinse.

COMMERCIAL BRINING

Sometimes commercial brines like the ones in bacon and hams also include phosphate, a functional ingredient that alters the pH of meat to help it bind and hold water more effectively. Phosphates dissolve some of the protein cross-links formed during rigor mortis, allowing the muscle fibers to swell and retain more moisture. They also help slow spoilage and oxidation, which extends both shelf life and food safety. In Australia, you'll often see them listed simply as 'mineral salts.'

ENHANCED MEATS

You might also see 'enhanced' or 'solution added' on meat labels. These are products that have already been brined or injected at the processing plant. Despite what you might've heard, it's not just a sneaky way to pump up the weight; it's meat science at work – designed to help people enjoy juicier, more forgiving results at home. The label will usually tell you the percentage of added solution. Just remember, since the meat is already salted, you'll need to adjust any extra seasoning you add.

MASTER BRINE GUIDE

This master recipe is for a soaking equilibrium brine (sometimes called a 'wet brine') and is great for pork, chicken, turkey and even some seafoods like salmon. It's balanced with sugar to enhance flavor and promote browning without oversalting, but you can leave it out if you prefer.

To keep things consistent, the amounts of water given in the table below are based on weight (I just wanted to save you from having to weigh it). Simply measure out the volume and use the matching salt and sugar amounts.

Remember, it's important to measure any salt by weight, not volume. For example, 1 cup of rock salt has a completely different sodium content to 1 cup of table salt. In this case, I recommend using brining salt – the crystals are teeny-tiny and dissolve faster.

METHOD

1. **Mix the base:** Combine cold water, salt and sugar (if using) in a non-reactive container until dissolved. To speed it up, take a small portion of the measured water, heat it to dissolve the salt and sugar, then return it to the rest of the cool water so the overall volume stays the same.
2. **Stir through any add-ins:** These are the aromatic optional extras that help make it your signature brine.
3. **Chill thoroughly:** The brine must be below 40°F(4°C) before adding the meat. If using ice, make sure to take the appropriate amount of water out so the solution isn't diluted.
4. **Submerge the meat:** The brine needs to completely cover the meat. Use a plate or a resealable bag filled with water to weigh it down.
5. **Let the meat brine:** See the chart opposite for times.
6. **Drain and dry:** Discard the brine completely. Pat dry with paper towels before cooking.

Note: A quick rinse after brining can help reduce surface salt, and is recommended if you're planning to add a heavy rub or surface seasoning. On the downside, rinsing is an extra step that can wash away some of the surface flavor from the brine and work against skin crisping in poultry. You may have to try it both ways to find out what works best for you.

RECOMMENDED BRINING TIMES

Small (pork chops, chicken pieces): 2–4 hours

Medium (whole pork loins, whole chickens, ducks): 4–6 hours

Large (small whole turkeys, pork shoulder): 8–12 hours

Extra large (medium whole turkeys): 12–18 hours

Extra extra large (big ol' turkeys): 18–24 hours

Don't be tempted to exceed the recommended times. There comes a point when the brine will start making things mushy, not juicy.

OPTIONAL ADD-INS

• FRUIT & VEG •

Garlic cloves, onions, celery, citrus (whole or peel)

• SPICES •

Peppercorns, mustard seeds, juniper berries, allspice berries, coriander seeds, cloves, star anise

• HERBS •

Bay leaf, oregano, thyme, sage, rosemary

• SWEETENERS •

Maple syrup, honey, molasses, brown sugar

Try to avoid ground spices, delicate herbs and fresh chilies – you'd be surprised how little heat transfers in a cold brine.

Aromatic add-ins make your brine smell amazing, but flavor molecules are generally too large and hydrophobic to travel far into the meat. Salt and some small solubles get in, but volatile aromatic compounds mostly just sit on the surface. Think of them as a bonus aroma layer rather than a deep flavor infusion. If you want those flavors in the finished dish, add them again later in your rub or marinade, or during the cooking process.

BRINING FORMULA BY WEIGHT

WATER WEIGHT/VOL	SALT (AT 6%)	SUGAR (AT 3%)	SUITED FOR
1 quart (1 liter)	2.1 oz (60 g)	1 oz (30 g)	2–4 pork chops, small chicken pieces
2 quarts (2 liters)	4.2 oz (120 g)	2.1 oz (60 g)	Whole small chicken, rack of ribs
1 gallon (4 liters)	8.5 oz (240 g)	4.2 oz (120 g)	Large chicken, whole pork loin
2 gallons (8 liters)	16.9 oz (480 g)	8.5 oz (240 g)	Small to medium turkey, pork shoulder

MARINATION

Marinating meat started out as a way to keep it from spoiling, but over the years, it's shifted into something we do mostly for flavor. These days, a marinade is usually a mix of oil and something acidic, like vinegar, lemon juice or wine, with herbs, spices and other aromatics layered in. In home kitchens, we tend to call any mixture the meat soaks in a 'marinade', no matter the ingredients.

WHY MARINATE?

Acidic marinades primarily function as tenderizers. Some ingredients like orange oils and thyme can also add antibacterial properties to the meat, extending quality and shelf life.

But there's more to it. Stay with me on this one; we're going to jump between meat science and home application, because in this case, they are not the same thing. I want to make sure you understand how marinating works, but also that what most of us are doing at home is flavor coating, not marinating.

SOAKING AND TUMBLING

On a commercial scale, marinades are applied by soaking, injecting or tumbling. Soaking (immersion marination) works much like a brine, with the entire cut completely submerged. In modern production, this method has largely been replaced by vacuum tumblers – large metal drums that rotate and agitate meat under vacuum.

With an immersion marinade, salt, water and other small molecules slowly make their way into the meat, but larger aromatic compounds mostly hang out near the surface. In other words, you'll get a great transfer of aroma, but most of the deeper meat won't taste like the marinade itself. Vacuum tumbling changes that – it helps pull more of those flavor compounds further in, boosting the final taste. The vacuum and tumbling action help distribute the marinade more efficiently through the meat. Reduced pressure and constant movement allow the liquid to move deeper into the muscle, meaning it penetrates faster and more evenly than static soaking.

Ultimately, marinade uptake depends on the type and quantity of ingredients. As a general guide, immersion marinades typically uptake roughly 4–10% over 24 hours (depending on salt, pH and meat type). On the other hand, vacuum tumbling can achieve 12–20% uptake in as little as 60 minutes, and can even exceed that with longer cycles.

FLAVOR COATING

Most home 'marinades' are really just coatings of flavor, not true marinades. The meat often isn't fully submerged and the marinade only clings to the surface, with very little absorption into the meat- usually around 1–3% in 24 hours.

However, if your marinade contains an active tenderizing ingredient, like yogurt (lactic acid), pineapple or papaya (enzymes), or a strong acid in high quantities, the time frame changes. These acids work quickly at the surface level to break down proteins, and too much exposure can damage the outer texture. In those cases, it's best to keep the marination short, often just a few hours.

So if we're not really deeply tenderizing when we marinate at home, what's the point? It still adds flavor, just not in the way you might expect. In most cases, what we're tasting is the marinade itself. Those surface ingredients hit your taste buds first, then the flavor of the meat follows.

One way to boost effectiveness is to vacuum-seal the meat with the marinade. While it's nowhere near as powerful as a commercial tumbler, it can make a difference. Just be aware of this: you'll need a heavy-duty chamber vacuum sealer. Most small, clamp-style home units don't pull enough oxygen to create the strong seal needed to get the job done.

Whatever your method or ingredients, always marinate in the fridge – the meat still needs to stay cold.

WHAT IS SILVERSKIN?

Silverskin is the common name for the tough, collagen-rich fascia of connective tissue on the outside of muscles (epimysium is the official anatomical term). With very long cooking, it can break down, but as a general rule, you'll have a better eating experience if you remove it completely.

Sometimes, the silverskin has been removed by the butcher, but a few bits and pieces have been left behind. It's still worth cleaning it up and trimming them away. Cuts that often come with thick swaths of silverskin include pork loin, beef tenderloin, top blade roasts, skirt steaks, lamb loins, venison backstrap and beef top round.

• BE THE BUTCHER •

HOW TO TRIM SILVERSKIN

1. Use a boning or trimming knife with a sharp tip. I prefer a flex or semi-flex for best control. Insert the tip of the knife immediately under the silverskin, pushing it through. You should be able to clearly see the blade under the silverskin.
2. Angle the blade up slightly to ride along the underside of the silverskin (it's harder to cut than muscle), and gently glide the knife along. Make sure to cut away from you, and use your other hand to hold the meat and keep it taut.
3. Repeat on other strands until the majority of the silverskin has been trimmed away.
4. Discard the silverskin and prepare your beautifully trimmed meat.

VARIATION: Most skilled butchers and processors prefer to cut with the silverskin against the board (cutting down, instead of up), but that method is harder to control without experience.

1

2

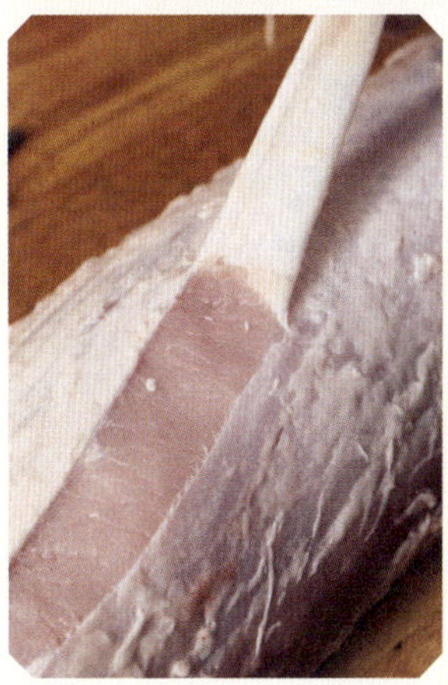

3

4

COOK IT

Cooking is the moment when everything you've chosen and prepped finally comes together. Time, temperature, technique and instinct all meet at the heat source. Whether you're searing, grilling or resting, there are lots of decisions that affect the flavor, texture and doneness of what ends up on the plate. This chapter is about understanding those decisions and cooking with intention, not guesswork.

CHASING THE ULTIMATE SEAR

I want you to approach the browning of meat as an extra ingredient because it kinda is. Browning meat creates new flavor and aroma compounds, which are literally like additional ingredients, enhancing the meaty experience.

The browning of meat is a phenomenon known as the Maillard reaction – the same thing that makes bread smell so fantastic as it bakes. Maillard is a chemical reaction between reducing sugars and amino acids. But for this reaction to start, conditions have to be just right, and one of the most important factors is water. Specifically, too much of it. When the meat is wet (usually from surface moisture or an added marinade), the water has to cook off before browning can begin.

One of the most important things you can do to kickstart the Maillard reaction is to pat the surface of your meat dry with a paper towel before cooking. It makes an enormous difference to crust success!

If you've struggled with getting ground beef to brown properly, it's that pesky moisture again. Insufficient heat or overcrowding causes water from the meat to pool instead of cook off, and you'll end up with sad, grey meat instead of a lovely browned surface. One of the best tips for ground meat is to place the whole block in a pan and leave it alone. Don't break it up until browning has started; then you can stir and crumble as needed.

Pan-sear like a pro (see opposite)

THE PAN-SEARING PRO TIP NO ONE EVER TELLS YOU ABOUT (BUT I WILL)

When you are cooking steak in a pan, always flip it onto a fresh section of the metal to maximize your sear (see pics opposite). This one simple step can make a huge difference to your sear and crust!

Temperature is everything when it comes to getting a great sear. And while it's possible to get things too hot and actually burn the surface rather than sear it, the most common issue people run into is that their pan temperatures just aren't hot enough.

Even if you preheat your pan, as soon as you place your steak down, the heat will rapidly transfer from the pan to the surface of the meat, cooling it off from the energy transfer. Most burners in domestic stoves are not powerful enough to recover the heat fast enough, so if you flip back onto the same spot, the second-side sear will be weaker. So, flipping it to a fresh, hotter section is the move.

That's another reason it's so much easier for steakhouses to create an incredible sear on their proteins. They have different equipment than us! Industrial stoves have more powerful burners that recover heat so well there's barely any dip in temperature. They also use specialty equipment like searing-hot salamanders, which can broil the steaks at temperatures above 700°F (370°C).

And of course, restaurants also have industrial exhaust fans and don't have to contend with setting the smoke detectors off. So, go easy on yourself if you're still struggling to get a crust quite as magnificent as your favorite steakhouse.

DON'T BUTTER BASTE 'TIL YOU READ THIS

Basting a steak with butter is a classic French preparation that adds richness to the sear. But *when* you add the butter to the pan makes all the difference between sizzling goodness and soggy, sad anti-searing. Butter is considerably high in water, and adding it to the pan before the Maillard reaction has started will only introduce more moisture and delay the reaction further. Save the butter for the end, and make sure you have a good amount of heat so the butter can foam and fry the surface. That foaming stage means the water is evaporating and the milk solids are starting to brown, giving that classic nutty, caramelized flavor.

TEMPERATURE

If I had better understood the importance of temperature-to-meat doneness, I probably would've cooked my own steaks years before I finally got up the courage to do it. I think a good-quality meat thermometer is about the most important tool a burgeoning meat enthusiast can have in their arsenal.

There are lots of variables when it comes to meat – the raw product itself, species, cut, cooking method, even the elevation and weather can impact your cook. But there's one thing that's a constant: internal temperatures. Measuring the temperature of your meat will tell you exactly when your steak is done, or exactly when your chicken is cooked, and take all the guesswork out of it.

DONENESS TEMPERATURES FOR STEAK AND RED MEAT

These temperatures are guidelines for culinary doneness. They reflect texture, color and flavor preferences.

Rare	120–125°F (48–51°C)
Medium-rare	130–135°F (54–57°C)
Medium	140–145°F (60–62°C)
Well done	155°F+ (68°C+)

FOOD SAFETY TEMPERATURES

While doneness is a personal preference, food-safe temperatures ensure harmful pathogens are killed, and should always be followed.

Chicken	165°F (74°C)
Pork	145°F (62°C)
Ground meat (except chicken)	160°F (71°C)

Food safety guidelines are designed to be foolproof, but they're not always nuanced. In reality, **time is just as important as temperature**. Food can be just as safe when cooked at a lower temperature, as long as it's held there for the right amount of time. The recommended food-safe temperatures above are designed for simplicity. But in controlled environments like sous vide, those rules can be safely bent. You're still hitting the same temperature targets to kill bacteria, just taking a different route to get there.

CARRYOVER COOKING

When it comes to temperature, one thing to be aware of is carryover cooking, where the meat continues to rise in temperature even after it's been removed from the heat source. This happens because the outer layers of the meat are hotter than the center, and that heat keeps moving inward even as the surface starts to cool. The larger the cut, the more noticeable the effect: a steak might rise just a couple of degrees, but a big roast could climb nearly twice that. That's why many people prefer to pull their meat a few degrees early, so it doesn't overshoot the doneness they're aiming for.

You may see conflicting advice about carryover cooking and temperature rise. In my own experience with steaks, I rarely see more than a 3–5°F increase. Yet, more and more articles and videos from food experts claim much larger jumps, sometimes 15–20°F. That speaks to the variability of 'experiments' in home kitchens, but I've noticed many of these newer findings use thick, metal, wireless thermometers designed to stay in the meat during cooking. That metal rod can conduct heat from the hotter exterior toward the cooler core, exaggerating the carryover. In more controlled tests, researchers use extremely thin wires or insert a probe only after the meat is off the heat to minimize conduction errors. Just another example of how every variable makes a difference, and why it's worth separating opinion from results.

WHY CAN YOU EAT STEAK RARE BUT NOT GROUND MEAT?

Intact cuts of red meat typically have bacteria on the surface, but not inside the muscle. When you sear a steak, the intense surface heat kills off those microbes, which is why it's safe to enjoy a rare or medium-rare center. But when meat is ground or mechanically tenderized, everything gets mixed together, so bacteria that were on the outside can end up distributed throughout the meat. That's why ground meat needs to be cooked thoroughly to ensure it's safe all the way through.

Poultry and pork are different: they can carry pathogens such as Salmonella and Trichinella within the meat itself, which is why they should be cooked to their recommended safe internal temperatures.

HOW IS STEAK TARTARE SAFE TO EAT?

Eating undercooked or raw meat is a calculated risk. Bacteria multiply over time, so the fresher the meat and the better it's been handled, the lower the chance of getting sick. There's always some risk, just like with raw seafood, but if the meat is from a reputable source, kept cold and properly prepared, the odds of getting sick are lower.

THE TWO-ZONE GRILL SETUP

You'll see me refer to a 'two-zone setup' a lot in this book. In fact, it's pretty much how I prepare my grill 95% of the time.

- **To set up your charcoal grill for two-zone cooking:** Light a chimney of coals and dump them out on one side of your grill. Use tongs or a shovel to move any stray coals to the main pile to create two definitive cooking zones - hot/direct and cool/indirect.
- **To set up a propane (gas) grill for two-zone cooking:** Light the two burners to the very left (or right - it doesn't matter), and leave all others off.

The two-zone setup is key to grilling with confidence because you control the heat and speed at which things are cooking.

Why the hot zone is great: On a charcoal grill, the concentrated heat of the coals all piled together gives you a really high temperature for developing crust and color. Think of it as a searing zone.

Why the cool zone is great: Some foods are prone to flaring up on the grill. Think bacon-wrapped anything, chicken wings and thick, fat-capped steaks. Having a cool zone allows you to move the proteins across and stop any flare-ups, slowing down your cook and maintaining control.

Using both zones during cooking: This setup is excellent for nailing doneness and safe temperatures. You can start your proteins over the hot zone to develop color and char, then move them to the cool side and close the lid, allowing them to cook gently until ready, without completely burning the outside (or your knuckle hairs!).

Using only one zone during cooking: There may be occasions where you set your grill up for two zones, but only end up using one side. If I'm only cooking steaks, I will use the hot zone and constantly flip the steaks until they are done. And if I want to use my grill like an oven with bonus flavor (for things like whole chickens, beef roasts, etc.), I'll cook them entirely on the cool side.

WHEN TO TAKE MEAT OUT OF THE FRIDGE

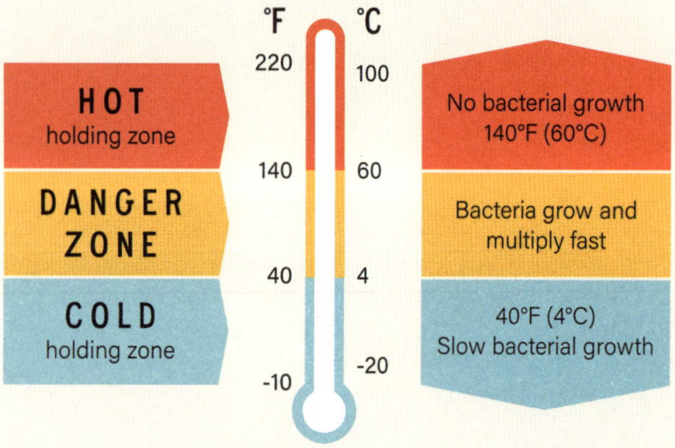

'Let it come to room temperature' is one of the most repeated pieces of cooking advice – and one of the most misguided.

DON'T LEAVE IT OUT FOR HOURS

Meat has a 'danger zone' between 40°F (4°C) and 140°F (60°C), where bacteria start to grow and multiply at a rapid rate. If you take a piece of meat out of your fridge (where it comfortably sat in the cold holding zone) and place it on the counter, it will take hours to actually come up to the ambient temperature of the room, and most of that time it'll be sitting in the danger zone. In fact, the core of the meat still won't reach room temperature at all. So, the idea of letting meat come up to room temperature isn't just ineffective – it's unsafe.

DON'T COOK IT STRAIGHT FROM THE FRIDGE

I try to avoid cooking meat straight from the fridge unless I'm short on time. Cooking it cold can drop your pan's surface temperature and cause internal moisture to release as steam. If your pan can't recover temperature quickly enough, that steam prevents you from developing a brown crust. The only exception is cooking on an exceptionally hot surface that can instantly vaporize water – something most home stoves just cannot manage. Until then, you're steaming, not searing.

THE SWEET SPOT

However, you should still take any meat you plan on searing out of the fridge about 20 minutes before cooking. As it sits, it will accumulate condensation on the surface from ambient humidity in the air, so you must pat it dry with a paper towel before you cook it. That's the key! This will help knock the chill off the surface, allowing the Maillard reaction to get rolling faster. And 20 minutes isn't long enough to push the meat into unsafe territory.

RESTING MEAT

We have long been taught that resting meat after cooking is a crucial step to retain the most moisture.

WHAT HAPPENS TO MEAT DURING COOKING?

Science tells us that as meat heats, the proteins within muscle fibers progressively denature, changing their structure. Myosin denatures first, causing fibers to shrink lengthways and squeeze out some of the immobilized water in the muscle. As temperatures climb and actin denatures, fibers contract in multiple directions, forcing out even more moisture. The connective tissue surrounding the fibers also contracts with heat, adding to the pressure that expels water.

WHAT HAPPENS DURING RESTING?

Resting meat after cooking falls into the realm of culinary technique rather than meat science, so there's not much formal research on the topic. Of the papers that do address it, there are conflicting results. One study that used beef (inside round cut) found that resting made no difference to moisture retention, whereas a Danish study that used pork, beef and veal loins found a higher amount of meat juices after a resting period.

Outside the lab, many chefs now believe the benefits of resting are really about carryover cooking and final target temperature, not juice redistribution. It seems we were focusing on time when perhaps we should have been focusing on temperature.

In my personal experience, resting meat does improve texture and appearance. We know that when it comes to Texas-style brisket, extended resting is crucial to the texture of the slice, and completely unrelated to the water content. So, while I cannot yet share the 'why' with you, I definitely prefer to rest my meat after cooking.

I rest proportionate to the cook time – for hot and fast steaks, perhaps 5–8 minutes, for large roasts, 15–20 minutes. And for long, low and slow cooks like brisket, you can rest for hours at a time. But truthfully, this is more holding than resting, and we'll talk about that more in the recipes.

SLICING MEAT

Cutting across the grain.

Cutting with the grain.

The easiest way to instantly make your meat more tender is to cut it against the grain. It's kinda crazy to think that one single action can have such a huge influence on the tenderness and enjoyment factor of your meat.

To understand why this is important, we're going to strip it right down to the building blocks of muscle structure. Singular muscle fibers are bundled together to form fascicles. These fascicles are then also bundled together to make even bigger bundles that make up the muscle –like a meaty fiber-optic cable. All these long strands of muscle fibers run together like long, meaty highways. If you took a knife and cut in the same direction (with the grain) as the fibers, the knife would have very little work to do, but when you then tried to eat that piece, your teeth and jaw would have more work to do, chewing through the still-intact fibers.

On the other hand, if you cut across the strands (against the grain), your knife would do the major work of severing the fibers. And when you take a bite, your teeth would feel less resistance, so you'd perceive it as being way more tender!

Of course, this whole 'how to slice' ethos only really applies to steaks, where you'd typically eat a larger piece, and becomes redundant when you finely dice meat (think taco fillings).

The top piece has been sliced against the grain, clearly showing the separation of the muscle bundles. The bottom piece is cut with the grain, in the same direction as the muscle fibers.

STORE IT

So, what happens when you're not cooking it? That's where smart storage comes in. Whether you're holding meat for a day, a week or a year, how you store it will make all the difference to how it tastes and feels when you finally cook or reheat it.

VACUUM-SEALING

One of the best tools you can invest in for home (and they're not actually that expensive) is a vacuum sealer. You don't have to be into ranching, homesteading or survivalism to get value from one, and they're far more useful than you might think.

Most bacteria on meat that cause spoilage need oxygen to grow, and vacuum-sealing removes that oxygen. It also slows oxidation (the cause of browning and rancid flavors) and helps meat hold on to its moisture. Without oxygen present, spoilage and oxidation are drastically slowed, which means vacuum-sealing buys you significantly more storage time in the fridge.

While a steak in paper or on a foam tray might only last 3–5 days before quality starts to drop, a vacuum-sealed steak can sit in the fridge for up to two weeks and still be in great shape. In fact, it's often even more tender by the time you're ready to use it (see the section on Aging on page 45).

Some situations where vacuum-sealing comes in handy:

- Portioning homemade bacon (page 68)
- Storing homemade jerky (page 168)
- Stocking up on meat when it's on sale: portion it to suit your use, vacuum-seal it and buy yourself a couple of weeks.
- Can't cook that roast tonight? Vacuum-seal it and keep it in the fridge or freezer until you're ready.

The only real downside to vacuum-sealing is a slight increase in moisture loss, known as drip loss, caused by the negative pressure of the vacuum. It's generally minimal, and a small trade-off for the extended shelf life and quality.

Vacuum-sealing is also fantastic for protecting meat in the freezer. Let's talk more about that ...

FREEZING

One of the best ways to store both raw and cooked meat is to freeze it. Freezing hits pause on the aging (and decaying) process, holding meat in a suspended state. It's preservation in action!

A common misconception is that meat in the freezer 'goes bad' after a certain amount of time. In reality, if it's kept consistently below 0°F (-18°C), meat can be held indefinitely without becoming 'unsafe.' It's tragic to think of all the perfectly good cuts that have been tossed because of this myth (and I say that as someone who recently ate an eight-year-old frozen steak).

The real concern with frozen meat isn't safety; it's quality. Over time, freezing can cause changes in texture, moisture and flavor. From a meat science perspective, freezing is a double-edged sword: it can improve tenderness, but it can also reduce water-holding capacity. The extent of these changes depends on the size and distribution of ice crystals formed during freezing. Many meat processors use flash or blast freezers, which chill meat extremely quickly and form smaller ice crystals. These cause less damage to muscle structure during thawing, so quality is better preserved than with the slower freezing that happens in a home freezer.

HOW FREEZING CAN AFFECT QUALITY

1. **Ice crystal formation:** Imagine tiny ice daggers forming inside the muscle fibers. They can physically break down structure (which works just like manual tenderization), improving tenderness but reducing juiciness.
2. **Freezer burn:** Extreme dehydration that causes discolored, firm patches. Safe to eat, but unpleasant.
3. **Lipid oxidation:** Fats can oxidize over long storage, creating rancid flavors. Still safe, but not enjoyable.

You can't completely prevent large ice crystal formation without specialty equipment, but you can manage the other two. If you find freezer-burned spots, simply trim them away before cooking.

MEAT SCIENCE

Meat science is a fascinating field that studies everything about meat. It covers how animals are raised and harvested, how muscle turns into meat and how meat is processed, stored and cooked. Ultimately, the field of meat science seeks to understand and improve meat quality and safety.

Meat scientists can be found in the classroom and major product development centers throughout the world.

A lot of people don't even realize meat science is a 'thing.' I didn't either, until I was invited to visit Texas A&M University's Meat Science department for the first time. Dr Jeff Savell was hosting a Friday class for freshmen called Barbecue 101. I drove down to College Station, walked into the classroom and watched as they rolled a whole side of beef into the room on a butcher's rail.

As the professors talked about brisket and showed where it came from on the carcass, I had a lightbulb moment – there was so much more to live-fire cooking than just the cooking itself. There was a whole world that explained the how and why of the raw product. That moment sparked my fascination with meat science, and I'm thrilled to share some of that world with y'all here.

WHAT QUALIFIES AS MEAT SCIENCE

Meat science uses controlled, repeatable methods to study everything about meat, from the animals it came from to how it is processed. Conclusions are drawn from data gathered under clearly defined and disclosed conditions, then analyzed and published in reputable journals as peer-reviewed research papers. Science is not absolute, but the only thing that can disprove it is better science. This is what separates formal scientific findings from one-off observations.

PEER REVIEWING

Peer reviewing is quality control. It's where other qualified experts evaluate a study before it's published. They scrutinize and check the methods, data and conclusions for accuracy, logic and reproducibility, and can request changes or reject the paper outright if it doesn't meet standards. This process helps ensure the research is credible.

WHAT IS NOT MEAT SCIENCE

Home experiments are not definitive meat science. Whether it's a viral social media cook or a well-known culinary website, most so-called experiments are still home cooking sessions, not scientific studies. They lack controlled environments, use uncalibrated, basic equipment, and skip repeat testing, which are the fundamentals of any real study. Without those controls, the results are just personal observations, not proven facts.

While meat science does address some aspects of cooking, many cooking-related meat topics fall under culinary technique, outside the boundaries of scientific research. So for questions like 'how to best cook a steak,' there are no definitive answers, just a variety of different approaches.

THE SCIENCE OF MEAT COLOR

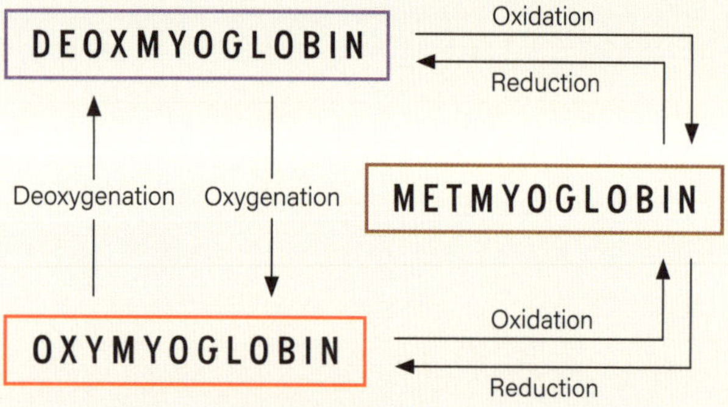

The most important thing you will learn in this section is that the color of meat does not indicate spoilage.

It sounds freaky, but from a chemical perspective, meat lives on past the point of slaughter. The cells that make up meat can still undergo biochemical and enzymatic changes, and the most obvious example of this is changing meat color.

The color of meat is determined by myoglobin, a protein that lies within the tissue cells. Myoglobin has a lifecycle of colors it can circle through, sometimes moving from one back to another. The change is most prominent in red meat.

In low oxygen, the meat pigment myoglobin is in a state called deoxymyoglobin, which gives meat a darker, purplish color. When the meat is exposed to air, oxygen binds to the pigment and it 'blooms' into oxymyoglobin, turning the meat bright red. Over time, normal exposure to oxygen causes the pigment to change again into metmyoglobin, which appears brown or grey. Early on (within 2–5 days of slaughter), meat can move back and forth between these color states, but as it ages and its natural reducing processes slow down, the change becomes permanent and the color stays brown.

Oxymyoglobin is also why we see a phenomenon called 'bloom.' When you cut into a freshly cooked medium-rare steak, you'll notice that the meat will intensify in red color as it sits on your plate. That's the oxygen working to convert the myoglobin into oxymyoglobin!

Color can also be influenced by other factors like the animal's age, species, diet and the type of muscle fiber. Meat from older animals is generally darker (veal is light pink while beef is more deeply red). There is also variation from one muscle to another, and the depth of color is usually determined by how much of a workout that muscle gets. That's why you can cut a cross-section of a pork shoulder, for example, and see both light and dark pink muscle types.

It's totally normal for there to be some change in meat color as you store it after purchase.

You can't rely on color alone to determine the freshness of your meat, so when in doubt, use your sense of smell. There's also an exception here, too. It's normal for some vacuum-sealed meats to have a slightly sour smell when they first come out of the bag, and with 5–10 minutes of sitting out in the air, this smell dissipates. Generally, meat shouldn't have any discernible odor at all, but meat that has spoiled will have a noticeably putrid smell.

To dive a little deeper into meat color, check out Troubleshoot It (page 48), which explains things like why your ground meat can be red on the outside but brown in the middle.

WATER-HOLDING CAPACITY

Muscle is made up of about 75% water. One of the most important attributes in meat quality is its ability to retain water, even when external pressures (gravity, cooking, etc.) are applied to it. This is known as water-holding capacity (or WHC). Water is what contributes to the 'juiciness' of meat and is a really important quality attribute.

Meat with good water-holding capacity keeps the water inside, staying juicier and losing less weight during cooking. Meat with poor water-holding capacity 'purges' moisture during storage and dries out faster when you cook it.

Water is locked into the muscle in different ways:

- **Bound water** (<5%) is tightly held at a molecular level. This water is basically glued in place and won't be lost under normal freezing or cooking.
- **Immobilized water** (~85%) is the water held in place by the muscle's structure and the slight natural electrical charge of its proteins (more on this shortly). This is the water lost during cooking.
- **Free water** (10%) is not bound or trapped, just hanging out in the crevices. This is the water most likely to be lost or seep out in the package. This is the water lost in cutting.

WHC is strongly connected to the pH of the meat. Muscle proteins like actin and myosin carry a net electrical charge, which repel each other slightly (kinda like the ends of a magnet pushing each other away). This charge creates space within the muscle structure – a perfect place for water to sit.

After slaughter, glycogen (the energy reserve of the muscle) is broken down into lactic acid, causing the meat's neutral pH to drop. As the pH approaches the isoelectric point of muscle proteins (which is 5.1), the proteins lose their net electrical charge and shift closer together, forcing water out of the space – much like wringing out a wet sponge! The closer the PH gets to 5.1, the lower the WHC. So, the aim is for the pH to decline steadily and stabilize at the ultimate pH further away from that isoelectric 'squeeze zone.'

But it's not just about the final number. The speed at which the pH drops has a massive impact on quality. If the pH drops too quickly while the carcass is still warm, it can create PSE (pale, soft and exudative) meat that is spongy and can't hold water. When the pH drops too slowly and stays above 6.0, it produces DFD (dark, firm and dry) meat. This meat feels sticky to the touch and holds onto its water so tightly that the surface looks dark and dry because no moisture is escaping, resulting in an odd, tight texture.

Though the pH change is a main factor in influencing WHC, there are also other factors that influence it, including animal stress, rigor mortis and processing methods.

For more on WHC, check out Brining (page 28) and Marination (page 30).

AGING

Aging is the act of holding meat for extended periods at refrigerated temperatures. It may seem counterintuitive, but when it comes to meat, fresher isn't always better. In meat, aging is employed to improve tenderness, and it works via the process of enzymatic autolysis (which is a nice way of saying 'controlled decomposition').

The moment an animal is slaughtered, its muscles begin a conversion into meat. Oxygen supply to the muscles ceases, which depletes cellular energy. As that energy runs out, protein bridges made up of actin-myosin form and tightly lock the muscle into a contracted state. That is what we call rigor mortis, and it makes the meat stiff and tough. Aging is a way to offset the stiffness of rigor, and tenderize meat.

Over time, aging allows natural enzymes, including a key group called calpains, to break down structural proteins. It's not breaking those actin-myosin bonds, per se, but rather softening the structure around them. This loosening reduces resistance and makes the meat less chewy and more tender.

Research tells us that aging will have the greatest effect on meat when done for 14–28 days, and it is also more noticeably effective on lower-quality beef. Since aging is primarily used for tenderness, it is not necessary for any cuts where the cooking method will also be a form of tenderization. For example, brisket is cooked for many hours until tenderness is achieved, so aging is redundant.

You'll notice it's almost always beef that gets aged. That's because beef varies the most in tenderness among the common proteins. Lamb, pork, chicken and veal are all a younger age, and potentially tender to begin with, and it usually takes bad cooking to make them tough!

Aging can be split into two main categories: dry and wet.

DRY-AGING

Dry-aging is both simple and complex. At its most basic, dry-aging is just leaving beef uncovered in a fridge. Even sides of beef hanging in a chiller after slaughter are actively aging, though this is just carcass aging. Specialty dry-aging takes place in carefully controlled environments with precise temperature and humidity levels to limit the growth of bacteria that cause spoilage.

As the meat ages, water evaporates, and there can be a significant loss of volume as the entire piece begins to shrink. Extended dry-aging forms a tough rind (sometimes called a pellicle) on the outside of the meat, which needs to be trimmed away. Because of the extended trimming, dry-aging is best suited to large pieces of bone-in meat like subprimals, rather than smaller cuts. And if you try to age a single steak, you'd probably end up with a mere sliver of usable meat after trimming.

Meat that has been dry-aged for an extended period, once the rind is cut away, is usually a deeper, darker red in color (because of the water loss), and will also cook a little faster. Because the meat is also firmer, it can be deceptive in terms of 'doneness', and will not spring back to the touch like a typical steak would.

While dry-aging is primarily about increasing tenderness, specialty dry-aging also enhances the flavor of the beef in several different ways:

- **The introduction of desirable bacteria and molds creates a unique microflora in the aging chamber (similar to blue cheese).**
- **Proteolysis (the breakdown of peptides into amino acids) leads to an increased concentration of free amino acids and compounds, which are significant flavor contributors to beef.**
- **The evaporation of water from within the muscle increases the flavor concentration.**

In recent years, dry-aging has become extremely popular at high-end steakhouses, and a variety of home dry-aging units have proliferated in the market. Mishandling and undertrimming of the dry-aged meat can lead to foodborne illness, and should only be attempted by those with some training in food safety practices. Messing with molds can also be potentially hazardous (due to microbial contamination), and the only way to know for sure if your microflora is safe is to have it tested. It's important to note that while bacteria can be cooked to a safe level, some molds remain toxic even with extended cooking. All that to say – don't just throw some ribeyes into your home fridge!

DRY-AGING TIME

Now, a word on aging time claims: when you see a steak labeled '30-day dry-aged,' don't assume that number is a universal flavor profile. In reality, a 30-day steak from your local butcher can taste completely different from a 30-day steak from a commercial distributor. This is because aging time is only one part of the story; the environment dictates the outcome. How fast the meat loses moisture depends on the setup: a massive commercial room packed with beef dries the meat slowly, while a single steak in a small locker evaporates moisture much faster.

The flavor is shaped by the 'microclimate,' too. A room rich with natural, beneficial molds will produce a deep, nutty funk completely different to a sterile fridge where UV lights zap all the microflora.

So, while '30 days' sounds like a precise measurement, it's more like a ballpark. If you want to better understand the variations between 30-, 45- or 60-day aging, it's as simple as trying to taste as many different kinds as you can. You'll quickly realize that the calendar is just a guide – it's the character of the specific fridge that actually ends up on your plate.

WET-AGING

Wet-aging is far more commonly practiced than dry, and is super accessible for anyone to do in their own home. The process of vacuum- or wet-aging was introduced in the 1970s and became widespread with the development of various vacuum films. The term 'wet-aging' simply refers to a product that is vacuum-packed, and therefore 'wet' from sitting in its own liquids. Any piece of vacuum-sealed meat is technically wet-aging right in the bag. The process is also significantly cheaper than dry-aging, not just because you don't need large specialty fridges, but because there's no shrinkage loss from water evaporating.

Wet-aged meat can have a pale, unappealing appearance and a sour smell when first debagged, but when exposed to air, oxymyoglobin is allowed to form. As a result, the meat will start to return to its signature red color, and the smell will dissipate. The downside to wet-aging is that because the product sits in its own 'juices' (find out more about those juices in Troubleshoot It on page 48), it can retain a minerally/serumy taste.

While dry-aged meat can be pushed to experimental limits, wet-aging has a natural limitation. If aged for too long, the proteins start denaturing and the meat can develop an unpleasantly mushy texture. Research suggests there is no significant benefit to wet-aging beyond 21–28 days.

Some modern variations on dry-aging are also starting to gain popularity. Many specialty butchers and high-end steakhouses use tallow to seal cut or 'facing' surfaces, allowing the bone and fat to create a natural protective layer that reduces trim loss and dramatically slows evaporation. Some go further and coat the entire subprimal in tallow, effectively sealing it in fat, though at that point, it's really more of a hybrid process than true dry-aging.

Aging should always take place in refrigerated conditions to keep the meat safe, but it's worth noting that the process pauses when frozen. If you place a vacuum-sealed steak in the freezer, enzymatic activity stops. And when you thaw it and return it to the fridge, the aging will actually resume.

QUICK COMPARISON CHART

WET-AGING	DRY-AGING
As simple as vacuum-sealing the meat.	Requires a depth of knowledge, possible microbial growth testing and dedicated fridges.
Lower price point, no loss of product during aging.	Higher price point and significant shrinkage during the aging process.
Can develop an unpleasant texture and minerally/serumy flavors if aged for too long.	Can develop deeper and more complex 'connoisseur-level' flavors with extended aging.
Primarily influences tenderness, with a minor effect on taste.	Can equally influence tenderness and taste, depending on the methodology.
Suited to individual cuts like a single steak.	Recommended for larger subprimal pieces.

HARDCORE
CARNIVORE

TROUBLESHOOT IT

Sometimes meat just ... does strange things. It has its own quirks – most are harmless, some are worth understanding – but they can definitely leave you wondering what's going on. This section takes the mystery out of those moments, explaining why they happen and what they mean. It's your guide to understanding what's normal, what's fixable and when (and if) you should actually be concerned.

WHY IS GROUND MEAT RED ON THE OUTSIDE AND GREY ON THE INSIDE?

Have you ever bought a tray or block of ground meat (especially beef), and when you got it home and cracked it open, the center was greyish brown?! This sometimes happens with chunky burger patties, too. There are some wild theories around this, like the grocery store taking fresh meat and wrapping it around old stuff, but I'm gonna burst your conspiracy bubble: it's actually completely normal. And there's nothing wrong with the meat.

You've already read about meat color and myoglobin (page 44), so you now know that meat can cycle through different color phases. When meat is ground, all of it is briefly exposed to oxygen, leading to the formation of oxymyoglobin, so it starts to turn red. But once it's shaped into patties or bricks for packaging, the meat in the middle doesn't get as much oxygen anymore. That low-oxygen environment encourages the formation of deoxymyoglobin, so the outside stays red while the inside can look brown.

WHY ARE THERE WEIRD SLIME BUBBLES ON MY BURGER?

Sometimes burgers can get weird, slimy bubbles bursting through the surface as they cook (I've even heard them referred to as burger pimples). It's actually a mixture of water, soluble protein (including albumin, the same protein in egg whites) and some fat. It's kind of like a meat geyser. As the patty heats from the bottom, water inside turns to steam, and once the bottom starts to sear, that steam pushes its way up and out. It might look a little odd, but it's completely safe to eat. To reduce bubbling, pat your patties dry before cooking, use freshly ground meat (not from a chub or roll) and avoid overcrowding the pan so moisture can evaporate more easily.

DOES PINK NEAR CHICKEN BONES MEAN IT'S RAW?

It's good to be cautious about food safety and thorough cooking when it comes to chicken, but seeing pink bones or pink meat near the bones doesn't always mean the meat is undercooked. Pigment from bone marrow can leach out and stain the meat around it, and this is particularly common with previously frozen or injected chicken. Marrow pigment can stay reddish-pink until it's heated past 180°F (82°C), well above the point where chicken is safely cooked. So as long as your thermometer reads at least 165°F (73°C), your chicken is safe to eat, even if the bones and surrounding meat are still rosy.

WHAT EXACTLY IS FREEZER BURN?

Noticing grey or discolored patches on some of your frozen meat? It's probably just freezer burn, caused by a process called sublimation, where ice turns straight into water vapor. It essentially causes the meat to dehydrate, resulting in dry, leathery patches. You'll notice it most when you have damaged, thin or unsealed packaging, but it can also happen when food is stored in the freezer for too long. The most important thing to remember is that you don't have to throw it out! Freezer burn is safe to eat; it's really only a quality issue, so you can just trim those spots away and the rest is good to go.

WHAT'S THE RED 'JUICE' COMING OUT OF THE MEAT?

One of the most common meat misconceptions is that any reddish liquid that seeps out of meat is blood. Whether we are talking about the juice that drips onto your plate from a cooked steak, or the liquid that sometimes pools in a vacuum-sealed bag (known as 'purge'), it is most certainly not 'blood.' Instead, it's mostly water mixed with myoglobin (that's the protein that gives meat its color, and you can read all about it on page 44).

WHY CAN I SEE A RAINBOW ON THE SURFACE OF SOME MEAT?

Ever noticed that thin slices of roast beef or turkey sometimes have a strange rainbow sheen? You might think it's due to dye or chemicals, or maybe a sign the meat has gone bad, but it's actually just an optical effect called iridescence, where light hits the surface and reflects back in different colors (kind of like a soap bubble). This happens most often with deli meats because they are made from tough, dense muscle fibers. When sliced thinly and cleanly, these fibers scatter light into a rainbow.

WHAT'S THE WHITE STUFF COMING OUT OF MY BACON WHILE I COOK IT?

When you pan-fry bacon, it's common to see a white ooze appear on the slices as they cook. It's not the most appetizing sight – it can look like bits of egg white – which makes sense, because it's made of the same type of protein (albumin). This white 'purge' is a mix of water, salt, liquefied fat and protein that is expelled during cooking as the proteins coagulate. It's often associated with 'pumped' bacon, the kind made on a commercial scale that's injected with brine to cure it as quickly as possible. It's completely safe to eat, but if you hate the visual, you can just wipe it away with a paper towel as it cooks.

I FULLY COOKED MY BURGER, SO WHY IS IT STILL PINK IN THE MIDDLE?

This phenomenon, called persistent pinking, refers to beef that stays pink even when it's fully cooked to well-done temperatures. Despite the appearance, it's not actually raw, but rather, the color is 'locked in' in a pink state. This is more common in meat with a higher natural pH level, but it can also be triggered or intensified by nitrogen oxides released from gas ovens or charcoal grills. As long as you use a meat thermometer to ensure the temperature reaches 160°F (71°C), it's safe to eat.

I SAW SOMEONE WASHING CHICKEN WITH DISH SOAP. SHOULD I DO THAT?

Some people rinse chicken because they believe it 'washes away' bacteria. In reality, scientific studies prove that washing chicken, even with lemon or vinegar, doesn't remove harmful pathogens like salmonella. In fact, food safety agencies advise against washing chicken because the practice is more likely to spread germs. Cooking is what makes the meat safe to eat, and proper temperatures will kill the bacteria (page 35). If you're trying to get rid of the 'slimy' surface (which is actually just wet protein), it's safer to simply pat it dry with a paper towel. And please – never, ever use dish soap.

PREFERRED GEAR

I get asked about my cooking setup all the time, so I wanted to share what I use most in my own (indoor and outdoor) home kitchen.

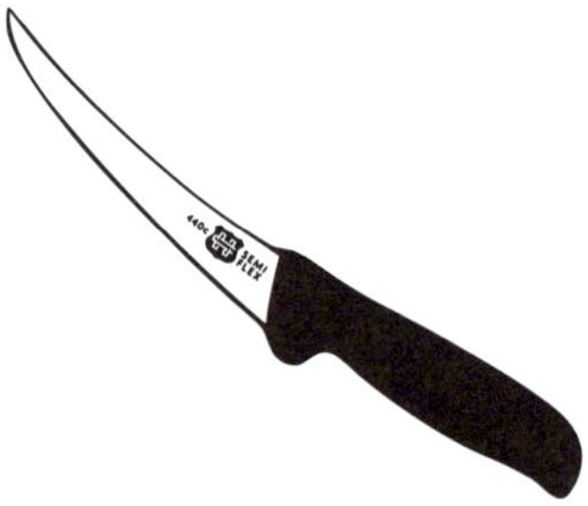

KNIVES

I'm sure it's no surprise that the knives I use the most are Hardcore Carnivore brand, because I literally created them based on what I prefer to work with. The 6-inch (15 cm) semi-flex boning knife is probably reached for more than anything else. I use a German steel 8-inch (20 cm) chef's knife as my primary, and have some very special reclaimed steel knives made by Texas Sage Forge and Iron Grove Tool Co. I am awful at sharpening knives, but I keep forcing myself to get better at it, and prefer to use a whetstone.

THERMOMETER

A good thermometer is another non-negotiable. Cheap ones are often inaccurate and end up being more frustrating than helpful. I recommend investing in a quick-read thermometer you can trust (I use Thermapen), because one solid purchase is worth far more than a heap of overcooked meat.

SPLATTER GUARD

There are a few tools and essentials I keep coming back to in my own kitchen, and while none of them are complicated, they make a world of difference. A splatter guard, for instance, is one of those simple mesh covers that sits over the skillet, and it's worth its weight in gold if you like cooking over high heat but hate the mess that follows. It won't make you love cleaning up, but it will definitely soothe your inner neat-freak.

VACUUM SEALER

A vacuum sealer is a big investment, but it earns its place quickly. I've already covered it in detail (page 42), but the short version is this: it will change the way you freeze food, dramatically improve the quality of your stored left-overs and allow you to experiment with wet-aging at home.

KITCHENWARE

In Australia, I learned to cook with an electric wall oven. I really struggled with the predominantly gas ovens in the US as they're less even in heat distribution, and much more finicky. So, I will always choose an electric when given an option. I buy cheap enameled Dutch ovens (because they're still sturdy), but spend money on cast iron. I use the Yeti skillets – they will last you a lifetime – and I season them with Crisbee Cream Iron. I always prep raw meat on a plastic board, and only use wood boards for cooked meat.

HEAVY-DUTY FOIL

Then there are the basics you don't usually think about until you've had the bad version. Heavy-duty foil, for example. Skip the flimsy stuff and just buy the quality roll. It's the same principle as cheap toilet paper … you'll only make that mistake once.

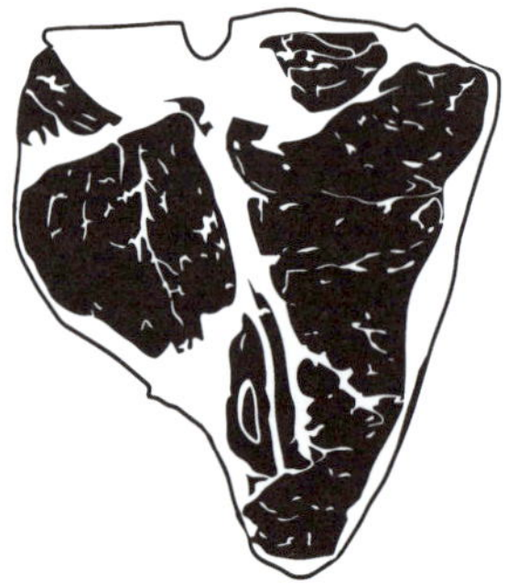

MEAT

Truthfully, the majority of the meat I purchase comes from H-E-B in Texas (arguably the greatest grocery store on earth). It's close, convenient and accessible, but also has an incredible selection, and if they don't have a certain cut, they will order it for you. H-E-B also generously supplied all the meat for the cookbook images.

I hunt my own venison and dove, but when it comes to other wild game, Hudson Meat Market in Austin is a great resource. For specialty steaks, I often order from smaller, boutique ranches or distributors like Herd & Grace (online) or Lone Star Meats (foodservice in Austin). And wherever possible, I'll try to source Aussie lamb.

OUTDOOR COOKERS

I have an assortment of grills for different occasions. Everything I cook in my backyard is fired by charcoal or wood (except for my griddle). It just tastes better that way! My primary is a PK Grill 360, and I use it most of the time. I also cook on a Pitts & Spitts Maverick pellet grill, Pitts & Spitts offset smoker and Chud Box. For charcoal, my go-to is always Kingsford Original.

HARDCORE CARNIVORE SEASONINGS

And yes, I use my own Hardcore Carnivore seasonings regularly (with some clear favorites). You may notice they're not written into most of the recipes here – and that's intentional. I wanted this book to be a true standalone guide, useful to anyone, anywhere, without relying on special products. That said, if you're familiar with Hardcore Carnivore, you'll have no trouble spotting the recipes where one of the rubs would take things to the next level.

PORK SHOULDER BUTT

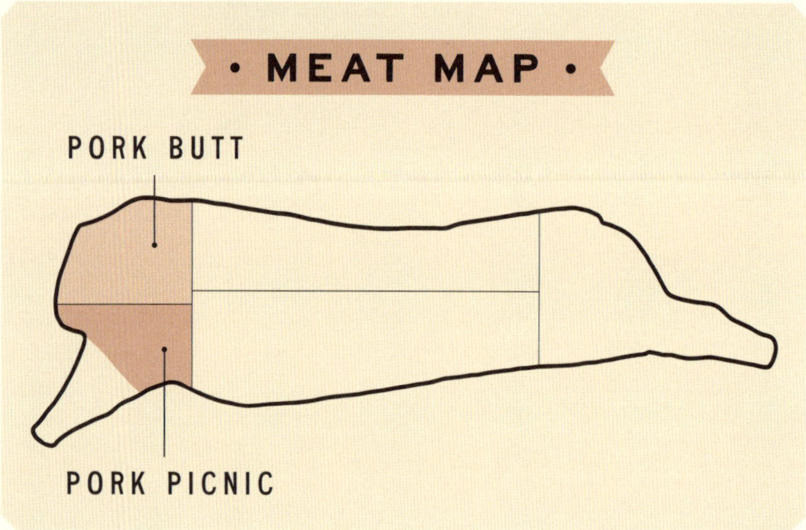

Let's just address the awkwardness upfront ... the pork butt is not the rear end of the pig. In fact, it's cut from the opposite end, up in the shoulder.

It's commonly accepted that the name 'Boston butt' originated from colonial New England, where inexpensive cuts like shoulder were packed into large wooden storage barrels (aka 'butts'). BBQ historian Robert Moss tends to disagree, having found no historical references to this name at any time during the colonial period, nor in the years that followed. He hypothesizes that since 'butt' is simply a term that refers to any large or thicker part of something, in this case, it meant the thicker end of the pig's shoulder.

Much like the beef chuck, the pork shoulder houses a jumble of different muscles, some tougher than others, and some more flavorful than others. Overall, it's a cut that needs to be cooked long, low and slow. But as with any cut of meat that is on the tough side, you can always slice it thinly to cook it quickly as I have done with my Night Market Skewers with Lemongrass (page 62).

Pork butt is cut from high on the shoulder, just above the picnic. The two cuts are quite similar, though the picnic often includes the hock, has slightly less fat and contains more connective tissue. While the picnic isn't as commonly found in stores or butcher shops, it can easily be substituted in any pork butt recipe in this book – and it's often more affordable, too.

As for the butt itself, it's home to a host of other cuts, so let's check them out.

Inside this versatile shoulder piece you can find the following cuts:

BOSTON BUTT: An alternative name for the pork butt.

BONELESS BUTT: Literally the same as the butt, with the scapula removed. Though the butt will be lighter with the bone removed, you will always pay more if the butcher does more work, so boneless butts tend to be more expensive.

BONE-IN PORK STEAKS: Also known as pork forequarter chops, they use a bandsaw to slice through the bone and create steaks that can be cut thin or thick (the thick, chunky ones are great for low-and-slow cooking).

PORK COLLAR/PORK SCOTCH/COLLAR BUTT: This is a smaller portion of the whole butt, roughly one-third of the whole piece. It's also the same collection of muscles that is used to make dry-cured coppa.

CELLAR TRIM/CELLAR TRIMMED: An American cut specification where the boneless pork butt is further trimmed of lean muscle and fat overlying the shoulder blade.

COLLAR BUTT STEAKS: Boneless steaks cut from the collar.

COUNTRY-STYLE RIBS: Shockingly, country-style ribs aren't ribs at all. And they're not even cut from the rib primal. They're just thin strips cut from the pork butt or the blade end of the pork loin. Sometimes they are 'bone-in', where the 'ribs' may contain a piece of the scapula (shoulder blade bone).

PORK SHOULDER BUTT

• MEAT NERD FACT •

The most winningest muscle in competition BBQ

Ever heard of the money muscle? It's perhaps the most prized part of the pork butt, revered by competition barbecuers worldwide. This muscle is trimmed out from the butt, smoked to perfection, then gently pulled and tucked into the presentation boxes, ready for judging. Supposedly, this is the best part of the butt, and using it can help you win competitions and prize money. Hence the name 'money muscle.'

But the thing is, the money muscle is not one single muscle but rather a tube-shaped collection of several muscles. It's the same collection that capocollo/coppa (a dry-cured Italian delicacy) is made from.

It takes a steady hand and some practice to seam out the money muscle as it can be hard to figure out where to stop cutting and trimming back. But if you want to get started and know where to find it, just look for the 'tiger stripe' muscle on one side of the pork butt. The one that kinda looks like the diagonal stripes on an old-school barber's pole. That's the *semispinalis capitis* muscle, and the very outer edge of the money muscle!

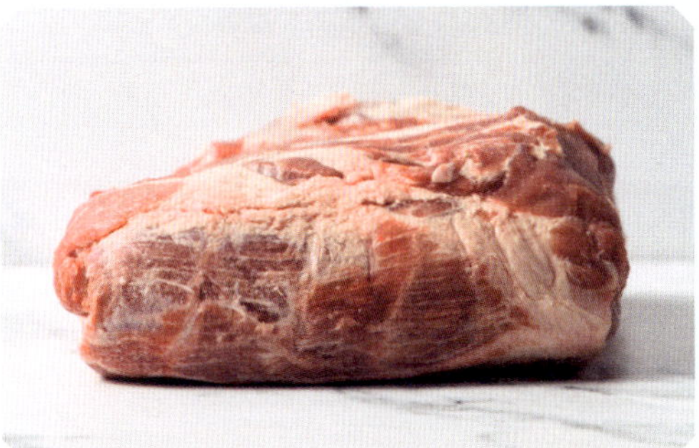

POZOLE ROJO WITH TOASTED HOMINY

SERVES 8–10

This stew is known as *pozole*, which is the Spanish word for hominy, a plump and tender corn kernel that has been nixtamalized (a soaking process that uses an alkaline solution to remove the outer hull). I was first introduced to this comforting, brothy stew during a Texas winter (which usually only lasts a month or two), but this Mexican staple is served year-round, especially for holidays and celebrations.

STEW

3 lb (1.3 kg) boneless pork butt/shoulder

2 tablespoons lard or olive oil

8 cups (2 liters) water

½ onion

1 tablespoon salt

6 garlic cloves

2 bay leaves

2 x 30 oz (850 g) cans hominy (white or yellow)

CHILI SAUCE

6 guajillo chilies

2 ancho chilies

3 chile de árbol (optional)

4 garlic cloves

1 teaspoon salt

2 cloves

1 teaspoon dried Mexican oregano or regular oregano

¼ teaspoon ground cumin

GARNISHES

Shredded cabbage, fresh radishes, diced avocado, queso fresco, crushed tortilla chips, chopped onion, lime wedges, scallions (spring onions), fresh chili slices, etc.

1. Cut the pork into medium-sized pieces, about 2 inches (5 cm).
2. Heat a heavy-based pot (like a Dutch oven) over high heat. Add the lard and allow to melt, then brown the pork, working in batches to avoid overcrowding.
3. After the final batch is done, pour ½ cup (125 ml) water into the pot and scrape up all the browned bits from the bottom. Return all the pork to the pot, then pour in the remaining water. It should cover the pork completely, so add more as needed. Add the onion, salt, garlic and bay leaves.
4. Bring to a boil, then reduce the heat to a simmer. During the first 20 minutes of cooking, use a spoon to scoop off and discard any scum that rises to the surface. Simmer the pork for 2–3 hours until completely tender.
5. For the chili sauce, remove the stems and seeds from the chilies, then place them into a heatproof container. Cover with hot water and allow to steep for 10–15 minutes until the chilies are softened.
6. Place the chilies into a blender along with ½ cup (125 ml) soaking water, and add the garlic, salt, cloves, oregano and cumin. Blend until smooth, then set aside.
7. Prepare the hominy by draining and rinsing under cold water. Lay the kernels out on a paper towel and pat dry. Spread the hominy out on a sheet pan (baking sheet) in a single layer, then place under a broiler (oven grill) on high for 4–8 minutes to blister and char. Allow to cool until it's time to add it to the stew.
8. Once the pork is tender, remove and discard the onion, garlic and bay leaves from the pot.
9. Using a slotted spoon, transfer the pork from the broth to a board. Shred the meat with your hands using heatproof gloves, or use two forks.
10. Pour the chili sauce into the broth through a strainer, using a spatula to force through as much as possible.
11. Return the meat to the pot, along with the hominy, and stir everything together. Simmer over low heat for an additional 30–60 minutes to let all the flavors mingle together.
12. Serve with the fresh garnishes so everyone can customize their preferred toppings. (I like adding them all!)

YETI

LOW-AND-SLOW PORK STEAKS WITH S'CHUG

SERVES 2–4

This is my interpretation of BBQ icon Tootsie Tomanetz's legendary pork steaks, which she serves every Saturday morning at Snow's BBQ in Lexington, Texas. Clay Cowgill, another pitmaster at Snow's, shared that one of the secrets to their tender/crispy steaks is a six-hour cook over direct coals, and a lard-laden mop sauce. The tricky part is that their industrial cooker has the meat sitting at least 24 inches (60 cm) away from the coals, which is way more distance than you find on a backyard grill, so I have adapted a recipe for home cooks. Although completely untraditional, I love serving these with a bright, spicy and herbaceous Israeli hot sauce called s'chug, which cuts through the smoky richness.

S'CHUG

6 jalapeños

1 bunch cilantro (coriander)

1 bunch flat-leaf parsley

3 garlic cloves

½ teaspoon ground cardamom

¾ teaspoon ground cumin

¼ teaspoon ground black pepper

½ teaspoon caraway seeds

1 teaspoon salt

2 tablespoons olive oil

MOP SAUCE

4 cups (1 liter) water

1 teaspoon onion powder

¼ cup (60 ml) white vinegar

2 tablespoons worcestershire sauce

2 tablespoons yellow mustard

2 tablespoons pork lard (see Notes)

PORK

1 teaspoon salt

2 teaspoons coarse black pepper

2 x 1.5 lb (680 g) thick-cut bone-in pork shoulder steaks

1. To make the s'chug, place all the ingredients into a blender and blend until smooth.
2. To make the mop sauce, place all the ingredients except the lard into a saucepan over low heat. Once the mixture is warm, add the lard and whisk until melted into the sauce. You will need to keep the pan warm to ensure the lard stays liquefied.
3. Preheat a smoker or pellet grill to 225°F (110°C).
4. To prepare the pork, combine the salt and black pepper in a bowl, then sprinkle generously over the pork steaks.
5. Place the pork steaks into the smoker and cook for 3 hours. Baste with the mop sauce every 30 minutes as they cook.
6. After 2 hours and 45 minutes, light half a chimney of charcoal. Once lit, place into a grill, scattering to create low-medium direct heat. The temperature of the grill should be around 225–250°F (110–115°C). You also need to keep the steaks as physically far from the coals as possible, so use a grill extender/expander rack if possible. They need to be sitting at least 12 inches (30 cm) away from the coals.
7. Remove the steaks from the smoker, place them directly above the coals on the grill, then close the lid. Cook for 60–90 minutes, mopping and turning the steaks every 20 minutes. Refill the charcoal as necessary to maintain the heat.
8. Serve the pork steaks with generous spoonfuls of s'chug.

NOTES

The steaks should be at least 1½ inches (4 cm) thick. They have a lot of cooking to do, so make sure they're nice and chunky. Unfortunately, you can't cut your own bone-in steaks without a bandsaw, but you can always buy a boneless pork butt and cut your own steaks.

Tootsie originally used lard in her mop, but later switched to butter. I wanted to bring back the full animal version, but you can sub the lard with butter or oil if you prefer.

If you don't have a small cotton BBQ mop to apply the mop sauce, just use a baster or silicone brush.

You need charcoal for this recipe to work. You will not get the same flavor or texture on a propane (gas) grill.

HICKORY-SMOKED PULLED PORK

SERVES 8–10

I shared a classic pulled pork recipe in my first book, *Hardcore Carnivore*, but it wouldn't feel right to cover pork butt without including one of its most iconic preparations. This is the traditional – and arguably best-tasting – smoked version, kissed by hickory smoke and flecked with lots of dark bark (see Notes).

- 8–10 lb (3.5–4.5 kg) bone-in pork butt
- ½ cup (125 g) yellow mustard
- 2 tablespoons brown sugar
- 4 teaspoons paprika
- 2 tablespoons salt
- 1 teaspoon ground black pepper
- ½ teaspoon ground cumin
- 2 teaspoons ground chili powder
- 1 teaspoon onion powder
- 2 teaspoons garlic powder
- 1 teaspoon mustard powder
- ⅓ cup (80 ml) apple cider vinegar
- ⅓ cup (80 ml) water
- 1–2 cups (160–320 g) BBQ sauce (optional)

1. Preheat a smoker or pellet grill loaded with hickory wood to 250°F (115°C). While it comes up to temperature, remove the pork from the fridge.
2. Use a knife to score the fat cap on the pork butt by making shallow cuts about 1 inch (2.5 cm) apart across the surface. Rotate the pork and repeat the cuts in the opposite direction to form a crosshatch pattern.
3. Spread the yellow mustard over the pork in a thin, even layer.
4. In a bowl, combine the sugar, paprika, salt, pepper, cumin, chili powder, onion powder, garlic powder and mustard powder. Stir with a spoon to blend evenly, then spread liberally all over the pork butt, being generous with the application so it's well coated.
5. Place the pork into the smoker to start the cooking process.
6. In a clean spray bottle, combine the vinegar and water and spritz the pork butt every 40–60 minutes as it cooks.
7. Smoke the pork until it reaches an internal temperature of 150–160°F (70–71°C). This will take 5–7 hours. By then, it will have developed a deep mahogany color.
8. Remove the pork from the smoker and wrap it tightly in two layers of foil, then return it to the smoker.
9. Cook for a further 3–4 hours, or until it reaches an internal temperature of 203–205°F (95–96°C).
10. Remove the pork from the smoker and rest for an hour. You can wrap it in a towel to insulate it while it rests, or put it into a cooler.
11. Unwrap the pork carefully and pour the juices into a cup or container.
12. Shred the meat with your hands using heatproof gloves, or use two forks.
13. Pour the reserved cooking liquid a little at a time onto the pork, tossing through until the meat is well saturated and nicely moist. Discard any remaining liquid. If desired, add BBQ sauce to taste and toss again to coat evenly.

NOTES

I like to start this recipe first thing in the morning to enjoy a pulled pork feast for dinner that night.

In BBQ terms, 'bark' refers to the dark outer crust that forms on smoked meat during low and slow cooking, and it's something pitmasters actively aim for.

When checking for internal temperature, avoid inserting the probe close to the bone as the reading can be inaccurate. Aim for the thickest part of the meat.

NIGHT MARKET SKEWERS WITH LEMONGRASS

MAKES 8 SKEWERS

Laden with ginger, garlic and lemongrass, the smell of these skewers cooking will whisk you away to a South-East Asian night market. I do have a secret and perhaps unexpected ingredient in this marinade – Sprite. The acid in the soda tenderizes the pork, while the sugar helps it to caramelize on the grill. It's a win/win. People are usually surprised to see pork butt grilled this way, but slicing your meat thin enough will tenderize even the toughest cut.

2 lb (1 kg) boneless pork butt (see Notes)
3 knobs fresh ginger
3 garlic cloves
2 stalks lemongrass
2 teaspoons salt
1 tablespoon fish sauce
1 shallot
2 cups (500 ml) Sprite or 7UP
2 limes, cut into wedges

MOP GLAZE

1 cup (250 ml) Sprite or 7UP
1 tablespoon soy sauce
1 teaspoon fish sauce
2 tablespoons peanut oil (see Notes)

1. Slice the pork into thin pieces. It's okay if the pieces aren't the same size, as long as they're no more than ¼ inch (6 mm) thick. Place into a large, non-reactive bowl and set aside.
2. Peel the ginger and place into a blender along with the garlic. Cut the woody green ends of the lemongrass and discard. Roughly chop the white bases and add to the blender with the salt, fish sauce and shallot. Blend until a rough paste forms. Pour in the Sprite, swirling around to loosen the paste, then pour the mixture over the sliced pork. Stir the marinade through the pork to make sure it's well coated, then refrigerate for 2–6 hours.
3. Light a grill for medium heat, about 350°F (175°C).
4. Remove the pork from the fridge and drain the marinade. Thread the pork slices onto skewers so they're tightly packed together.
5. Combine the mop glaze ingredients in a bowl and stir lightly.
6. Place the pork skewers on the hot grill and baste with the mop glaze. Cook for 20 minutes, turning them every 3–5 minutes and basting after each turn.
7. Serve with lime wedges.

NOTES

You can also use pork shoulder or collar for these skewers.

If possible, try to find soda that is made with cane sugar rather than corn syrup.

You can also substitute the peanut oil with canola, olive or your preferred oil.

Use thicker wooden skewers as they hold up better than their thinner counterparts and are less likely to burn and break.

PORK BELLY

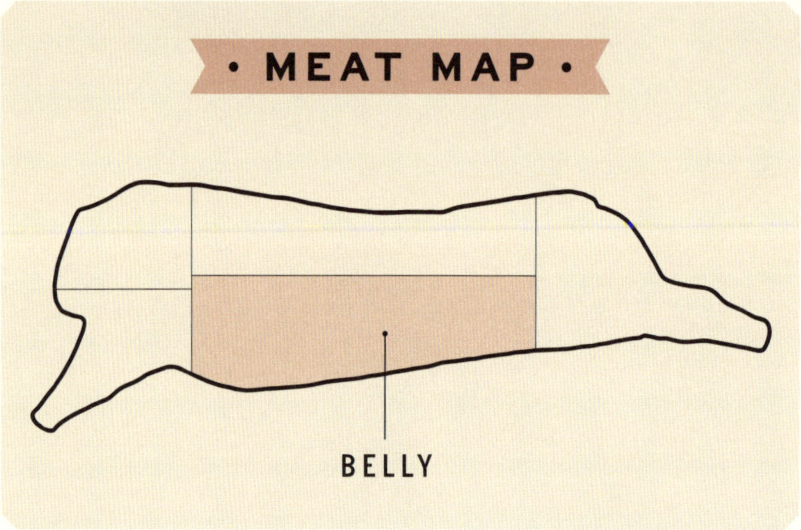

It's not only the ratio, but the actual composition of the meat and fat that makes pork belly so marvelous. If you had to compile a list of the most universally loved, used and recognized meat cuts, pork belly would be pretty high up there. It's the protein star in Japanese chashu ramen, Filipino lechon kawali, Italian porchetta, French rillons (arguably the first pork belly burnt ends) and classic English roast pork, among many others. And, of course, it's the essential starting point for one of the world's most beloved savory treats – bacon.

MAKIN' BACON

Depending on where you live, 'bacon' can look quite different. It's prepared in the same way, but the main variable is the part of meat it's made from. Commonly, a single slice of bacon is called a 'rasher' in the UK and Australia, whereas it's simply called a 'strip' in the US. There are four main cuts of bacon.

BACK OR LOIN BACON: Made only from the pork loin, it's easily recognizable from the singular circle of muscle. This is also known as Canadian bacon.

MIDDLE BACON: This cut has the loin plus a big strip of the belly attached. Sometimes it's also sold with the rind (skin) on.

SHORTCUT BACON: This cut consists of the loin plus a small 'tail' or portion of the belly attached. It's also known as Irish or Wiltshire bacon.

STREAKY BACON: Definitely the most common type of bacon in the world, it's made entirely from pork belly. The seams of fat running the entire length make this the crispiest of the bacons (see below).

BACON CROSS-SECTION

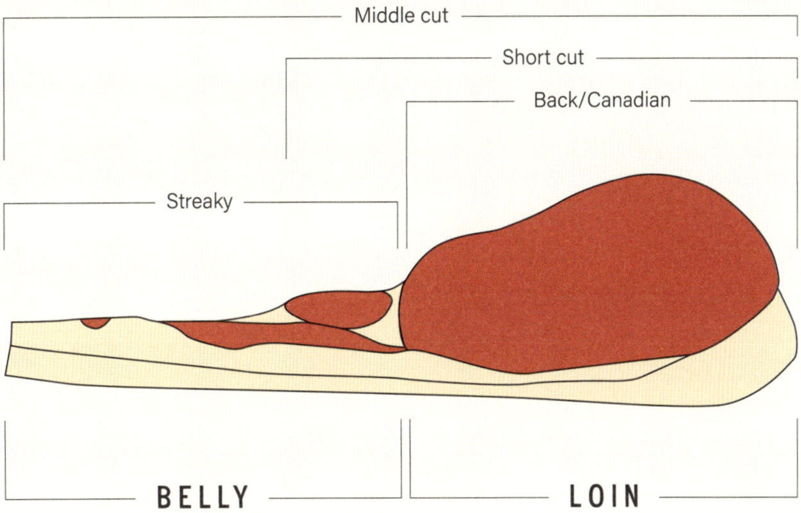

HOW TO MAKE YOUR OWN BACON

Making your own bacon is more of a science than an art. Curing meat requires precise measurements and weights to ensure the finished product is safe. And for bacon, that means having enough nitrites to make sure it's cured, while making sure they're at safe levels to consume.

This is another area where using weight, not volume, is extremely important. Different types of salt have different densities. For example, a tablespoon of kosher salt and a tablespoon of flake salt have different sodium levels, and one will taste saltier than the other. But if you measure according to weight rather than volume, you'll have a consistent result.

I've provided a bacon dry-curing 'calculator' so you can use it to cure any size of pork belly. (You can also make bacon out of other parts like the loin and shoulder, but they need a longer cure time.) The two main ingredients we're calculating are sodium nitrite ($NaNO^2$), which is the curing agent, and sodium chloride (NaCl or salt).

Accepted levels for nitrites in dry-cured bacon are between 150 and 200 parts per million (ppm). In the European Union, 150 ppm is the maximum accepted, while the US allows up to 200 ppm. It's important to make sure you stay within that bracket. The ideal ratio for salt is 2.5% of the meat weight.

Again, this calculator only addresses meat weight, salt and nitrites, which are functional ingredients that relate to the curing process. Everything else (e.g. garlic, sugar) is merely a flavor ingredient and can be adjusted to taste.

Caution: This calculator is designed to work with Pink Curing Salt #1, a specialty ingredient that is commonly used for curing. It's a combination of regular salt blended with 6.25% of sodium nitrite, and is sometimes called Prague Powder #1 or Insta Cure #1. Here are some more tips for making sure you're using the right stuff.

- Do NOT substitute pink curing salt with pink Himalayan salt, which is just regular flavoring salt.
- Do NOT use Curing Salt #2, which also has nitrates in it, and is used for meats that are cured for over 30 days, like salami and prosciutto.
- Do NOT substitute Pink Curing Salt #1 in this calculator with pure sodium nitrite. A lethal dose of $NaNO^2$ is as small as 1 gram. That's why they created pink salt in the first place. The dilution is to prevent overdose, and the color was added to make sure it would never be confused with regular salt.

NaCl: sodium chloride (salt)

$NaNO^2$: sodium nitrite

PS: Pink Curing Salt #1

PPM for $NaNO^2$: Between 150 and 200 ppm. In the example provided, I'm using 175 ppm, which you'll see referenced in Step 3.

• MEAT NERD FACT •

Commercial bacon is not made with a dry cure; rather, it is injected with cure to speed up the process. Injected bacons also have added ascorbic acid (vitamin C), which is a reductant that helps to prevent the formation of a volatile compound called nitrosamine. It's not essential to include ascorbic acid in dry-cured bacons, but if you would like to add it to your bacon, you should calculate it for 150 ppm. Ascorbic acid is available from specialty food supply stores and online retailers like Amazon.

TOO MUCH MATH?

Don't worry, I have a ready-to-go recipe for ya on page 68!

THE DRY CURE BACON CALCULATOR

STEP 1

Convert the meat weight to grams.

(e.g. a 5.5 lb piece of pork belly = 2494.76 g)

STEP 2

Calculate the NaCl required for 2.5% with the following equation:

0.025 x [meat weight in grams] = required NaCl in grams

(e.g. 0.025 x 2494.76 g = 62.37 g of NaCl)

STEP 3

Calculate the total $NaNO^2$ required with the following equation:

[preferred ppm ÷ 1,000,000] x [meat weight in grams] = required $NaNO^2$ in grams

(e.g. [175 ÷ 1,000,000] x 2494.76 g = 0.436 grams of $NaNO^2$)

STEP 4

Calculate the amount of PS you need (based on 6.25% nitrite concentration) with the following equation:

[total $NaNO^2$ required] ÷ 0.0625 = grams of PS needed

(e.g. 0.436 ÷ 0.0625 = 6.98 grams of PS)

STEP 5

Calculate how much NaCl the PS will contribute (based on 93.75% NaCl concentration within PS) with the following equation:

[required PS in grams] x 0.9375 = amount of NaCl in the PS

(e.g. 6.98 x 0.9375 = 6.54 g)

STEP 6

Subtract the NaCl in the PS from the overall NaCl needed.

(e.g. 62.37 g - 6.544 g = 55.82 g)

So, for 5.5 lb of pork belly, you need 55.82 g of salt and 6.98 g of Pink Cure #1.

HOMEMADE MAPLE BOURBON BACON

MAKES AROUND 24 THICK-CUT SLICES

One of the benefits of making your own bacon from scratch is the opportunity to create some unique flavors. Once you have your cure ratio figured out, you can play around with the rest of the ingredients to develop your own signature style. This maple bourbon is a great starting point for flavor inspiration.

55.82 g salt

6.98 g Pink Curing Salt #1

1 tablespoon freshly cracked black pepper

¼ cup (60 g) brown sugar

5.5 lb (2.5 kg) skinless pork belly

¼ cup (60 ml) maple syrup

¼ cup (60 ml) bourbon

1. Combine the salt, curing salt, black pepper and sugar in a small bowl.
2. Rub this seasoning all over the pork belly, then place it inside a large resealable bag. If there is excess seasoning left where you rubbed the pork, scoop it up and add it to the bag.
3. Pour in the maple syrup and bourbon, then seal the bag and massage the liquids to distribute them evenly.
4. Place the pork belly in the fridge to cure for 7–10 days. Turn the bag over once every day so the cure is evenly distributed, briefly massaging the liquid into the belly.
5. Preheat a smoker or pellet grill to 225°F (105°C).
6. Remove the pork belly from the bag and discard the liquid. Rinse lightly with water, pat dry, then place into the smoker to cook for 2½–3 hours until the internal temperature measures 150°F (70°C).
7. Allow to cool, then place in the fridge to firm up completely before slicing. Store slices in plastic wrap for up to 2 weeks. Alternatively, you can freeze them in batches and use as needed.

NOTES

If you end up making this frequently, consider investing in a deli slicer. You'll get a super-thin cut, which is helpful if you like your bacon extra crispy.

You can also enhance the flavor of the bacon through your wood selection. Maple, apple, cherry and hickory are all great wood pairings.

If you don't have a smoker, you can cook the bacon in your oven until it reaches the same internal temperature (but it won't have that signature smoky flavor).

GRILLED PORK BELLY BÁNH MÌ

SERVES 4

Vietnamese hot bread shops hawking fresh and cheap bánh mì rolls are super common in my hometown of Melbourne, Australia. The internet is rife with 'best bánh mì in Melbourne' lists, and everyone has their own favorite vendor. Though I love the crispy roast pork belly version, grilling takes the flavor to a new level, with a smoky char that marries with the rich fat, fresh veggies and fiery chilies.

- 2 tablespoons salt, divided
- 2 lb (1 kg) skinless pork belly
- 6 garlic cloves, crushed
- 1 cup (250 ml) soy sauce
- 2 cups (500 ml) water, divided
- 2 tablespoons fish sauce
- 2 tablespoons honey or jaggery (palm sugar)
- 2 tablespoons toasted sesame oil
- 2 large carrots
- ¼ cup (55 g) granulated (white) sugar
- ½ cup (125 ml) rice wine vinegar
- 4 crusty French bread rolls
- ¾ cup (175 g) chicken or pork liver pâté
- 2 mini (Lebanese) cucumbers, sliced thinly lengthways
- 12–15 sprigs cilantro (coriander), roots removed
- 2 bird's eye chilies, finely sliced

1. Place a large pot of water over high heat and bring to a boil. Add 1 tablespoon salt to the water.
2. Slice the pork belly lengthways into ½-inch (1 cm) strips. Gently place the strips into the boiling water, cover with a lid and boil for 20 minutes. You may need to decrease the heat so it doesn't boil over.
3. Drain the water and allow the meat to cool slightly, then place it in a container or resealable bag. Add the garlic, soy sauce, 1 cup (250 ml) water, fish sauce, honey and sesame oil. Massage or shake so the marinade is combined, then refrigerate for 2–4 hours.
4. Peel and julienne the carrots, then place in a bowl. Add the remaining salt and the sugar and massage well into the carrots. Pour in the remaining water and rice wine vinegar and allow to sit for at least 2 hours. If using on the same day, cover and place in the fridge.
5. Light a grill on medium heat for two-zone cooking (page 36), about 350–450°F (175–230°C).
6. Drain the pork belly, discarding the marinade.
7. Lay the pork belly strips down onto the direct heat. Grill for 1–3 minutes, turning frequently, until seared and slightly charred. If you experience a fat flare-up, move the piece to the indirect heat side of the grill until the flames die out, then return to sear. Once the pieces have a nice charred color and the fat has rendered even more, move them to the indirect side of the grill. Close the lid and cook for a further 5–7 minutes. Remove from the grill and slice into small pieces. (In a sandwich, I find it's easier to eat small pieces than a whole slice.)
8. To assemble the bánh mì, slice one of the bread rolls lengthways, not cutting all the way through. Smear 2–3 tablespoons of pâté across the bottom of the roll. Nestle a generous amount of sliced belly on the pâté. Top with the carrots, a slice or two of cucumber, fresh cilantro and a few slices of chili. Repeat until all the sandwiches are assembled.

NOTES

Boiling helps to soften and remove a lot of the thick fat in the pork belly, so when it grills, you get a more rendered, pleasant bite that doesn't feel fatty and overly rich.

I prefer using a resealable bag for marinating. You have more flexibility to arrange the meat so it's fully immersed in the liquid. Using a rigid container means that not all the meat will make contact with the marinade, so you have to keep turning it (which is, frankly, a PITA).

ROLLED PORCHETTA WITH CRACKLING

SERVES 8–10

This roast is an absolute showstopper. The method includes all my secrets to crispy crackling, but the most important one is planning ahead. The skin needs an overnight stay in the fridge to properly dry out. A word of caution: your fridge matters more than you think. If it's too full or running humid, the skin won't dry effectively and may remain damp on the surface, even after several hours. If that happens, blot it regularly with paper towel to remove excess moisture.

5–6 lb (2.3–2.7 kg) skin-on pork belly
1½ tablespoons fennel seeds
1 tablespoon black peppercorns
8 garlic cloves, crushed
2 teaspoons salt, plus ¼ cup (35 g) extra
1 tablespoon finely chopped oregano leaves
1 tablespoon finely chopped sage leaves
zest of 1 orange
2 teaspoons avocado oil or other high-heat oil

1. The night before you wish to serve the porchetta, prepare the pork belly by piercing the skin with a pork skin tool or sharp knife, making dozens of small pricks all over. Next, score the skin with a knife. You can make cuts in the same direction, or in a diamond pattern; just make sure you aren't cutting deeper than the skin layer.
2. Flip the belly over so it's lying on the skin, meat side up, and prepare the seasoning.
3. In a small dry skillet over medium heat, toast the fennel seeds and peppercorns until fragrant, about 1–2 minutes, swirling the pan so the seeds don't burn. Use a mortar and pestle or spice grinder to turn them into a powder.
4. Spread the garlic across the surface of the meat, then season with 2 teaspoons salt and the spice powder. Scatter the oregano, sage and orange zest on top.
5. Prepare five lengths of butcher's twine (it's handy to have it ready). Have the long side of the belly positioned horizontally in front of you, then roll the belly tightly away from your body.
6. Secure the belly so it remains tightly rolled by tying the twine in knots along the roll.
7. Place a wire rack onto a sheet pan (baking sheet), then position the porchetta on the rack. Pour ¼ cup (35 g) salt over the top of the roast. It will only sit on the top; it may not cling to the sides. Place the salt-laden porchetta in the fridge, uncovered, overnight.
8. In the morning, brush the salt off the top (it should be damp from all the moisture it absorbed) and let the porchetta continue drying in the fridge.
9. Preheat the oven to 450°F (230°C). If you have a convection setting, use it.
10. Remove the porchetta from the fridge. You can cook it on the tray and rack it dried on, or you may use a deeper roasting pan with a rack (because a lot of fat will accumulate).
11. Brush the porchetta lightly with the avocado oil. Place into the oven and roast for 30–40 minutes to kickstart the crackling, then reduce the heat to 325°F (165°C).
12. Continue to cook the porchetta at low heat for about 60–90 minutes, or until it reaches an internal temperature of 140–145°F (60–62°C).
13. If the skin is not as crisp and bubbly as you'd like, crank the heat back up to 450°F (230°C) and cook for a further 15–20 minutes, keeping an eye on it to ensure the skin doesn't burn. Don't worry, it definitely won't dry out!
14. Remove the porchetta once crispy and slice to serve, removing and discarding the twine as you go.

AIR FRYER CHICHARRÓN

SERVES 4–6

One of the most memorable meaty bites I ever had was my first taste of chicharrón in Monterrey, Mexico. They're found all over the *carnicerías* (meat markets) of the city, and are crescents of fried pork belly with impossibly crispy flesh. This air fryer version feels slightly less sinful, but it still has a big flavor payoff. I recommend pairing them with fresh guacamole and using the chicharrón as a dipper.

2–3 lb (1–1.3 kg) skinless pork belly

2 teaspoons salt

½ teaspoon chili powder

1 lime, cut into wedges

1. Slice the pork belly lengthways into 1-inch (2.5 cm) strips. Take each strip and make additional slits by slicing every ½ inch (1 cm), but don't cut all the way through.
2. Sprinkle the pork belly with salt on all sides.
3. Place into the basket of the air fryer and spread each piece into a slight arc so there's space between each cut. Depending on the size of your air fryer, you may need to cook in batches.
4. Cook for 25 minutes on 390°F (200°C), then turn over and cook for another 25 minutes on the other side.
5. Flip the pieces one more time, then increase the heat to 400°F (210°C) and cook for 5–7 minutes until crispy.
6. Place the pork belly pieces onto a cutting board and allow to rest for 2–3 minutes. They will continue to firm and crispen while resting.
7. Dust with the chili powder and squeeze over lime juice immediately before eating.

NOTE

If you don't have an air fryer, I've got good news – you can still make this recipe on the stovetop. Place the strips in a pot and cover with water. Simmer for an hour, letting the water boil off and leaving the rendered fat in its place. Let the chicharrón cook in their own fat until crispy (which makes quite a mess as they sputter and splatter!). In short, the air fryer version is way easier and lets some of the fat drain off, so borrow one from a friend.

DESSERT BACON WITH PECAN PIE CRUMBLE

SERVES 2–4

You don't have to eat this as dessert (although let's acknowledge bacon's superpower as one of the few meats that can feature in an appetizer, main or dessert). It actually makes for a fun breakfast or brunch item, too. For this recipe, bacon gets a luxe upgrade with the addition of a streusel-like pecan crumble – for the ultimate salty-sweet collab. It's definitely what I would call a 'sometimes food', but you gotta treat yourself every now and then.

12 oz (350 g) bacon strips (about 12)

⅓ cup (50 g) all-purpose (plain) flour

⅓ cup (75 g) brown sugar

⅛ teaspoon ground cayenne

2 tablespoons melted and cooled salted butter

½ cup (60 g) roughly chopped pecans

1. Preheat the oven to 365°F (185°C).
2. Line a sheet pan (baking sheet) with foil and place a wire rack on top. Lay the bacon strips on the rack, ensuring they don't overlap.
3. Place in the oven on the middle rack and bake for 25 minutes.
4. While the bacon is in the oven, prepare the pecan pie crumble. Combine the flour, brown sugar and cayenne in a bowl, then add the melted butter and stir with a fork. Add the pecans and use your fingers to finish crumbling the dough, which should look like damp sand.
5. Remove the bacon from the oven. It should be almost cooked. Sprinkle 1–2 teaspoons of the pecan pie crumble across each bacon strip.
6. Return the bacon to the oven for 10–15 minutes until the crumble has melted slightly and the edges of the bacon are crispy.

PORK RIBS

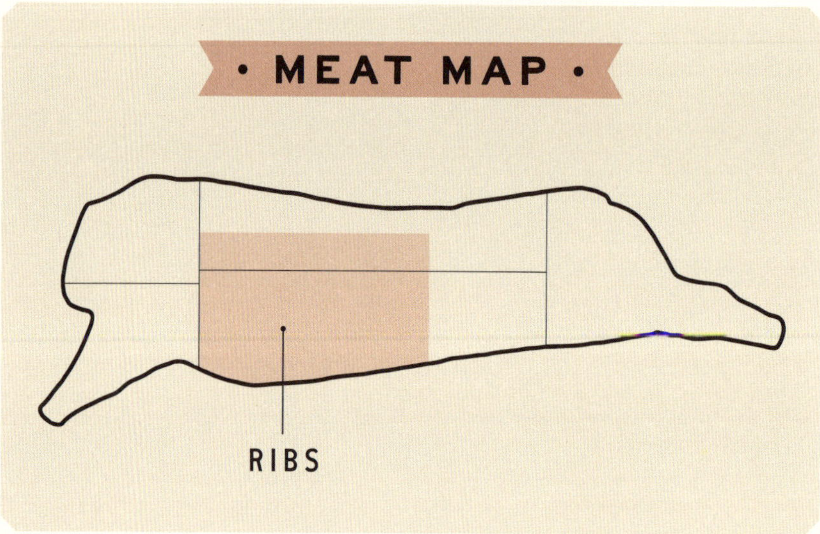

It's the cut that needs no explanation to understand where it comes from, but one rack of ribs can produce at least four different variations. To best understand how different rib configurations are cut, it's easiest to view them from the side.

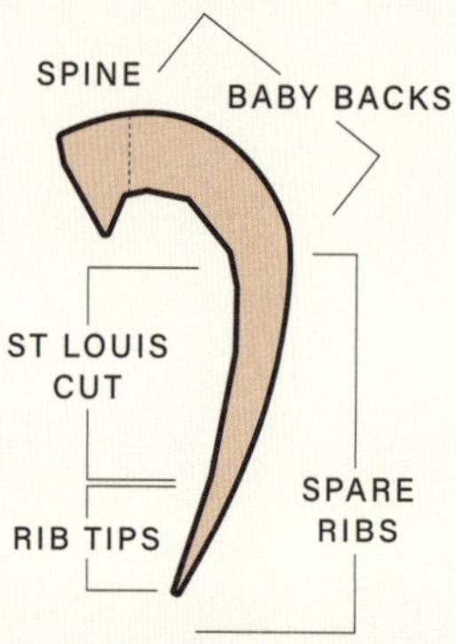

PORK RIB TYPES

SPARE RIBS: This is the entire section of rib plate left after baby backs are cut off.

ST LOUIS CUT: This is a squared-off portion of spare ribs.

COUNTRY-STYLE: These aren't ribs at all but sections of boneless pork (usually shoulder or loin) sliced into rib shapes.

RIB TIPS: This is the left-over bottom portion once the St Louis is cut. Popular in Chicago-style BBQ.

INTERCOSTALS: This is the meat between the rib bones.

WHY DOES MEATINESS VARY?

Sometimes you'll get a rack of ribs where parts of the meaty surface have been trimmed back so far that the tops of the bones are left exposed. They're called 'shiners.' So why is rib meatiness so inconsistent? Genetics, age and feed all play a role in the overall size of the animal, but in most cases it comes down to butchery decisions – and those are driven by which cuts are most valuable.

Take Australia, for example, where smoked ribs aren't nearly as popular as in the US. There, the meat over the rib bones is often removed and used for middle bacon, a product that commands a higher price and has stronger demand. That's why racks Down Under are rarely left with much meat on them.

You see the same thing with baby back ribs. Baby backs are actually a collection of several muscles, including the *iliocostalis*, *serratus ventralis* and *levatores costarum*, but the only way to get truly meaty ones is if the butcher leaves some of the pork loin (*longissimus*) attached. Processors will do this because baby backs trade at a higher price than loin alone. If they make the cut just right, they will leave a strip of loin on the ribs and still have a pretty decent chunk of loin left to sell separately.

Check out the difference:

BABY BACKS: These come from the very top of the rib, which attaches to the spine.

TWICE-COOKED CRISPY BABY BACKS WITH SHICHIMI TOGARASHI

SERVES 6–8

The texture of these ribs is really surprising. First, they are braised in a soy, ginger and garlic stock until tender, then battered and fried until crispy. The result is a firm crunch that gives way to tender, porky goodness. Shichimi togarashi is a Japanese chili powder loaded with mouth-tingling sansho pepper. If you prefer something less spicy, you can finish with furikake instead (another Japanese seasoning blend made with seaweed).

BRAISING LIQUID

4 cups (1 liter) chicken stock

4 cups (1 liter) water

6 garlic cloves, smashed (see Notes)

2-inch (5 cm) piece fresh ginger, roughly sliced

1 cup (250 ml) soy sauce

⅔ cup (170 ml) mirin

2 star anise

2 tablespoons granulated (white) sugar

2 teaspoons salt

1 teaspoon MSG (optional; see Notes)

PORK RIBS

1 x 3.5 lb (1.5 kg) rack baby backs

6–8 cups (1.5–2 liters) frying oil (peanut, canola, vegetable or another neutral oil)

½ cup (60 g) cornstarch (cornflour)

½ cup (75 g) all-purpose (plain) flour

½ teaspoon salt

1 tablespoon shichimi togarashi

1. Place all the ingredients for the braising liquid in a large pot and bring to a boil.
2. Slice the rack of ribs in half between the two middle bones, then slowly immerse the sections in the liquid. Reduce the heat to a strong simmer and braise for 1.5–2 hours until tender.
3. Remove the ribs from the liquid and place onto a board to cool. Reserve ½ cup (125 ml) braising liquid, discarding the rest.
4. Heat the oil in a deep-sided pot until it reaches 350°F (170°C).
5. While the oil heats, and once the ribs are cool enough to handle, slice them between each bone, then place them in a resealable plastic bag. Add the cornstarch, flour and salt, then seal and shake the bag to coat the ribs thoroughly. Add the reserved braising liquid to the bag and shake again to form a slurry.
6. Working in batches (so as not to overcrowd the pot), fry the ribs for 3–5 minutes until golden brown. Remove the ribs from the pot and drain on a paper towel, then sprinkle with the togarashi while still hot. Repeat until all ribs are fried, allowing the oil to come back up to temperature before starting a fresh batch.
7. Serve immediately.

NOTES

'Smashing' the garlic means placing the flat side of a knife over each clove and hitting it firmly to break its shape and release the flavor.

MSG doesn't deserve the bad rap it's gotten over the years – and it's a shame considering how delicious it is. It's the sodium form of glutamic acid, an amino acid naturally found in foods like meats, mushrooms, tomatoes and seaweed. But if you don't wanna use it, just leave it out.

CLASSIC BBQ PORK RIBS

SERVES 6–8

Let's talk about rib texture, because it's deeply personal. Some people prefer their rib meat to fall off the bone, but others want a bite that comes away cleanly from the bone, without dragging other meat away. I prefer the latter, which is also a little harder to nail, because there's a smaller window for this kind of doneness. But if you prefer your ribs to fall off the bone, throw another hour or two onto the clock during the wrapped part of the cook.

- 2 teaspoons salt
- 2 tablespoons paprika
- 1 teaspoon chili powder
- 1 teaspoon onion powder
- 1 teaspoon garlic powder
- 2 tablespoons brown sugar
- ½ teaspoon mustard powder
- 1 teaspoon black pepper
- 2 x 3.5 lb (1.5 kg) St Louis cut ribs
- ¼ cup (60 ml) apple cider vinegar
- ½ cup (125 ml) water
- 4 tablespoons salted butter
- 4 tablespoons honey
- ⅔ cup (180 g) BBQ sauce

1. Preheat a smoker to run between 225°F and 250°F (110°C–130°C).
2. In a small bowl, combine the salt, paprika, chili powder, onion powder, garlic powder, brown sugar, mustard powder and black pepper. Mix to incorporate the ingredients.
3. Lay the ribs bone side up on a large cutting board. If the skirt steak is still present on the back, use a trimming knife to remove it completely.
4. Using a teaspoon or butterknife, push underneath the membrane and loosen it off one of the bones in the middle. Grip the loosened portion of the membrane with a paper towel, then pull the rest away and discard.
5. Sprinkle the seasoning over the racks. Start with a light application to the bone/underside, then apply as evenly as possible to the meat side, making sure everything is covered. Let sit for 15 minutes to allow the seasoning to mingle with the surface moisture of the ribs and become a paste.
6. Place the racks into the smoker, bone side down, and cook for 2 hours.
7. In a spray bottle, combine the apple cider vinegar and water. Spritz the ribs lightly every 30 minutes.
8. Remove the racks from the smoker and place onto a large sheet of foil. Cut the butter into small cubes and gently stud them across the surface of the meat, spreading them evenly. Drizzle half the honey in a zig-zag across the top, then seal the foil package tightly. Repeat with the other rack.
9. Place the ribs back into the smoker, bone side down, and cook for a further 2 hours.
10. Remove the ribs from the smoker and gently open one end of the foil package. Use caution as a lot of liquid will have pooled. Gently pour out and discard the liquid. Open the rest of the package, scrunching the foil around the sides of the rack so the top of the ribs is exposed. Gently paint the top of the racks with BBQ sauce, then return to the smoker for 10–15 minutes so the sauce sets.
11. Slice the ribs between the bones to serve.

NOTES

You can collect the trimmed pork skirt steaks in your freezer until you have enough to grill them up and have a feast.

If you have a favorite BBQ rub (I use a combo of Hardcore Carnivore Red and Sweet BBQ), use it instead of the homemade spice rub.

I recommend doubling up the foil wrap. The bones have a way of piercing it, so a second layer gives you extra insurance.

STICKY-ROASTED APRICOT SRIRACHA COUNTRY-STYLE RIBS

SERVES 4

If you don't know what boneless 'country-style' ribs are, you can read all about them on page 77. The good news? If you can't find them, it's easy to just cut your own. Just grab a boneless pork shoulder (also called pork butt) and cut it into thick, finger-shaped strips. Just like that, you've got DIY boneless ribs. I wanted to include an oven-roasted recipe within the rib category, so if you don't have a grill or a smoker, you can still enjoy the goodness.

- 1 tablespoon paprika
- 1 teaspoon garlic powder
- 1½ teaspoon salt
- ½ teaspoon black pepper
- 3.5 lb (1.5 kg) country-style boneless pork ribs
- ¾ cup (250 g) apricot preserves (jam), divided
- ½ cup (125 ml) hot beef or chicken stock or water
- 1½ tablespoons sriracha sauce
- 1 tablespoon worcestershire sauce

1. Preheat the oven to 325°F (165°C).
2. Combine the paprika, garlic powder, salt and black pepper in a small bowl. Mix to create a seasoning rub.
3. Place the ribs into a roasting pan, then sprinkle the rub on top. Make sure they are well coated in the rub, then spread them out in a single layer in the pan.
4. In a small cup, stir together ¼ cup (85 g) apricot preserves and the stock until the preserves are mostly dissolved in the hot liquid. Pour the mixture over the ribs, then seal the pan tightly with foil.
5. Place in the oven and roast for 1 hour. Carefully remove the pan from the oven, remove the foil and use some tongs to turn the ribs over. Reseal with the foil and return to the oven to roast for an additional hour.
6. In a bowl, combine the remaining preserves with the sriracha and worcestershire sauce.
7. Remove the ribs from the oven, uncover them and carefully pour out and discard the liquid that has accumulated in the pan. Using a basting brush, generously brush the ribs with the apricot sriracha mixture, then return to the oven, uncovered, for 15–20 minutes until the glaze is set.

PORK LOIN

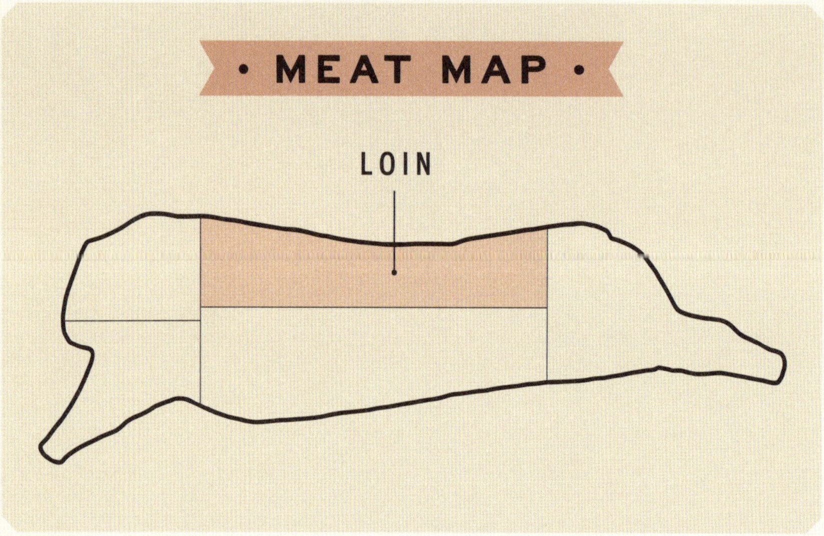

Would you believe me if I told you that the pork loin is the same muscle as the largest part of the ribeye? Yup, it's the *longissimus*! It runs right along the spine of the animal along its back (while we're at it, it's also the same muscle in a lamb or venison backstrap).

The loin is sometimes called the loin eye, and it's actually really versatile, lending itself to a variety of different cuts. It's used to create roasts and boneless pork chops, and it can even be cut to bulk out baby back ribs (page 77). The loin can be notoriously dry and often benefits from brining, which forces water into the meat to make up for the water lost during cooking (page 28).

HOW CAN THESE ALL BE PORK CHOPS?

I reckon this is one of the most confusing parts about meat – all the visual variables of the cuts! How can one pork chop look so different to another? It all comes down to the 'spec' or specification that the processor is working with, which is usually dictated by the customer (the stores buying them). What these chops have in common is that they all contain the pork loin as the starting point. The loin is surrounded by several smaller muscle groups, and pork chops can include various combinations of these muscles, with varying configurations of the bone, too!

PORK CHOPS

• BE THE BUTCHER •

HOW TO CUT YOUR OWN PORK CHOPS FROM BONELESS LOIN

You can purchase entire lengths of pork loin from some grocery stores and butchers, and this gives you tremendous flexibility and control of how thick you want your chops. It's also a more economical way to purchase, since buying in bulk will always save you some coin. With a little know-how, you can create any of the following from a single loin.

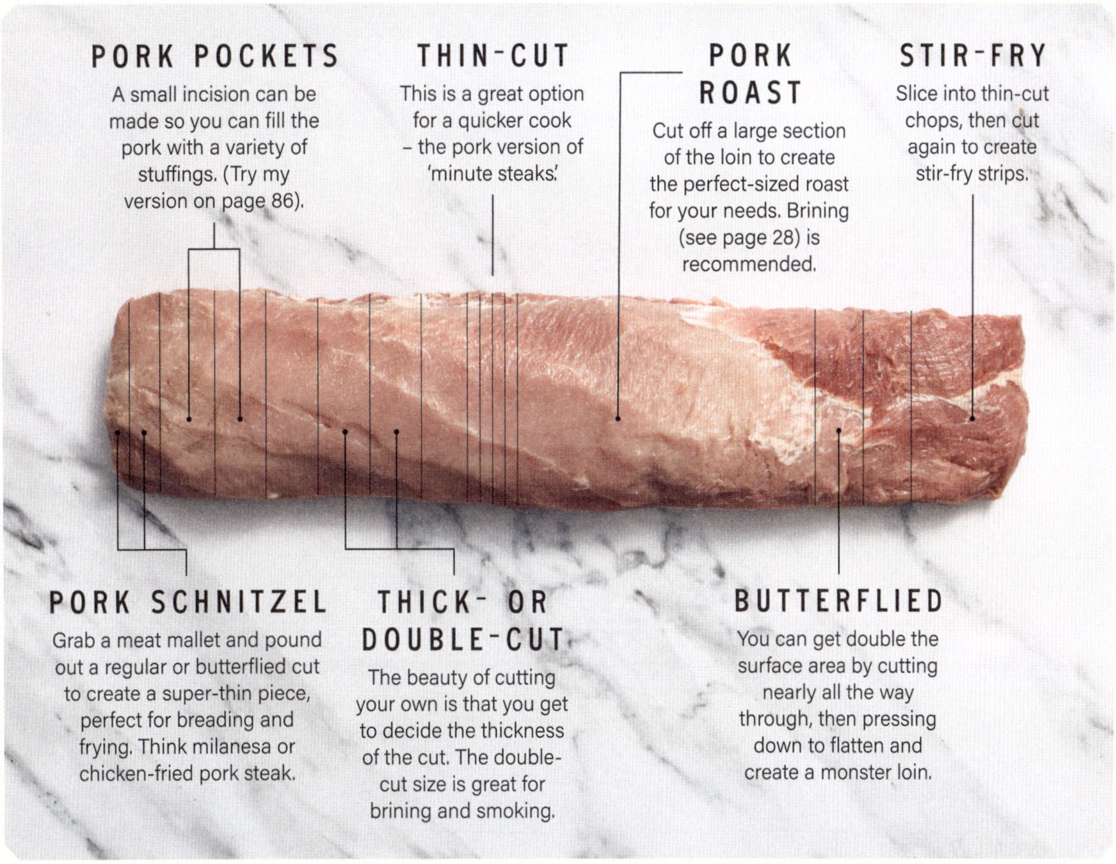

PORK LOIN

STUFFED PORK CHOPS WITH LEMONY RICOTTA AND SPINACH

SERVES 6

Here's the real secret to stuffed pork chops – you gotta use thick-cut ones so the pork doesn't dry out. I'm talking at least 1½-inch (4 cm) chunkies. This recipe will work with bone-in or boneless chops, and if you're having trouble finding the right size, cut your own from a boneless loin (page 85).

- 6 thick-cut pork chops, about 1½ inches (4 cm) thick
- ½ cup (100 g) finely chopped cooked spinach (drained of excess liquid)
- zest and juice of 1 lemon
- ½ cup (115 g) ricotta cheese
- ½ cup (120 g) cream cheese
- ½ cup (50 g) finely grated parmesan cheese
- ¾ teaspoon garlic powder, divided
- ½ teaspoon ground nutmeg
- 2½ teaspoons salt, divided
- 2 teaspoons smoked paprika
- 1 teaspoon finely ground black pepper
- 2 tablespoons olive oil

1. Preheat the oven to 350°F (170°C) and remove the chops from the fridge.
2. In a bowl, combine the spinach, lemon zest and juice, ricotta, cream cheese, parmesan, ¼ teaspoon garlic powder, nutmeg and ½ teaspoon salt. Mix with a spatula or wooden spoon until combined.
3. Use a sharp knife with a fine point to cut a slit into each pork chop. The aim is to cut evenly down the middle of one side, going about three-quarters of the way into the meat, being careful not to cut all the way through. Think of it like a pita pocket!
4. Place spoonfuls of the creamy filling into the pork chop. Scrape along the opening so that the stuffing is roughly level with the meat. If it's overstuffed, it will melt out into the cooking pan.
5. Combine the remaining garlic powder and salt with the paprika and pepper. Sprinkle over the pork chops on both sides.
6. Place a large, oven-safe skillet over high heat. Once hot, add the olive oil.
7. Lay the pork chops in the skillet and cook for 4–5 minutes on each side.
8. Place the skillet in the oven to cook for a further 10–15 minutes, or until the filling registers at least 140°F (60°C) on a meat thermometer.

NOTE

Make sure you're using traditional loin chops (bone-in or boneless). They have the whole loin muscle, so you can make a neat pocket for stuffing. Shoulder chops are comprised of several muscles, so it'll be hard to make a nice cut (plus, they're kinda tough).

BACON-DRAPED PORK WITH APPLES, HAZELNUTS AND SAGE

SERVES 6–8

So, with bacon, pork and sausage, does this dish actually count as an all-swine version of turducken? Maybe not. But it's a great recipe to concoct during the cooler months, when you're looking for hearty comfort with harvest flavors. The bacon 'drape' also helps protect the delicate pork loin from drying out by shielding it with a fatty barrier.

- 1 tablespoon olive oil
- ½ onion, peeled and finely diced
- 1 sweet apple (I prefer Envy or Fuji), peeled and finely diced
- ¼ cup (10 g) finely chopped sage leaves
- ⅓ cup (40 g) toasted and chopped hazelnuts
- 2 tablespoons dry breadcrumbs
- 1 x 3 lb (1.5 kg) boneless and skinless pork loin
- 2 teaspoons salt
- 8 oz (225 g) fresh sausage (filling only, no casing)
- 8–10 belly bacon slices

1. Preheat the oven to 375°F (190°C).
2. Place the olive oil in a saucepan over medium heat.
3. Add the onion and apple and cook for 10–15 minutes until they have softened. Stir in the sage leaves and hazelnuts and cook for a further minute. Remove the saucepan from the heat, stir through the breadcrumbs and allow to cool.
4. Butterfly the pork loin by slicing down through the middle of the eye, three-quarters of the way through. Push the sides down (like opening a book) so it lays like one large flat piece.
5. Season the opened loin with salt, then spread the sausage across the entire surface to create a thin, even layer.
6. Spoon the cooled stuffing mixture down the long center of the loin (pictured page 90). Prepare a sheet pan (baking sheet) with a wire rack on top. ›

NOTES

You can use breakfast sausage or any kind of fresh sausage filling for this – even the ones in the casings. Just split the casing open and use the delicious innards. This sausage layer is also a great way to add extra flavors, so don't be shy about choosing a sage or Italian sausage!

A serrated brisket or bread knife is best for cutting this roast and making that initial slice through the bacon nice and clean.

7. Close the loin up like a book, rolling it around the filling. Bring both sides together to touch, rather than rolling it into itself. Gently turn the loin over and place it seam side down on the wire rack. Tuck the loin in a little to ensure it's safely holding in the stuffing; the sausage will act like mortar to keep everything together.
8. Drape the bacon slices over the loin one at a time, slightly overlapping, and tuck the ends in under the loin.
9. Place in the oven and roast for about 60 minutes. Check the internal temperature around the 45-minute mark so you don't needlessly overcook it. The pork roast is ready when the internal temperature reads 140–145°F (60–62°C) on a thermometer inserted into the thickest part of the meat.
10. Remove from the oven and slice to serve.

TEA-SOAKED PORK CHOPS WITH BLACKBERRY LEMON RELISH

SERVES 8

Loin can be notoriously dry, and that's where brining makes all the difference. It enhances both the texture and juiciness of the pork (in case you missed it, I give a full rundown of how brining works on page 28). While a basic brine will suffice, I reckon it's a great opportunity to infuse extra flavor, like the subtle floral aroma and tartness the tea brings.

BRINE

- 3 cups (750 ml) boiling water
- 5 Earl Grey tea bags (see Note)
- ¼ cup (72 g) salt
- 4 cups (1 liter) apple juice
- 2 cups (500 ml) cold water

PORK

- 8 x 6 oz (175 g) thick-cut pork chops, about 1–1¼ inches (2.5–3 cm) thick
- 1 teaspoon salt
- 2 tablespoons olive oil

RELISH

- 1½ cups (210 g) frozen blackberries
- zest and juice of 1 medium lemon
- ¼ cup (60 ml) balsamic vinegar
- ½ teaspoon freshly ground black pepper
- ¼ cup (60 g) brown sugar
- ½ teaspoon five-spice powder

1. Start by making the brine. Pour the boiling water into a large, heatproof container, add the tea bags and steep for 10 minutes. Add the salt and stir to dissolve. Stir in the apple juice and cold water, then allow the mixture to cool completely.
2. Once cool, place the pork chops in the brine to soak and refrigerate for 2–4 hours.
3. Remove the chops from the brine and pat dry with a paper towel. Season lightly on both sides with salt.
4. Place a large skillet over medium-high heat and add the olive oil. Once the pan has heated up, place the pork chops in the skillet and cook for 6–8 minutes on one side.
5. While the pork is cooking, add all the relish ingredients to a saucepan. Place over medium heat and simmer until the blackberries soften. Use a wooden spoon to crush them against the side of the saucepan and break them down into a jam-like consistency. Reduce the heat to low and simmer.
6. While the sauce is simmering, flip the pork over and cook for a further 5–7 minutes on the other side, or until the internal temperature of the meat reaches 145°F (60°C).
7. Remove the pork from the pan, cover loosely with foil and rest for 5–10 minutes.
8. To serve, slice the pork chop, then spoon a generous amount of relish over the top.

NOTE

If Earl Grey is too strong for you, just swap it out for your preferred tea variety.

RIBEYE

• MEAT MAP •

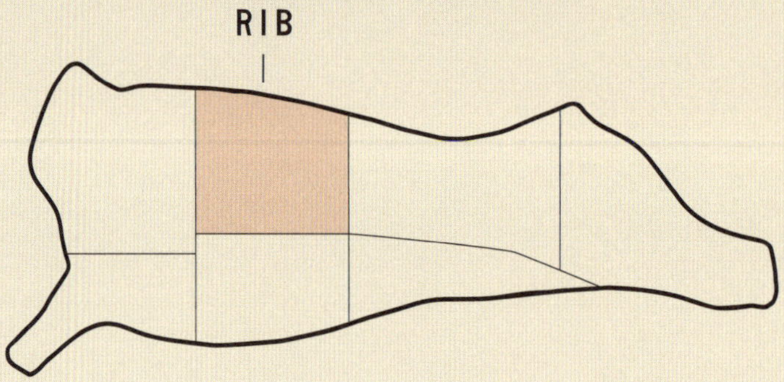

The ribeye sits at that perfect intersection of flavor and indulgence – a legendary cut that no steakhouse would ever dare omit from the menu. Cut from the rib primal, it's known for consistent tenderness and generous marbling. It's one of the most popular steaks for a reason: it reliably delivers a full, beef-forward eating experience.

MEET THE RIBEYE FAMILY

Who'd have thought that one steak could have so many not-so-secret identities? There's a pretty good chance that some of your very favorite steaks are actually the same, but in different variations. Check these out.

PRIME RIB/STANDING RIB ROAST: The whole rib primal is trimmed down to make a prime rib roast. Outer layers like the lifter muscle are removed and the bone is cut down. Bones may be frenched, cut away and tied back on, or left intact. It's basically a huge log of uncut ribeye steaks.

BONELESS RIBEYE ROLL: This is the same as prime rib, but with no bone. It's a whole roll of ribeyes, just waiting to be cut, with the rib bones completely removed. These can come in a variety of lengths, and sometimes you'll see them sold as boneless prime rib.

CATTLEMAN'S STEAK/COWBOY: If you took a prime rib roast and sliced it between the bones, you'd be cutting cattleman's steaks. These are bone-in ribeyes with a 2–3-inch (5–7.5 cm) bone tail.

BONELESS: The classic meat-only ribeye steak. In Australia and New Zealand, it's called a 'scotch fillet' (a lot of Aussies don't realize scotch and ribeye are the same thing!). It's also known by its French moniker – entrecôte.

TOMAHAWK: This is the same as a cattleman's steak but with a long bone! Yes, they look ridiculously cool. But you're paying more for a couple of extra lengths of bone you can't consume.

BONE-IN: This is a basic ribeye with the bone still attached, but without any extension on the bone. So, it's essentially a cattleman's steak, but shorter. When thickly sliced, it can be referred to as côte de boeuf.

PRIME RIB/ STANDING RIB ROAST

BONELESS RIBEYE ROLL

CATTLEMAN'S STEAK/COWBOY

BONELESS

TOMAHAWK

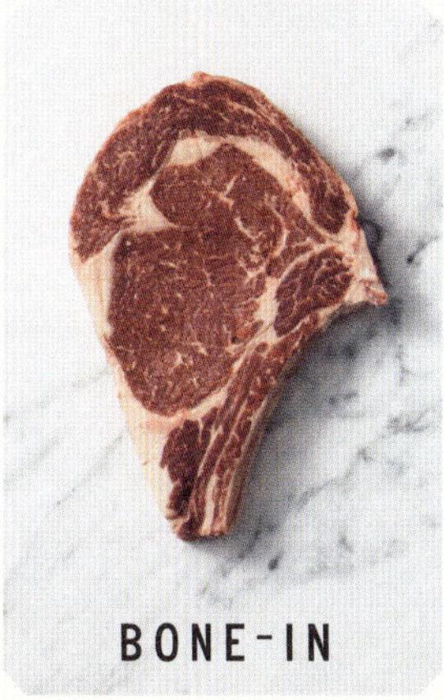

BONE-IN

ANATOMY OF A RIBEYE

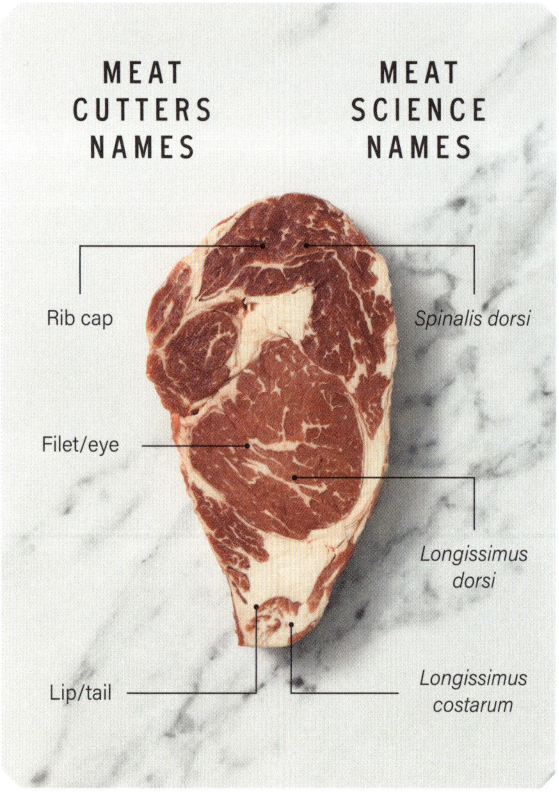

Most hardcore beef aficionados consider the *spinalis dorsi* (ribeye cap) to be the king of all steaks. It's far more tender than its neighbor, the *longissimus dorsi*, and has a wonderfully pure beef flavor. The problem is, it's very hard to find the *spinalis dorsi* on its own. You have to ruin a whole ribeye to get it out. But if you're game to try and cut your own, see my guide on page 97.

HOW TO CHOOSE THE BEST RIBEYE

The *spinalis dorsi* gets thinner as it spans along the rib primal, so as you cut along the ribeye roll, the amount of cap in each steak gets smaller and smaller. So, for maximum bang for your buck, always choose ribeyes that have a thick and prominent amount of cap muscle.

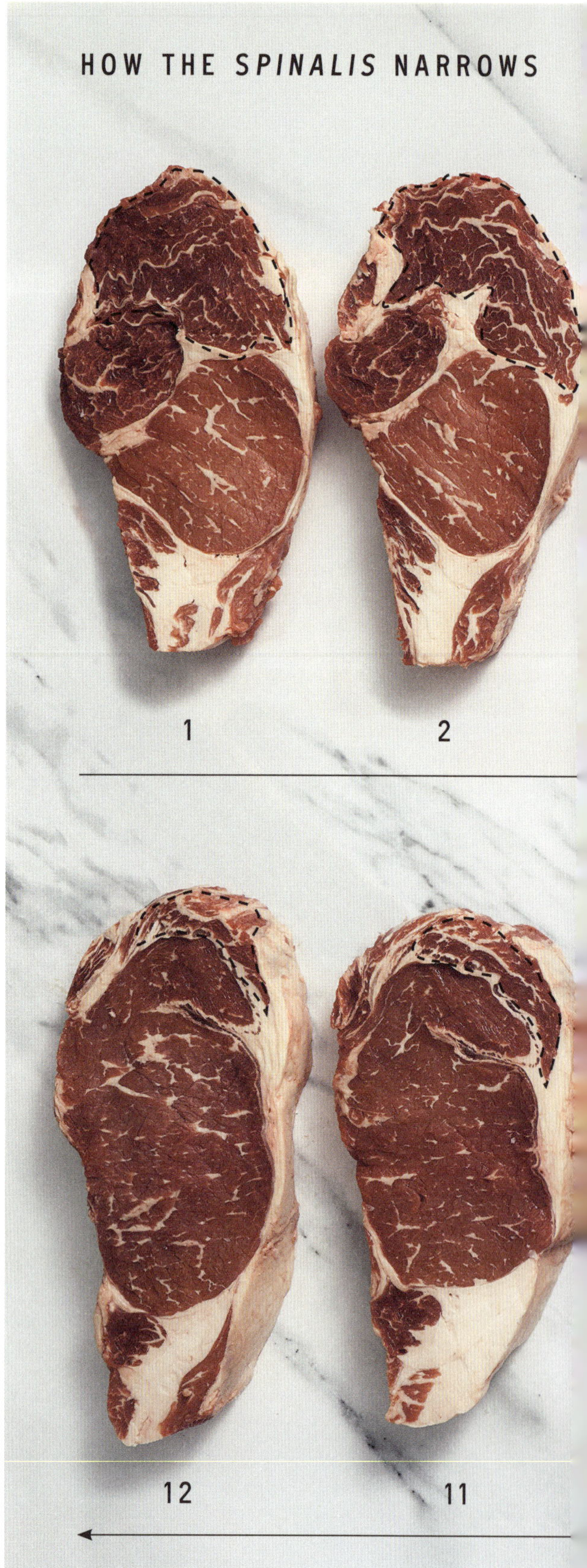

When an entire ribeye roll is broken down into steaks, it's easy to see how the cap becomes smaller as it tapers off.

THE KING OF STEAKS

As I mentioned earlier, it's exceptionally rare to find *spinalis* sold on its own. The good news is you can simply cut it yourself.

Whole boneless ribeye rolls (also known as cube rolls in Australia) are often available at large bulk stores like Costco, and lots of grocery stores have them sitting out the back (since that's where they cut their steaks from). You just need to ask, and if they don't have them, they can order them in for you.

Once you cut away the flat *spinalis dorsi*, you can keep it whole or cut it into smaller steak portions. Then, take the remaining *longissimus* and cut it into thick 'ribeye filet' steaks. Here's my step-by-step guide to cutting your own *spinalis*: the king of steaks.

• BE THE BUTCHER •

HOW TO CUT YOUR OWN *SPINALIS DORSI*

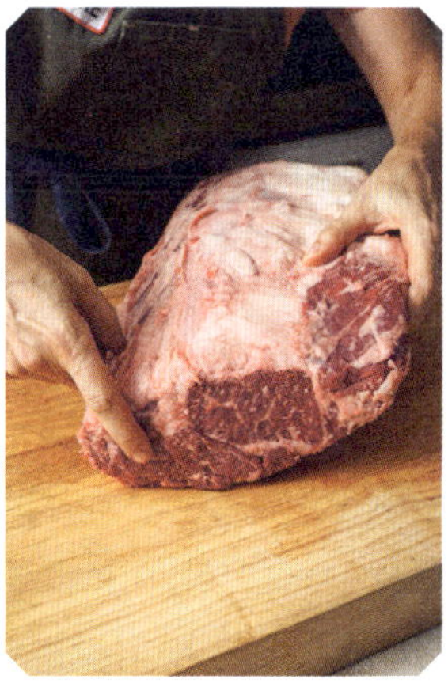

1

2

3

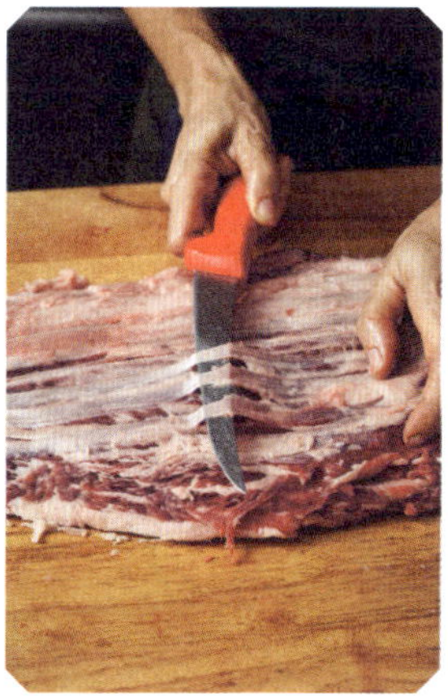

4

5

1. Take a look at each cut end of the whole ribeye roll and find the one with the larger *spinalis dorsi*.
2. It's easiest to start by separating the natural seam between the muscles. Start by putting your thumb or finger in the seam underneath the *spinalis dorsi*, digging it in and moving side to side to start opening up the seam.
3. Work with your hands to slowly pry the cap muscle off the eye, using a sharp boning knife (page 26) where necessary to make small cuts and release any stubborn connections until the whole cap muscle is separated.
4. Trim any excess silverskin and fat from the *spinalis dorsi* and cut into smaller steaks if preferred.
5. Use a knife to slice thick sections of the remaining eye and create 'ribeye filet' steaks.

If you don't plan on using the steaks right away, vacuum-seal them for later. Once sealed, they will keep for up to 14 days in the fridge, or throw them in the freezer until you're ready.

SMOKED AND SEARED TOMAHAWK STEAKS

SERVES 6–8

This method is technically a 'reverse sear', which is cooking over low heat to start and finishing with a high-heat sear. With the smoke/sear combo, you get all the goodness of smoky flavoring, without missing out on the crust and sear from a direct flame. Oh, and your food already comes with a built-in handle.

2 x 2.5 lb (1 kg) tomahawk steaks, at least 1½ inches (4 cm) thick

½ tablespoon salt

1 teaspoon ground black pepper

½ teaspoon garlic powder

2 tablespoons melted salted butter

1. Preheat a smoker to 250°F (120°C) and remove the steaks from the fridge while the smoker heats.
2. Combine the salt, black pepper and garlic powder in a bowl. Coat the steaks liberally with the seasoning on both sides of the meat, then place into the smoker.
3. Cook for 60–75 minutes, or until an internal temperature of 125°F (52°C) is reached. Start monitoring the temperature around the 45-minute mark in case your cook is moving quickly.
4. Remove the steaks from the smoker and cover with foil to rest.
5. Light a grill for searing. For gas, light two burners to high heat. For charcoal, light half a chimney of coals. Once lit, dump them into one spot so they are piled and concentrated in heat.
6. Brush the surface of the steaks with melted butter and sear for a minute on either side.
7. To serve, slice the bone away from the meat and cut into slices.

NOTES

The 'sear' can be done in any number of ways. Whatever method you use, sear for a minute or so on each side, and that's it! Aside from the grilling method, you can also sear in a hot skillet, crank your smoker up, use a chimney of charcoal for the 'afterburner' effect, or even blowtorch the meat.

One benefit of the 'reverse sear' is that the meat has already rested between the low cook and the sear, so you can chow down right away.

THE JKF STEAK

SERVES 2

JKF stands for 'just keep flipping', a phrase I created to describe my preferred way of cooking a steak. Yeah, flipping your steaks constantly while they cook is a bit controversial, but I stand by it. Using really high heat is key, which is why I love to cook over charcoal. Each time you expose the surface of the meat to the heat, you're drying it out, which kickstarts the Maillard reaction. But because you're constantly turning the meat, it doesn't overcook on one side, so you end up with 'coast-to-coast' doneness and one helluva crust that's ready in mere minutes. #JustKeepFlipping.

2 x 1.5 lb (700 g) boneless ribeye steaks, at least 1½ inches (4 cm) thick (see Notes)

1½ teaspoons salt or your preferred steak seasoning

1. Remove the steaks from the fridge 20–30 minutes before cooking.
2. Prepare a grill for high-heat cooking, about 500°F (250°C). If using charcoal, pile it up together to form a really intense mound of heat.
3. Pat the steaks dry with a paper towel and season them well on both sides with salt.
4. Place the steaks onto the hot grill over direct heat. Begin to flip the steak every 30–45 seconds. The first one or two flips will be pretty underwhelming, but trust the crust! It will build as you continue to cook it. The flame will also build as the fat renders from the steak, so the cooking intensity will increase as time goes on.
5. The steaks should take around 8–10 minutes to cook to medium-rare, but start monitoring the temperature from the 6-minute mark onwards. When it reaches 128–133°F (53–56°C), remove it from the grill. Rest for 5 minutes, loosely covered with foil, before slicing and enjoying.

NOTES

You can also use a bone-in ribeye if you prefer! I just like the way the boneless ones sit on the grill. A quick reminder: if you're in Australia or New Zealand, the 'boneless ribeye' is called a scotch fillet.

Always buy the best quality meat you can afford, but if you're using a leaner steak, you may want to give it a thin coating of oil before seasoning, to encourage the sear.

My preferred seasoning for this is, of course, Hardcore Carnivore Black.

GRILLED WHOLE RIBEYE CAP WITH THYME BROWNED BUTTER

SERVES 4–6

You'll notice by the short ingredient list that I'm keeping this one simple. While eating *spinalis dorsi* is not unusual (I mean, it's part of ribeye steaks after all), eating a meal of ONLY *spinalis dorsi* is a very special treat. For a cut like this, you need to taste the purity of the beef, which is why I season it with salt only. But every few bites, I like to slather on this insanely moreish browned butter to really send things over the top.

½ cup (4 oz/125 g) salted butter

2 teaspoons thyme leaves

1 whole ribeye cap (see page 94)

2 tablespoons avocado oil or beef tallow (page 244)

1½ teaspoons salt

1. Melt the butter in a small saucepan over medium heat, swirling the pan regularly. The butter will foam as it cooks, then the milk solids will start to separate and brown. Keep stirring until the butter is a dark golden brown color. This step happens very quickly, so keep an eye on it to ensure it doesn't burn. It should smell toasty and fragrant.
2. Remove from the heat and cool for 2–3 minutes. Toss in the thyme leaves and stir through. As the butter cools, the milk solids will sink to the bottom, so you need to keep stirring. To do this, pour the butter into a metal bowl and place it over a larger bowl filled with ice. Stir the butter until it firms and turns opaque, with the milk solids and thyme leaves evenly distributed. Store in the fridge until ready to use.
3. Remove the ribeye cap from the fridge and light a grill for high-heat grilling, about 500°F (250°C).
4. Pat the steak dry with paper towels, then drizzle the avocado oil on both sides, massaging to coat the steak evenly. Season both sides with the salt.
5. Place the steak directly on the hot grill and cook, turning every 1–2 minutes until it reaches an internal temperature of around 130–135°F (54–57°C), about 8–10 minutes all up.
6. Remove the steak from the grill and cover loosely with foil. Rest for 5–8 minutes.
7. Slice across the grain and dot with a generous amount of browned butter to serve.

BEEF RIBS

• MEAT MAP •

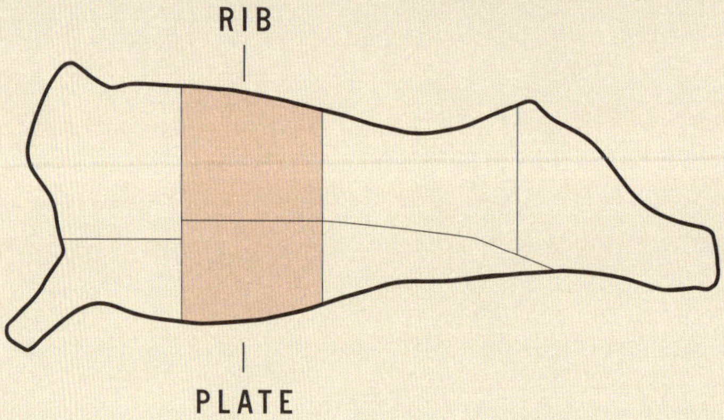

Beef ribs are a true chameleon. They can go hot and fast on the grill or low and slow in the smoker, and both approaches deliver incredible results. Thin cuts thrive over high heat, while thick slabs reward patience with rich, tender meat. Few cuts offer that kind of range.

Beef ribs go by many different names, depending on where they're cut from and how they're portioned. They span two separate primals on the carcass, and can be cut across or between the bones, left as large slabs or separated into individual ribs. That's why there are so many variations available.

What they share is the same basic structure: rib bones surrounded by the *serratus ventralis* and intercostal muscles. These are hard-working muscles with plenty of connective tissue, which makes ribs incredibly flavorful but best suited to either very hot, fast cooking in thin slices, or low-and-slow methods that allow the collagen to break down. Thin cuts like flanken or galbi are ideal for grilling, while thick-cut ribs shine when smoked, braised or slow-roasted.

To make things more confusing, not every 'short rib' actually comes from the rib primal – many boneless versions are cut from the chuck. And so-called 'finger ribs' are simply the meat between the bones, also known as intercostals.

QUICK GUIDE TO BEEF RIB CUTS

PLATE RIBS/DINO RIBS: Cut from the plate primal – specifically ribs 6, 7 and 8 – and sold as a three-bone slab. These massive, meaty ribs are often called 'dino ribs', made famous by Texas BBQ.

CHUCK RIBS: Taken from ribs 2, 3, 4 and 5 in the chuck primal. Usually sold as a four-bone rack, they're smaller than plate ribs but still great for smoking or braising.

ENGLISH CUT/SHORT RIBS: Ribs cut lengthways between the bones, then halved into individual portions, each with a thick block of meat sitting on top. Ideal for braising, but also excellent when smoked or slow-roasted.

BACK RIBS: Cut from the rib primal after the ribeye is removed – they're the baby backs of the beef world. Most of the meat sits between the bones rather than on top, so they can be a bit light on the meat-to-bone ratio.

FLANKEN CUT/GALBI/ASADO RIBS: Ribs cut straight across the bones into thin strips, so each piece contains several small cross sections of bone. Perfect for hot, fast grilling.

FINGER RIBS/INTERCOSTALS: The strips of meat found between the rib bones, sometimes removed when fabricating boneless short ribs.

PLATE RIBS

CHUCK RIBS

ENGLISH CUT RIBS

BACK RIBS

FLANKEN CUT RIBS

FINGER RIBS

SMOKED SICHUAN PEPPER BEEF RIBS

SERVES 6–8

Plate ribs are typically the largest type of rib section and have three giant bones. Can't find plate ribs? No problem. You can also use chuck ribs or even individual short ribs, but the cooking time will be significantly shorter. Massive Texas-style smoked ribs are known for their coarse black pepper bark, but my version has the added oomph of fragrant, mouth-tingling Chinese Sichuan pepper.

- 1 x 5–6 lb (2.5–3 kg) rack of beef plate ribs
- 2½ tablespoons Sichuan peppercorns
- 1½ tablespoons coarse salt
- 1½ tablespoons coarse black pepper
- ½ teaspoon five-spice powder
- 2 tablespoons olive oil
- ½ cup (125 ml) water
- ¼ cup (60 ml) worcestershire sauce

1. Preheat a smoker to 300°F (155°C). Remove the ribs from the fridge 20–30 minutes before cooking.
2. Place the Sichuan peppercorns in a spice grinder (or use a mortar and pestle). Pulse or grind until the peppercorns are a mixture of powder and coarse pieces. Combine with the salt, black pepper and five-spice powder to create the rub.
3. Pour the olive oil onto the ribs, using your hands to spread it over the entire surface, making sure it is well coated.
4. Spread the rub all over the ribs, pressing it firmly against the meat surface. Ensure all surfaces, including the sides, are well coated.
5. Place the ribs into the smoker, bone side down. Close the lid and allow to cook.
6. In a spray bottle, combine the water and the worcestershire sauce. Spritz the ribs with this mixture every 45–60 minutes as they cook.
7. Smoke the ribs for a total of 5–6 hours, or until they are completely tender. To check, insert a skewer or thin meat thermometer at several points. You should feel no resistance at all when pushing against the meat. If some areas are still tight, continue to cook.
8. Once tender, remove the ribs from the smoker and wrap them tightly in butcher's paper or foil. Leave for 30 minutes to rest. They will retain plenty of heat.
9. Slice between the bones to serve.

NOTE

I recommend oak, mesquite or hickory wood to pair with the beef.

RED WINE RAGÙ WITH PAPPARDELLE

SERVES 6–8

I'm including two different recipes for this hearty, meat-laden pasta sauce, so you can choose your own adventure. One uses the bones to first make the bone broth (page 256), then the meat is repurposed for this ragù. But if you want to dive straight in, I've included a version for making it from scratch.

3 tablespoons olive oil, divided

1 x 3.5 lb (1.5 kg) rack of beef back ribs or 4 cups (500 g) shredded left-over bone broth meat (page 256)

1 onion, diced

2 carrots, peeled and diced

2 garlic cloves, crushed

2 tablespoons tomato paste

1 tablespoon dried oregano

2 teaspoons freshly cracked black pepper

2 teaspoons salt

1 cup (250 ml) red wine

2 cups (500 ml) beef stock

28 oz (810 g) crushed canned tomatoes

2 bay leaves

1 lb (450 g) pappardelle pasta (see Notes page 110)

parmesan cheese, to serve

basil leaves, to serve

METHOD #1: MAKING IT FROM SCRATCH

1. Place a heavy-based pot (like a Dutch oven) over medium-high heat and add 1 tablespoon olive oil.
2. Slice the back ribs between the bones to separate into individual ribs.
3. Brown half the ribs in the pot for 5–10 minutes on each side, then remove and set aside. Add another tablespoon of olive oil and repeat with the remaining ribs.
4. Pour the last tablespoon of oil into the pot, then add the onion, carrot and garlic. Cook until softened, about 5–7 minutes, stirring frequently with a wooden spoon. Use the spoon to scrape up all the browned bits from the bottom of the pot as the veggies cook.
5. Add the tomato paste, oregano, black pepper and salt, stirring to combine. Cook down for another minute or two.
6. Pour the wine into the pot and turn the heat down to medium. Keep scraping the sides to loosen and dislodge all the browned bits.
7. Add the beef stock and crushed tomatoes, along with the browned beef ribs. Reduce the heat down to a simmer, cover and cook for 2 hours, stirring occasionally, or until the meat is tender.
8. Use tongs to remove the ribs from the liquid. Discard the bones and any membrane and shred the remaining meat, then return it to the pot.
9. Stir the meat into the sauce, then taste and add additional salt if desired. Simmer for a further 15 minutes, then remove from the heat.
10. Prepare the pasta according to the package directions. You can either add it to the pot and stir through the ragù, or plate the pasta, then spoon generous amounts of sauce over the top – whichever you prefer. To serve, top with parmesan and basil leaves. ›

METHOD #2: USING LEFT-OVER MEAT FROM THE BONE BROTH

1. Place a heavy-based pot (like a Dutch oven) over medium-high heat and add the olive oil.
2. Add the onion, carrot and garlic to the pot. Cook until softened, about 5–7 minutes, stirring frequently.
3. Stir in the tomato paste, oregano, black pepper and salt. Cook down for another minute or two.
4. Pour the wine into the pan and turn the heat down to medium, then add the beef stock and crushed tomatoes. Reduce the heat down to a simmer, cover and cook for 2 hours, stirring occasionally, allowing the sauce to reduce and concentrate in flavor.
5. Add the shredded meat to the sauce, stir through and simmer for a further 15 minutes. Season with additional salt if desired.
6. Prepare the pasta according to the package directions. You can either add it to the pot and stir through the ragù, or plate the pasta, then spoon generous amounts of sauce over the top – whichever you prefer. To serve, top with parmesan and basil leaves.

NOTES

If you can't find beef back ribs, you can also use short ribs, which have more meat on them.

You can substitute the pappardelle with any type of pasta you prefer, but try to choose one that can really grip the sauce, like fusilli or penne. The rougher the surface, the better!

CARAMELIZED GOCHUJANG-GLAZED BEEF RIBS

SERVES 6–8

This superfast recipe makes a great appetizer to precede a grilled main course. It takes only five or so minutes to cook, so your grill is freed up very quickly. For a big crowd, cut between the bones to create smaller bite-sized riblets.

6 x 1.5 lb (700 g) flanken cut rib strips, cut ¼ inch (6 mm) thick

2 tablespoons gochujang paste

2 teaspoons sesame oil

¼ cup (60 ml) rice wine vinegar or apple cider vinegar

1 tablespoon honey

2 tablespoons soy sauce

1. Remove the beef from the fridge.
2. Light a grill for medium-heat cooking, about 400–450°F (210–230°C).
3. In a small saucepan, combine the gochujang, sesame oil, vinegar, honey and soy sauce. Place over low heat and stir to combine. Simmer and reduce for 2–4 minutes, or until it thickens slightly.
4. Lay the ribs on the grill, then immediately brush the top with some of the glaze. Cook for 1 minute, then flip over. Brush the other side with more glaze, leaving the ribs to cook for 1–2 minutes. Flip them over one final time and cook for 1–2 more minutes until they start to char around the edges. Ensure each glazed side is exposed to direct heat at least once so the sauce can caramelize.
5. Remove from the grill, allow to cool for a minute, then serve.

NOTE

Believe it or not, you don't need to salt the ribs before you glaze them. The soy sauce and gochujang provide plenty of salty flavor for such a thin cut of meat.

SHORT RIB RAMEN WITH BLACK GARLIC OIL

SERVES 4

We've all had those late-night bowls of instant ramen, but this is what happens when it grows up. Fall-apart short ribs step in as the star, and a deep, flavorful broth replaces the packet. Then comes the real magic – a drizzle of smoky black garlic oil that ties everything together. It's cozy, slurpable and just the right kind of extra.

2 tablespoons olive or avocado oil

3 lb (1.5 kg) bone-in short ribs (see Notes)

4 cups (1 liter) chicken or beef stock or bone broth (page 256)

6 cups (1.5 liters) water

1 bunch scallions (spring onions)

2-inch (5 cm) piece fresh ginger, peeled and chopped into 3 pieces

8 garlic cloves

½ cup (125 ml) soy sauce

2 star anise

1 cinnamon stick

1 tablespoon sambal (chili garlic sauce)

1 tablespoon salted butter

8 oz (85 g) enoki or shimeji mushrooms

½ teaspoon salt

4 ramen noodle cakes

spray oil

2 soft-boiled eggs, halved

1 tablespoon sesame seeds

BLACK GARLIC OIL

¼ cup (60 ml) canola or vegetable oil

¼ cup (60 g) crushed garlic

¼ cup (60 ml) sesame oil

1. Place a large, heavy-based pot over high heat and add the olive oil. Once shimmering, add the beef ribs. Cook for 5 minutes without moving or disturbing them, then turn and brown the other side.
2. Add the stock and water to the pot, along with two of the scallions. Add the ginger, garlic, soy sauce, star anise, cinnamon and sambal. Bring to a boil, then reduce the heat to a simmer and cook for 2–3 hours until the beef ribs are extremely tender.
3. While the beef is cooking, prepare the black garlic oil. In a small saucepan, heat the canola oil and crushed garlic over medium-low heat. Cook, stirring or swirling the pot regularly, until the garlic is sticky and blackened, about 15 minutes. Allow to cool slightly, then place in a blending cup along with the sesame oil. Blend with an immersion blender until combined, then set aside.
4. Place a skillet over high heat and add the butter. Once the butter is melted and foaming, add the mushrooms and salt. Cook for 5–7 minutes, stirring occasionally, until the mushrooms are browned. Set aside.
5. Prepare the noodles according to the package directions. I like to cook them for 30–60 seconds less than recommended for a chewier result. Split them evenly into four bowls.
6. Finely slice the remaining scallions and set aside.
7. From the large pot, fish out and discard the ginger, garlic, scallion, star anise and cinnamon. Using tongs, remove the beef ribs and place them on a sheet pan (baking sheet).
8. Spritz the beef ribs with a little spray oil, then place under the broiler on high for 3–4 minutes until browned and somewhat crispy.
9. To assemble the ramen bowls, nestle some of the cooked mushrooms on the noodles in each bowl, along with half an egg. Loosely shred the rib meat and split between the bowls.
10. Ladle some of the hot broth into each bowl. It should be hot enough to warm the egg, noodles and mushrooms. Sprinkle the sesame seeds over the top and add the sliced scallions to finish. Drizzle with a spoonful of the black garlic oil and serve immediately.

NOTES

If you can't find bone-in short ribs, use boneless short ribs. You'll end up with a little extra meat (which no one is gonna complain about).

Between the stock and the soy sauce, this dish doesn't need any extra salt, but if you're a major salt fiend, feel free to add 1 teaspoon salt to the meat before you brown it.

BRISKET

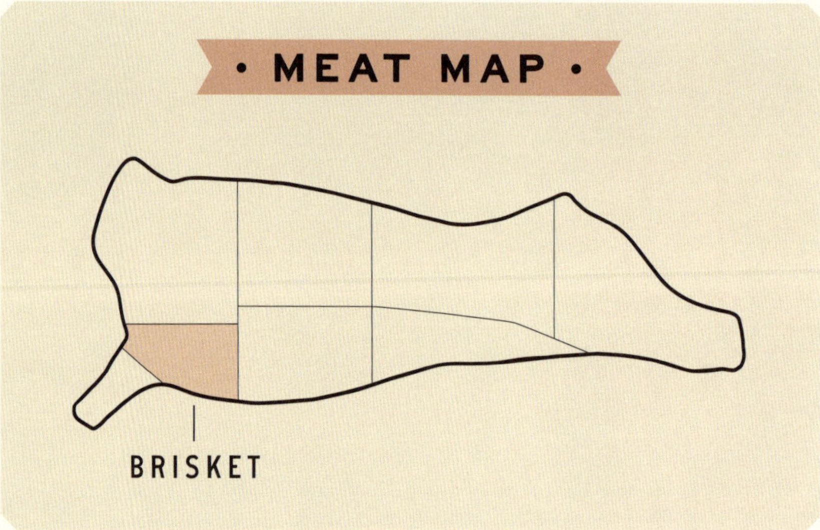

The brisket primal is comprised of locomotive muscles, meaning they are used for movement. Muscles that move more and work harder are always tougher, so brisket needs to be cooked for a long period of time to make it tender. Long cooking methods include braising, sous vide or even slow cooking. The exception to this rule is if you slice it extremely thinly, which is how it's used in Vietnamese pho and Korean hot pot. But of course, the most famous way to prepare a brisket is smoking it low 'n' slow – Texas-style.

Brisket is famously tough because it's packed with collagen, the ultra-strong protein that holds muscle fibers together. Collagen is the rope-like protein that makes hardworking muscles tough in their raw state. With steady low heat over a longer cooking period, those collagen fibers can transform into gelatin. But it's not merely temperature that gets the job done – moisture is crucial to the conversion. In a completely dry environment, collagen fibers simply contract and become chewy. With moisture available, the collagen can loosen and dissolve rather than seize up.

That process, driven by heat, time and hydrolysis, breaks collagen's structure into smaller, sticky pieces we recognize as gelatin. These gelatin molecules then form a loose network that can trap both water and fat, which is why properly cooked brisket feels simultaneously juicy and rich. To be clear, gelatin won't magically catch the majority of the rendering brisket fat (that is lost as it melts off), but it can hold and stabilize smaller amounts of fat that are in immediate proximity to where the gelatin forms.

Two major muscles make up the brisket:

- *pectoralis profundus* (flat)
- *pectoralis superficialis* (point).

Low-and-slow BBQ uses a 'packer cut' brisket, named for the rough, untrimmed versions that came straight from meatpacking plants. This is the whole brisket primal in 'diamond in the rough' form. All the fat cap is left intact, so the pitmaster can choose to trim it to their liking. More manageable brisket portion sizes are also available in the store, usually pieces of lean, trimmed flat, which are suited to corned beef or pot roast.

One of the biggest challenges of cooking a whole packer brisket is its irregular shape and shifting grain. At one end, it's thick and chunky, while the other tapers off, making it tricky to cook evenly without drying one side or undercooking the other. Adding to the challenge is the orientation of the muscles, with the point draping over the flat, and its fibers running diagonally to the flat's grain. While this doesn't change the way you cook a brisket, it does mean you need to know how to slice it properly to get the best results.

Before we dive into the recipes, let's do some quick meat myth-busting – the truth about the 'left brisket'. For years, a rumor has floated around that choosing a left-sided brisket yields better results. This idea was based on the falsehood that cattle favor one side when they lay down to rest, making one side more tender than the other. For the record, cattle alternate the side they rest on, which evens out pressure and blood flow. So let's put this myth to rest.

PACKER CUT BRISKET

TEXAS-STYLE OVERNIGHT BRISKET

SERVES 12–24

This is perhaps the holy grail of all smoked foods. People have moved across continents and oceans for this prized meat (it's me – I am people). Brisket is a BBQ enigma. The challenge of cooking this irregularly sized primal to tender perfection seems to be part science, part art and lots of patience. But the real trick is repetition – the more you cook, the better you'll get.

While not traditional, I wanted to make this as easy and accessible as possible, so this recipe is designed specifically for pellet smokers or any smoker that can regulate its own temperature, so you can get some sleep. If you don't have one like that, you can still follow these directions. You'll just have to keep getting up to manage your fire/temperature.

1 x 14–15 lb (6.5–7 kg) whole packer cut brisket

3 cups (750 ml) water

brisket rub (see Notes)

½ cup (125 ml) apple cider vinegar

1. Starting around 11 pm, trim the brisket according to the instructions on page 119.
2. Preheat a pellet smoker to 200°F (90°C).
3. Fill a foil pan or heatproof container with 2 cups (500 ml) water inside the cooking chamber.
4. Season the brisket generously with the brisket rub, actively pressing it into all surfaces.
5. Place the brisket, point side up, into the pellet smoker. I always put mine on the top rack because the radiant heat from the deflector plate on the bottom shelf is too much for the brisket flat.
6. Close the lid and go to bed!
7. At 7 am the next morning, mix the remaining water with the apple cider vinegar in a spray bottle. Liberally spritz the top and sides of the brisket to rehydrate.
8. Increase the pellet smoker temperature to 250°F (120°C).
9. Monitor the internal temperature of the brisket for the next 2–3 hours, spritzing lightly every 30–45 minutes.
10. Once the brisket reaches an internal temperature of 165°F (73°C), wrap it tightly in butcher's paper (like swaddling a baby – snug, with no gaps) and return to the smoker.
11. Cook until the thickest part of the point reaches 205°F (96°C), usually another 4–6 hours.
12. Remove the brisket from the smoker and let it rest for at least 1–2 hours at ambient room temperature. The key here is to let the temperature drop before slicing or holding. It just needs to stay above 150°F (65°C), but it'll take hours to drop that low.
13. If you want to serve the brisket later, you can hold it by placing it in a cooler. If the weather is cold, 'preheat' the cooler by filling it with some hot water for about 10 minutes, then drain before you put the brisket in. Hold the brisket in the butcher's paper and do not slice before holding.
14. When you're ready to serve, slice the brisket. Start by cutting the brisket in half where the flat meets the point. Slice the flat across the grain into pencil-width slices. For the point, rotate 90 degrees before slicing.

NOTES

Truthfully, I don't measure my brisket rub. I use a 1:2 ratio of salt to coarse black pepper and apply it generously. Some use a binder like mustard or add garlic powder, but salt and pepper is classic.

Pepper size matters. A 16-mesh coarse grind (about sesame-seed size) is standard for Texas BBQ and essential for proper bark.

You'll need a smoker for this recipe – it can't be replicated in an oven.

THE TEXAS BRISKET PLAYBOOK

Some musings and valuable takeaways I have learned through trial and definitely some error.

TAKE ADVICE WITH A GRAIN OF SALT

This may be controversial, but I'm just gonna say it: there is a lot of nonsense floating around in BBQ. I've heard pitmasters claim they can 'smell hormones' in raw beef, or flat out lie about where their meat is sourced from. Some overcomplicate the process or toss in pointless steps, and honestly, I think a few just enjoy messing with people (e.g. the left brisket rumor). Don't get me wrong, there are incredible pitmasters who share knowledge without the gatekeeping. But the field is crowded, and not all advice is worth following. The truth is simple: the best way to get good at brisket is practice.

WOOD CHOICE

Texas has several different BBQ regions (they use mesquite down south, and hickory in the east). Wood selection wasn't a culinary choice – pitmasters defaulted to whatever species was plentiful in their region. Central Texas is the most famed style, and the wood of choice is post oak.

BIGGER IS BETTER

Larger briskets are naturally more forgiving in the smoker. They hold a greater reservoir of internal moisture, which means they stay juicy long enough for collagen to fully break down into gelatin. Smaller briskets dry out faster, leaving less water available for that conversion. Their lower thermal mass makes them more prone to overshooting doneness, meaning you're more likely to end up with something leathery and dry.

FAT IS FLAVOR

Always use the highest quality briskets you can afford. The more intramuscular fat, the easier (and more forgiving) they are to cook. It's just that simple.

COOKING TIME

A true Texas brisket takes time – at least 10–12 hours on the pit, in my experience. Competition cooks might hot-shot one in 6 hours, but the result is a whole different animal: roastier flavor, firmer bite and none of that slow-smoked, melt-in-your-mouth texture that defines Lone Star brisket. You just can't rush perfection.

BINDERS

Binders like mustard are sometimes used as a base layer to 'glue' the seasoning to the meat. If you want to use one, go for it, but you don't actually need one to get the seasoning to adhere. Some folks get fancy with their binders, using niche ingredients like pickle juice. And hey, if you can taste 2 tablespoons of pickle juice under a ton of pepper and 12 hours of smoke, I'm impressed.

SMOKER TYPES

An offset smoker (regular or reverse flow) is the traditional pit of Texas BBQ. It's completely analogue and the temperature is manipulated by controlling the airflow through the firebox and out the chimney. While I believe that the best-tasting briskets do come from this type of smoker, I'm a big fan of the convenience of automated smokers like pellet grills, which make BBQ more accessible to busy lifestyles.

TALLOW

In recent years, there's been a trend of finishing brisket with melted tallow. Sometimes it's brushed on top of the resting brisket. Sometimes it's painted onto the butcher paper before wrapping. Either way, the main effect is cosmetic – tallow gives the bark a glossier finish and can soften it slightly, making slicing easier. It doesn't make the meat juicier. Fat can't penetrate the water-filled muscle fibers or connective tissue. It only coats the surface and doesn't reach the interior.

PAPER, NOT FOIL

The 'Texas crutch' (wrapping brisket in foil) has long been used to push meat through the stall, that frustrating phase when surface moisture evaporates, cooling the brisket and stalling the internal temperature. The downside of impermeable foil is that it creates a completely sealed environment, trapping both steam and heat, which can ruin bark and overcook the brisket during the resting or holding phase. Peach paper, on the other hand, is uncoated but treated for extra-wet strength. Because it's porous, it allows steam to escape, helping preserve bark while still keeping the brisket protected.

HOLDING IS NOT RESTING

Did I write that loudly enough? In the 'brisket renaissance' of recent years, pitmasters have pushed the technique of long holding, producing a distinct and highly prized texture. It's not the same as resting. The key difference is letting the brisket cool significantly before the active holding phase begins. What likely started as a way to keep briskets service-ready has now become one of the hallmarks of modern brisket.

INJECTIONS

Competition teams often inject briskets with beef stock, MSG or other boosters because judges often only take one bite per entry. But that's not traditional Texas BBQ. If you cook a brisket properly, the natural collagen-to-gelatin conversion delivers all the moisture and tenderness you need – no injections necessary.

TEMPERATURE PROBING

Once the brisket is wrapped, I check the internal temperature by jamming my thermometer straight through the paper. I prefer not to use leave-in temperature probes. I find them fiddly and prone to inaccuracies.

• BE THE BUTCHER •

HOW TO TRIM A BRISKET – TEXAS BBQ STYLE

I was taught to trim briskets by pitmaster Evan LeRoy of LeRoy and Lewis Barbecue in Austin, Texas. More than just a talented chef, Evan is a good mate of mine, and it's been incredible watching him hone his craft and earn industry-wide accolades, and even a Michelin star.

1. Place the brisket flat side up, and cut into the thick piece of fat on the side, following the natural seam to remove it.
2. Trim off any excess fat and silverskin. Use your hand to push the brisket up from beneath to even up the cutting surface.
3. Flip the brisket over and trim back the 'mohawk' on the top of the brisket to create an aerodynamic shape.
4. Cut away any overly thin pieces by making a large cut along one side, then curving the cut across the front (think of a giant J shape, or reverse J, depending on which side brisket you have).
5. Remove the thick band of fat running along the other side by feeling for it with your fingers and trimming through the bulk of the fat seam.
6. Shave down any sharp points or edges so the whole brisket is left with a smooth, aerodynamic shape. Trim any excess fat cap down to about ¼ inch (6 mm).

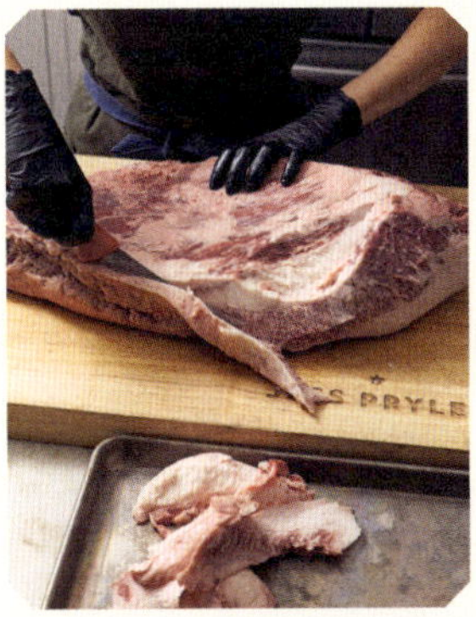

1

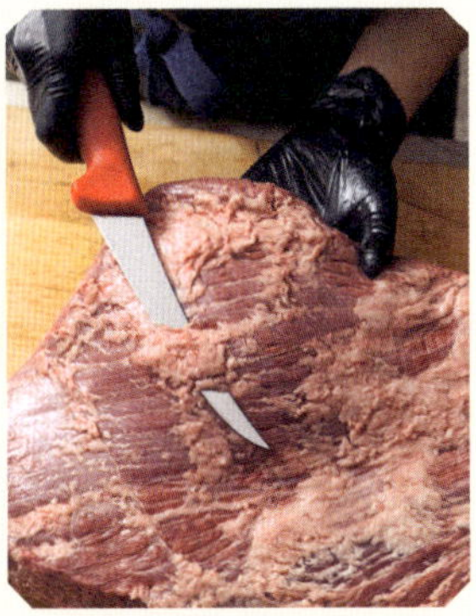

2

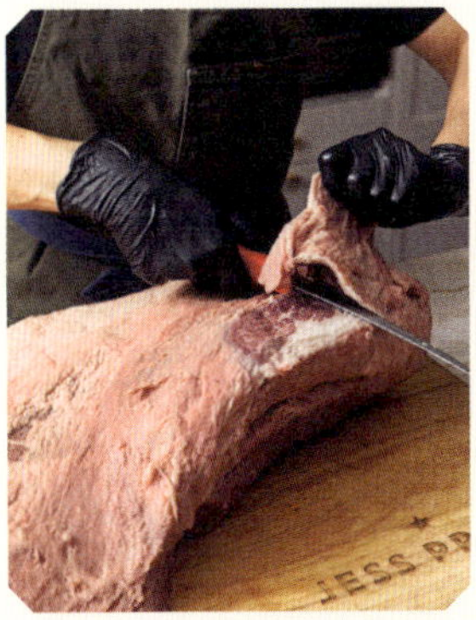

3

4

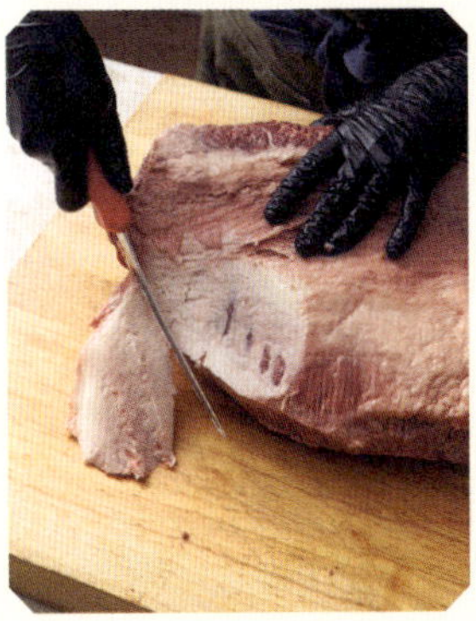

5

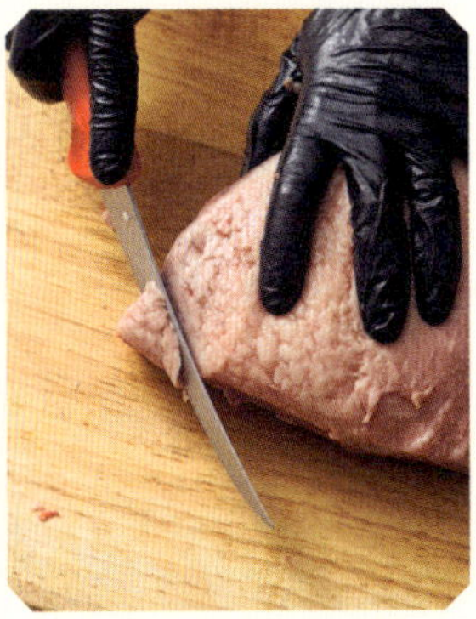

6

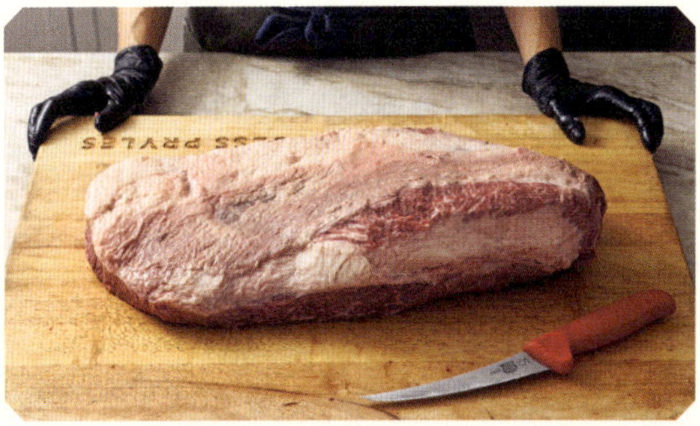

CHEESY BRISKET MELT

SERVES 2

If you smoke a whole brisket and don't have a crowd to feed, you're bound to end up with left-overs. I like to chop any extra meat into smaller, more usable pieces that can be repurposed in all kinds of dishes – breakfast tacos, quesadillas, shepherd's pie, fried rice – anywhere you'd usually use ground (minced) beef. Of course, there's nothing wrong with keeping it classic. Pile that brisket between two slices of thick 'Texas toast' (see Notes) with a generous amount of cheese, and you've got yourself an all-star sandwich.

- 1½ cups (250 g) chopped brisket left-overs (page 116)
- 4 slices thick-cut white bread
- 3–4 tablespoons softened salted butter
- 4 slices cheddar cheese
- ¼ cup (60 g) BBQ sauce
- 6–8 pickle slices
- 1 cup (100 g) shredded (grated) Monterey Jack or tasty cheese

1. Reheat the brisket in a small saucepan or skillet over medium-low heat, or in the microwave until warmed through.
2. Spread the bread with butter on one side only, making sure to coat right to the edges.
3. Place a skillet over medium-low heat. Add one slice of bread, butter-side down. Layer with a slice of cheddar, half the brisket, half the BBQ sauce, 3–4 pickle slices, half the shredded cheese and another slice of cheddar. Top with the second slice of bread, butter-side up. Repeat for the second sandwich.
4. Press down gently and cook for 3–4 minutes, or until golden brown. Flip carefully and cook for another 3–4 minutes on the other side.
5. Remove from the pan, let rest briefly, then slice in half to serve.

NOTES

'Texas toast' is just a fancy name for thick-cut white bread – because everything's bigger in Texas.

If you can, buy a block of Monterey Jack or tasty cheese and shred as needed. The pre-shredded stuff has a coating that prevents it from reaching maximum meltability.

You can also use a large griddle to make these. Warm the meat first, layer on the shredded cheese and pickles, then scoop the filling into the bread and finish toasting.

AUSSIE MEAT PIES

MAKES 8 INDIVIDUAL PIES

There's something drool-worthy about biting into a buttery, flaky pastry layer and hitting a rich, gravy-smothered beef filling. While traditional meat pies are made with ground (minced) meat, I think the rich flavor profile of brisket (and the long, slow braising process) makes it the perfect cut for this classic Aussie recipe. The trick is to allow plenty of time for the browning of the meat at the start of the recipe – this step is key to getting a deep brown gravy with more complex flavor.

- 4 tablespoons olive oil, divided
- 3–4 lb (1.5–2 kg) beef brisket flat or rolled brisket, cut into 1-inch (2.5 cm) cubes
- 1 onion, finely diced
- 1 tablespoon tomato paste
- 1 tablespoon Vegemite (optional; see Notes)
- ½ cup (75 g) all-purpose (plain) flour
- 4 cups (1 liter) beef stock
- ¼ cup (60 ml) worcestershire sauce
- 2 teaspoons salt, plus more to taste
- 4 sheets ready-made pie crust (shortcrust pastry), thawed
- 4 sheets ready-made puff pastry, thawed
- 1 egg, beaten

1. Place a Dutch oven over high heat. Add 1 tablespoon olive oil, then add one-third of the beef cubes. Working in batches to avoid overcrowding the pot, brown the meat until it develops a dark crust, then remove it using a slotted spoon. Repeat this process two more times, adding 1 tablespoon oil before each batch until all the beef is browned.
2. Add the remaining tablespoon of olive oil to the pot, then cook the diced onion for 6–8 minutes or until softened. Stir occasionally to scrape the browned bits from the bottom of the pot. You can add a couple of tablespoons of water to help this process.
3. Stir in the tomato paste, Vegemite (if using) and flour. It will form a thick, messy paste.
4. Add the beef stock a little at a time, stirring constantly until the mixture turns to a sauce. Add the browned beef, worcestershire sauce and salt. The liquid should just cover the meat. If necessary, you can top up the liquid with water so the meat is fully immersed.
5. Bring to a boil, then reduce the heat to a simmer. Place a lid on the pot and cook, stirring occasionally, for 2–3 hours, or until the brisket is completely tender.
6. Preheat the oven to 375°F (190°C) and line eight 5-inch (13 cm) individual pie tins.
7. Cut the pie crusts slightly larger than the diameter of the tins so that there is a slight lip. This is necessary so the pastry lid can be sealed. Gently press a pie crust into one of the tins. You can also trim and press pieces of the crust together to fit the tins. Layer with a sheet of parchment (baking) paper, then fill with baking weights, uncooked rice or dried beans. This is known as 'blind baking' and it stops the crusts from puffing while you're cooking them. Repeat until all tins are filled, then bake for 10 minutes. Allow to cool, then remove the weights and paper.
8. Once the meat is tender, allow to cool, then use heatproof gloves or two forks to break it up.
9. Fill the pie shells with a heaping amount of meat mixture. Cut the puff pastry sheets into circles large enough to seal each pie, then place on top of the meat mixture. Gently press the puff pastry onto the rim of the baked shell to form a light seal.
10. Make 2–3 holes in the pastry to form steam vents, then brush the tops with the beaten egg.
11. Place in the oven and bake for 35–45 minutes until the pastry is golden brown.

NOTES

This is a great recipe for a tougher cut like brisket, because the long, slow cooking process really lets the meat tenderize and break down to become one with the gravy. You could also substitute the brisket for chuck or any stew meat, but the leaner it is, the less rich the filling will be.

Vegemite is the oft-misunderstood national condiment of Australia. While it's traditionally eaten as a breakfast spread on toast, it's extremely concentrated and salty, almost like beef bouillon paste. It's also the perfect hit of umami to add to dishes just like this.

There are two different pastries used in this recipe. The base of the pie uses shortcrust, while the top has puff pastry. Since you're working with square sheets of pastry, you may have to piece together some sections so they fit.

CHUCK

MEAT MAP

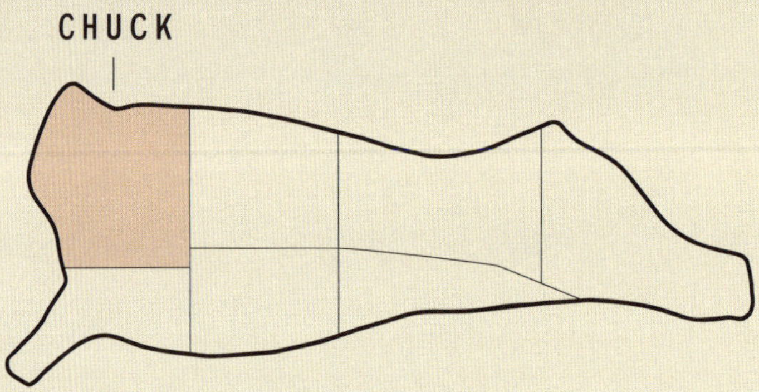

If there's a primal that overdelivers, it's chuck. This single shoulder section of the steer is packed with variety. It gives us sleeper steaks like flat iron and Denver, deeply beefy roasts, and has enough collagen to power braises that stay moist and rich when shredded. It also happens to be one of the most economical primals, which is why it turns up in everything from ground (minced) beef to classic pot roast.

Historically, the chuck subprimal was traditionally left whole. Not because it lacked potential, but because early butchery prioritized speed, yield and uniformity. Breaking the chuck into individual muscles required more time and skill, with little commercial incentive to do so. As consumer demand shifted towards better eating quality, seam-butchery revealed that the chuck is incredibly versatile – capable of yielding dozens of distinct steaks and roasts, including the chuck eye, flat iron, Denver, *teres major,* blade steak, seven-bone, arm steak, clod and more.

You won't see all of them here, and that's intentional. Old-school cuts like the seven-bone slice went straight through a jumble of muscles, some tender, some tough. Modern butchery follows a different blueprint, separating muscles along natural seams so the hidden gems can take center stage. In this chapter, we'll focus on the greatest hits – the cuts that show why chuck is one of beef's most rewarding primals.

THAT 'BEEFY' FLAVOR

Many cuts from the chuck are described as deeply 'beefy,' which raises the question: why don't all muscles taste the same? A big part of that comes down to how much a muscle is used. Muscles that do more work (like those in the chuck) develop higher levels of myoglobin, along with a denser network of proteins and connective tissue. That increased activity doesn't just change texture, it also concentrates flavor, giving these cuts a deeper, more pronounced beefiness compared to more passive muscles.

There's also a difference in the types of muscle fibers. Hardworking muscles tend to have more oxidative fibers, which rely on sustained energy use and are associated with stronger, more developed flavor. By contrast, less-used muscles are made up of more glycolytic fibers, which are naturally more tender but milder in taste. This is why a flat iron or Denver cut from the chuck can deliver more intensity than a filet, even when cooked the same way.

Finally, connective tissue contributes more than just toughness. Muscles with more collagen often start out tougher, but they also carry more flavor potential. When cooked properly, that collagen converts to gelatin and integrates into the meat, enriching both mouthfeel and overall taste. The result is a cut that doesn't just taste like beef – it tastes *more* of it.

• MEAT NERD FACT •

The name 'chuck' comes from an old English term meaning a thick chunk of meat. Long before muscle-specific cutting, butchery relied on heavy cleaver work to divide carcasses into coarse but manageable portions. The shoulder was treated as a single piece, taken off in one 'chunk.'

THE RIBEYE'S NEIGHBOR

Perhaps one of the most confounding steaks out there is the chuck eye steak. The internet is littered with 'here's the secret cut you need to know about' videos, touting this as a holy grail steak. They seem to suggest that, if you're lucky enough to find one at the store, it's akin to finding an original van Gogh at a flea market.

Here's the deal: while the beef primals are a roadmap full of nice straight lines, that's just not how muscles work. They twist and turn, with rounded edges and tapering ends. And where some muscles end, others start to form. And some of those primal dividers end up slicing right through some of the muscles. In this case, where the rib is separated from the chuck, it slices right through what meat nerds consider the very best muscle of all – the *spinalis dorsi* (page 96), or ribeye cap.

So, the first two steaks from the chuck end do contain some of the same meat you'd find in a ribeye, and at a much cheaper price. But you can really only cut about two truly special chuck eye steaks – after that, the *spinalis dorsi* tapers off to barely a bite-sized piece, surrounded by other muscles that are far less tender. Pick the right chuck eye and it's a bargain. The others are just average chuck steaks.

The chuck eye has a couple of aliases. It's also known as 'poor man's ribeye' or the 'Delmonico' (although some folks use 'Delmonico' to refer to a regular ribeye steak).

The takeaway here is that it's a good steak at a good price, but don't drive yourself crazy scouring the grocery shelves trying to pick the perfect one. Most supermarkets don't even stock them regularly, so you may be searching in vain. If you can't find it, just use a ribeye steak instead!

TENDER SHREDDED BEEF

MAKES ABOUT 4 CUPS (640 G)

MAIN RECIP

Chuck is the ultimate cut for braising and shredding, with an ideal ratio of fat and meat.

Knowing how to make tender shredded beef is something of a core kitchen competency. It's a simple technique, but it's the starting point for so many other recipes. I've created three recipes that use this one as the foundation (see following pages) to show you how easy it is to get inspired.

- 1 x 2.5–3 lb (1–1.5 kg) chuck roast
- 2 tablespoons olive oil
- 1½ teaspoon salt
- ½ teaspoon onion powder
- 1 teaspoon garlic powder
- 1 teaspoon ground black pepper
- 2 tablespoons soy sauce
- 2 tablespoons worcestershire sauce
- 3 cups (750 ml) beef stock

1. Slice the chuck roast into 4–6 large chunks. Pat the pieces dry with a paper towel.
2. Place a heavy-based pot (a Dutch oven is perfect) over high heat. Add the olive oil to the pot.
3. Nestle the chuck pieces into the pot for 6–8 minutes to brown. Use tongs to turn the pieces over and brown the other side for a further 6–8 minutes.
4. Sprinkle the salt, onion powder, garlic powder and black pepper over the meat, then add the soy sauce and worcestershire sauce. Finally, pour in the beef stock.
5. Bring to a boil, then reduce to a simmer. Cover and cook for 3–4 hours until tender, turning the beef 1–2 times during cooking.
6. Remove the chuck pieces with tongs and allow to cool slightly, then use heatproof gloves or two forks to shred the meat.
7. Ladle ⅓ cup (80 ml) cooking liquid over the meat to keep it moist. If you prefer a super-juicy finish, return the meat to the pot and stir. It will soak up most of the liquid!

BEEF DEBRIS PO'BOYS

SERVES 4

The po'boy is a famous sandwich hailing from New Orleans, Louisiana. And while the most well-known varieties are packed with fried seafood, the beef debris was said to have been invented when a customer asked for roast beef offcuts to be added to his sandwich gravy.

4 cups (640 g) **Tender Shredded Beef** (page 126), with some adjustments to base recipe (see Step 1)
1 teaspoon Cajun seasoning
2 tablespoons tomato paste
4 x 6-inch (15 cm) sections of French bread or soft baguette
½ cup (120 g) mayonnaise
6 tablespoons dijon or stone-ground mustard
½ iceberg lettuce, finely shredded
hot sauce, to serve

1. Make the Tender Shredded Beef, but reduce the salt by 1 teaspoon, and add the Cajun seasoning and tomato paste.
2. Slice each of the bread sections lengthways, then spread with mayonnaise on both sides.
3. Prepare a skillet over medium heat and, working one at a time, place the bread mayo side down to toast lightly for 1–2 minutes.
4. Spread one side of a toasted bun with mustard.
5. Load the bun with a cup of the shredded beef, then pile on a generous portion of iceberg lettuce.
6. Finish with a couple of dashes of hot sauce, and repeat the process to assemble the remaining po'boys.

LOADED BEEFY NACHOS WITH JALAPEÑO RANCH

SERVES 4–6

The essential building blocks of chips and cheese are taken to the next level with this fully-loaded recipe. The key to great nachos is building flavor without adding too many ingredients that may threaten the structural integrity of the chip. The braised shredded beef and homemade jalapeño ranch intensify the nachos experience, while still making sure you're not left holding a broken, toppingless chip!

1 tablespoon olive oil

3–4 cups (480–640 g) **Tender Shredded Beef** (page 126)

½ teaspoon ground cumin

1 teaspoon chili powder

½ teaspoon dried oregano

15 oz (425 g) tortilla chips (see Note)

8 oz (225 g) shredded (grated) Mexican or cheddar cheese

¼ cup (25 g) chopped cilantro (coriander) leaves

½ cup (95 g) diced avocado

JALAPEÑO RANCH

1 cup (115 g) pickled sliced jalapeños, divided, plus 2 tablespoons pickling liquid

¼ cup (60 ml) buttermilk

¼ cup (60 g) sour cream

¼ cup (60 g) mayonnaise

zest and juice of 1 lime

¼ teaspoon onion powder

1 garlic clove

½ teaspoon dried dill

½ teaspoon dried chives

¼ teaspoon salt

¼ cup (7 g) cilantro (coriander) leaves

1. Place a large skillet over medium heat and add the olive oil. Add the shredded beef, along with the cumin, chili powder and dried oregano. Stir the spices through the meat, then continue to stir every so often while the beef reheats, about 5–7 minutes in total.
2. Prepare the jalapeño ranch by combining all the ingredients, except half the pickled jalapeños, in a blender. Blend until smooth. Let sit for at least 30 minutes before using.
3. Preheat the oven to 350°F (175°C).
4. Arrange the tortilla chips on a large sheet pan (baking sheet). Spoon the beef across the top of the chips, then scatter the remaining pickled jalapeños over. Spread the cheese generously over the top.
5. Place the pan in the oven for 6–8 minutes until the cheese is melted and bubbly.
6. Top with the cilantro leaves and diced avocado. Drizzle the jalapeño ranch over the top. Serve immediately.

NOTE

If you can't find tortilla chips, corn chips are a near-identical substitution. You can't really get the quantity wrong – you just need enough to generously fill the bottom of a large sheet pan (baking sheet).

THE NATIONAL BEER of TEXAS

BRAISED CHUCK WITH GOUDA AND CHIVE BISCUIT CRUST

SERVES 6–8

This is the kind of rib-sticking comfort food built for cold nights and empty stomachs. Tender braised chuck is nestled beneath a golden crust of cheesy drop biscuits, which soak up all those rich, beefy juices. It's hearty, cozy and completely satisfying.

4 cups (640 g) **Tender Shredded Beef** (page 126)

2 cups (300 g) all-purpose (plain) flour

2 teaspoons baking powder

1 teaspoon salt

8 oz (225 g) gouda cheese, shredded (grated)

2 tablespoons finely chopped chives

4 oz (115 g) salted butter

1–1¼ cups (250–310 ml) milk

1. Arrange the shredded beef at the bottom of a 9 x 13-inch (23 x 33 cm) baking dish, ladling over extra juice to keep it nice and moist.
2. Preheat the oven to 400°F (210°C).
3. In a mixing bowl, combine the flour, baking powder, salt, cheese and chives. Shred (grate) the butter using a large shredder and place into the bowl. Toss briefly with your hands to coat the butter shreds in flour and distribute them through the mixture, being careful not to overwork it or heat it with your hands too much.
4. Stir in 1 cup (250 ml) milk and work it through until it just comes together. If the mixture is still dry, add the remaining milk. You may not need all of it.
5. Using a scoop or large spoon, drop large portions of the mixture onto the shredded beef to form a crust. There will be small gaps between the spoonfuls, but try to cover as much of the surface as possible.
6. Place in the oven and bake for 15–20 minutes until the crust is golden brown.
7. Allow to cool slightly before serving.

DELMONICO AGUACHILE

SERVES 2

While traditional aguachile is made with shrimp, along the Texas/Mexico border (deep in the heart of beef ranching territory), you will find this meaty version. Aguachile literally translates to 'chili water' in Spanish, and this fiery marinade has plenty of acidic citrus to cut through the beef fat. Think of it like a meaty, spicy ceviche.

- 2 x 1 lb (450 g) chuck eye steaks
- ½ cup (125 ml) neutral oil (e.g. canola or peanut)
- 5 garlic cloves, finely sliced
- zest and juice of 2 limes
- juice of 2 oranges
- ½ cup (125 ml) soy sauce
- 1 tablespoon Maggi seasoning sauce
- 1 tablespoon worcestershire sauce
- 1 serrano pepper, finely sliced
- ½ teaspoon salt
- ¼ red onion, thinly sliced
- ¼ cup (7 g) finely chopped cilantro (coriander) leaves

1. Remove the steaks from the fridge.
2. Pour the neutral oil into a small saucepan over medium heat.
3. Add the garlic and fry until crisp, about 3–4 minutes. Make sure you keep an eye on it. The garlic crisps can turn from golden brown to burnt very quickly, and they have an unpleasant bitter taste if they are cooked too long. Once the garlic pieces are golden brown, remove them from the oil with a slotted spoon and place them onto a paper towel to drain. Reserve 4 tablespoons of the oil.
4. In a bowl, combine the lime zest and juice, orange juice, soy sauce, Maggi seasoning, worcestershire sauce, 2 tablespoons of the reserved oil and serrano pepper. Stir and set aside.
5. Place a heavy-based pan over high heat. Add the remaining tablespoons of the garlic oil to the pan.
6. Season the steak with salt on both sides and place into the hot pan. Cook the steak, turning it every 3–4 minutes until it reaches the desired internal temperature.
7. Remove the steak from the pan and place onto a board. Allow to rest for 5 minutes.
8. Add the red onion to the soy citrus mixture so it can soften slightly.
9. Slice the steak and arrange on a deep plate. Pour the soy citrus mixture over the top, spooning the onion and pepper over the steaks. Top with cilantro leaves, then finish with the fried garlic chips. Serve immediately.

NOTE

This dish makes for an excellent appetizer. It's a fun way to share a steak with a whole table of meat lovers.

MEET THE FLAT IRON

This cut is a double threat. It's the second-most tender muscle after the tenderloin, and it's also loaded with flavor. On top of that, it's one of the most myoglobin-rich muscles, so when cooked correctly, you'll get a gorgeous, blush-pink color payoff.

And yet, not many people recognize just how good it is. That may be because you've heard it called something else. The *infraspinatus* muscle goes by a long list of aliases: top blade roast, top blade steak, oyster blade roast, oyster blade steak, featherblade roast, featherblade steak, top chuck steak, book steak and butler steak.

Anatomically, the *infraspinatus* is a long, flattened cylinder, a little like the shape of a fish. Running straight through the middle is a gnarly seam of connective tissue – almost like the skeleton running through that fish. It takes a helluva lot of cooking to break down, and when it's underdone, it's not fun to eat.

This is how the flat iron evolved.

On the beef forequarter, the *infraspinatus* sits atop the scapula, in an unassuming spot on the shoulder where it transitions into the arm. During processing, it is removed whole in roast form.

You'll start to get an idea that this is indeed a mighty tasty cut when you remove the silverskin from the top and see all the marbling.

Traditionally, the roast was then cut straight down to make individual steaks, each with that nasty connective-tissue seam right in the middle. These are top blade or oyster blade steaks.

But then, they started cutting in the opposite direction, and created a whole new steak. To make a flat iron, the cut is made horizontally to the seam, filleting off a perfectly tender steak – no gristle, no tough stuff.

FLAT IRON STEAK SANDWICH

SERVES 2

Sometimes, simplicity is the smartest move when you've got great ingredients. Some sandwiches take hours to pull together because of fussy components, but this one's all low effort and high reward: medium-rare steak in a baguette, topped with a bright, chopped mix of parsley, capers and olives, and finished with lashings of butter. I spent far too long chasing the 'perfect' sauce – testing spreads and drizzles – before realizing the best answer was plain salted butter. A thick, unapologetic smear. Why complicate excellence?

- 1 tablespoon neutral oil (e.g. canola or peanut oil)
- 1 lb (450 g) flat iron steak (see Note)
- 1¼ teaspoons salt, divided
- 2 anchovies
- 1 cup (30 g) chopped flat-leaf parsley leaves
- 2 teaspoons finely chopped capers
- ⅓ cup (60 g) chopped pitted Castelvetrano olives or other pitted green olives
- 1 tablespoon red wine vinegar
- 3 tablespoons extra virgin olive oil
- 2 mini baguettes or sections of baguette about 6 inches (15 cm) long
- 1–2 tablespoons softened salted butter

1. Heat a skillet over high heat and add the neutral oil.
2. Season the steak with 1 teaspoon salt on both sides and place into the hot skillet. Sear on one side for 5 minutes undisturbed, then flip and cook on the other side for a further 5 minutes.
3. Remove the steak from the skillet and place on a plate to rest.
4. Finely dice the anchovies, sprinkle over the remaining ¼ teaspoon salt and work them together on the board. Alternate between mincing with the knife and dragging the flat side across the mixture until it forms a paste.
5. Place the anchovy paste into a medium bowl along with the parsley, capers, olives, vinegar and olive oil. Mix with a spoon until all ingredients are incorporated.
6. Cut open the baguette and generously smear the butter on both sides.
7. Slice the steak thinly across the grain, then lay the pieces onto the bread.
8. Top with a generous spoonful of 'the green stuff' and serve immediately.

NOTE

Depending on where you purchase your meat, the flat iron may be in one long section of steak or cut into 2–3 portions. Either will work, but if you have one larger whole steak, add an extra minute to the cooking time.

BEEF LOIN

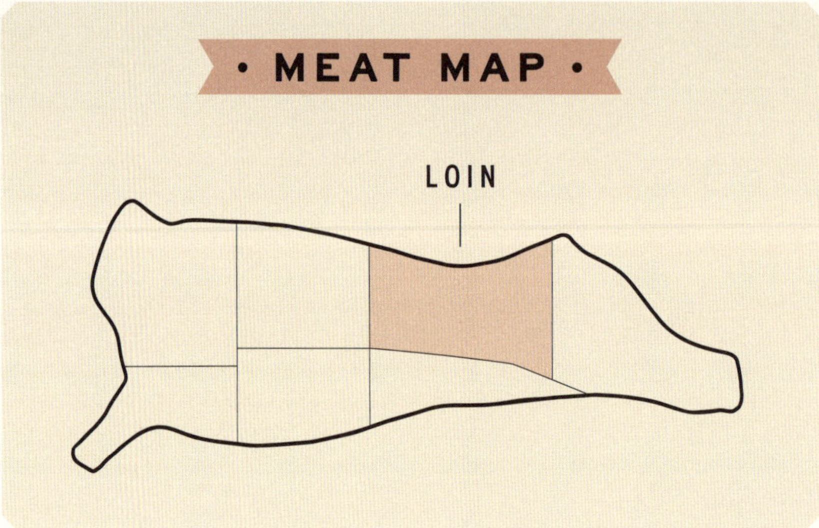

The loin is where the hindquarter begins. Often overshadowed by the big boys of the forequarter, like chuck and ribeye, it actually contains some of my very favorite steaks. The loin can be further split into two subprimals: the short loin and the sirloin.

SHORT LOIN
(SIRLOIN: AUSTRALIA, NZ, UK)

The short loin is comprised of the *longissimus* and *psoas major* muscles. They lie next to each other, separated by the transverse process bone. Sounds complicated, but you might recognize it a little better in the photo.

And if it looks a little familiar ... yes, the short loin is also where T-bones come from! But hang in there, we're about to get into all sorts of naming chaos. In the US, this steak is actually called a porterhouse. It's only a T-bone if there's less than 1¼ inches (3 cm) of tenderloin. Meanwhile, if you order a porterhouse in Australia, you'll only get the steak from the right-hand side of the picture, which Australia and the UK also call a sirloin. In the US, it's a strip steak. It's a lot to memorize! And since the tenderloin is such a prized steak, it's got its own section on page 152.

SIRLOIN
(RUMP: AUSTRALIA, NZ, UK)

The sirloin is a hefty collection of some big hitters. In this cut, you'll find the flap/bavette (page 171), ball tip, tri tip (page 171) and the top sirloin butt (called a D rump in Australia, NZ and the UK).

Within the top sirloin is where you'll find one of my all-time favorite steaks – the picanha (*biceps femoris*). That's the Brazilian name for it, but it also happens to be the most popular cut in Brazil, so the rest of the world has lovingly adopted the moniker. This cut is also known as the top sirloin cap (US), rump cap (Australia, NZ, UK) and sometimes coulotte (France).

Since the picanha has three sides, it's frequently confused with the tri tip steak (*tensor fasciae latae*, sometimes called the bottom sirloin triangle). In fact, if you search for picanha on online grocery sites, sometimes they'll show you a tri tip instead. But that doesn't make it the same thing! Both cuts come from the sirloin, but they are two different muscles.

RUMP CAP (AUSTRALIA, NZ, UK)

SCORED AND ROASTED PICANHA

SERVES 6

If you've ever eaten in a Brazilian restaurant, you have likely seen picanha before – it's the C-shaped steak stacked onto skewers. And though it's usually cooked rotisserie-style, I reckon it's wonderful as a roast. The thick fat cap that covers the top of the picanha slowly renders as it roasts – a built-in baster!

1 x 3–4 lb (1.3–1.8 kg) whole picanha or top sirloin cap

1½ teaspoons salt

¼ teaspoon freshly ground black pepper

1 teaspoon smoked paprika (see Notes)

1 teaspoon ground coriander

¼ teaspoon garlic powder

1. Preheat the oven to 325°F (165°C).
2. Use a sharp knife to score the fat cap of the picanha in a crosshatch. Take care to only cut through the fat, stopping before you cut into the meat.
3. Place a large skillet over high heat. When the pan is hot, place the picanha fat side down for 3–5 minutes. Once the fat has browned and started to render, remove from the heat and place onto a board.
4. Combine the remaining ingredients to form a dry rub and massage into the meat on all sides, including the fat cap.
5. Place a rack over a sheet pan (baking sheet) and position the picanha fat side up. Roast in the oven for 1 hour, or until the internal temperature reaches 135°F (57°C).
6. Remove from the oven and cover loosely in foil. Allow the meat to rest for at least 15 minutes before slicing and serving.

NOTES

As I mentioned at the beginning of the chapter, some stores try to sell tri tip as picanha. It's definitely not the same thing. Tri tip is significantly smaller and thinner. If you suspect you have ended up with a tri tip, don't fret! Skip the fat cap scoring and just reduce the cooking time to account for the smaller cut size.

If you don't have smoked paprika, substitute with regular paprika.

• BE THE BUTCHER •

HOW TO CUT YOUR OWN PICANHA STEAKS

I've featured a lot of steaks in this book, and I've referred to a lot of them as my favorites. But the picanha steak is actually my favorite. Well, at least at the time of writing this book (it tends to bounce around a little). Each steak features a lovely piece of whole muscle nestled next to a perfect strip of fat.

It's uncommon to find picanha steaks available for retail sale, but it's super easy to cut your own.

1. Start by identifying the direction the meat fibers are running (grain). We are going to cut in the same direction as the grain.
2. Use a trimming, chef's or scimitar knife to cut the steaks. You can cut them as thick or as thin as you like. I recommend about 1¼ inches (3 cm). It's normal to end up with one small triangle steak due to the shape of the muscle. Consider that lil' one the chef's treat.
3. The fat on the picanha is harder than the muscle, so it can prop up on one side and prevent full contact with the pan or grill. To fix this, turn each steak onto its side, on the fat cap, and cut a bevel into each side to allow it to sit flat.
4. Finally, lay each steak on its side and cut the fat cap to even it out to about ¼ inch (6 mm).

1

2

3

4

HERB-MOPPED CHARGRILLED PICANHA STEAKS

SERVES 6

Basting steaks with an oil-based sauce or glaze is a great way to layer flavors on the grill. To add even more complexity, I like to bundle together fresh herbs to create a mop. The heat of the grill and the physical action of brushing or 'slapping' the herbs against the meat help to release their natural oils, adding extra flavor and aroma.

- 6 picanha steaks
- 3 teaspoons salt
- 1 teaspoon garlic powder
- 2 teaspoons paprika
- 2 teaspoons freshly ground black pepper
- 2 sprigs rosemary
- 3–5 sprigs thyme
- 2–4 sprigs oregano
- ⅓ cup (80 ml) olive oil
- ¼ cup (60 ml) red wine vinegar
- 2 tablespoons honey or agave nectar
- 2 tablespoons worcestershire sauce

1. Light a grill for medium-heat, two-zone cooking (page 36), about 300–400°F (145–200°C). Remove the steaks from the fridge.
2. In a bowl, make the rub by combining the salt, garlic powder, paprika and black pepper.
3. Next, take the rosemary, thyme and oregano, and use butcher's twine to tie them together to make a herb mop. Crush the herbs a little with your hands to bruise them and intensify the oil release.
4. In a bowl, combine the olive oil, vinegar, honey and worcestershire sauce. Stir or whisk to combine.
5. Season the steaks liberally with the rub, then place them onto the grill over direct heat. Dip the herb mop into the oil mixture, then slap the top of the steaks, re-dipping as necessary. Cook for 1–2 minutes, then turn and repeat on the other side. Repeat the turning, slapping and basting every 2 minutes until the steaks reach an internal temperature of 130–135°F (54–57°C).
6. Remove the steaks from the grill and rest for 5–8 minutes, covered loosely with foil, before serving.

NOTE

Picanha steaks can cause flare-ups on the grill from the thick fat caps. I always like to grill them over a two-zone setup (page 36), so if you do experience a flare-up, just move them across to the indirect side until the flames die down.

CENTER CUT TOP SIRLOIN STEAK WITH JALAPEÑO PECAN PESTO

SERVES 2

While not quite as tender as the cap it sits under, the top sirloin steak is the best 'bang for buck', especially if you're looking for size. I mean, these are simply physically large steaks! They have a wonderful toothsome texture and big beefy flavor – and they're also really budget-friendly. I pair this beef behemoth with a roasted jalapeño and pecan pesto, which I spoon over the top like a sauce. If you want to make it more of a meal, toss the pesto through your favorite cooked pasta, like spaghetti or gnocchi, then serve the steak on the side.

2 x 1 lb (450 g) center cut top sirloin steaks (see Note)

1-2 teaspoons salt

2 tablespoons olive oil or softened beef tallow (page 244)

PESTO

5 fresh jalapeños

2 oz (55 g) parmesan cheese, diced

½ cup (25 g) chopped cilantro (coriander)

½ cup (15 g) chopped flat-leaf parsley

½ cup (25 g) chopped arugula (rocket) leaves

¾ cup (90 g) chopped pecans

2 teaspoons salt

3 tablespoons olive oil

1. Remove the steaks from the fridge 20–30 minutes before cooking. Season generously with salt on both sides.
2. To make the pesto, arrange the jalapeños on a sheet pan (baking sheet) and place under a broiler (oven grill) set to high heat. Broil for 4–6 minutes per side, or until the skins are blistered and charred. Remove and allow to cool.
3. Place the parmesan cheese into a blender or food processor. Blend until it resembles coarse crumbs.
4. Remove the stems and seeds from the charred jalapeños and add the flesh to the blender, along with the cilantro, parsley, arugula, pecans and salt. Blend for 30–60 seconds until the mixture starts to become cohesive. You may need to use a spatula to push the mixture down for an even blend.
5. Add the olive oil and blend until a chunky, creamy pesto is formed, then set aside.
6. Place a large cast-iron skillet (or any pan large enough to fit both steaks without overcrowding) over high heat.
7. Once the pan is ripping hot, add the olive oil, then cook the steaks for at least 3 minutes. Repeat on the other side. Continue to flip the steaks every 1–3 minutes over high heat until the internal temperature reaches 135°F (57°C) on a meat thermometer.
8. Remove the steaks from the pan and rest under loose foil for 5 minutes.
9. Serve with a dollop of pesto on each steak, with more in a bowl for second helpings!

NOTE

Wherever possible, try to get thick-cut sirloin. Even if you're feeding two, it's better to share one thick-cut steak than to cook two thin ones. They are always easier to cook to a lovely medium-rare, whereas their thinner counterparts are more like minute steaks. We perceive well-done meat as being tougher because more water is lost in the cooking process. And when it comes to thin steaks, it can be challenging to cook them to anything but well done!

SIRLOIN STEAK (US)

RUMP STEAK (AUSTRALIA, NZ, UK)

TURKISH-STYLE KEBABS WITH SUMAC ONIONS AND YOGURT FLATBREADS

SERVES 4–6

The marinade for these kebabs pulls double duty: it has a citrusy flavor from the sumac and gentle heat from the Aleppo pepper. But the magic ingredient is the onion. It contains proteolytic enzymes (which act as meat tenderizers), so you get the functional benefit along with the flavor.

2.5 lb (1 kg) sirloin steaks
2 teaspoons salt
2 teaspoons ground cumin
2 teaspoons Aleppo pepper flakes
2 teaspoons sumac
2 teaspoons ground coriander
3 tablespoons olive oil
1 onion

SUMAC ONIONS

1 red onion
2 teaspoons sumac
2 tablespoons lemon juice
¼ teaspoon salt
½ cup (15 g) finely chopped flat-leaf parsley

FLATBREADS

2 cups (300 g) self-raising flour
2 cups (520 g) light plain Greek-style yogurt
2 teaspoons baking powder
1 tablespoon olive oil, plus extra for brushing
1 teaspoon salt

1. Slice the sirloin steaks into cubes about 1-inch (2.5 cm) wide.
2. Place the meat into a resealable bag or container. Add the salt, cumin, Aleppo pepper, sumac, coriander and olive oil. Peel the onion and grate with a box grater. Add the grated onion and onion juice to the bag, then massage the meat to combine all the ingredients. Seal the bag and place in the fridge for at least 2 hours or up to 6 hours.
3. Light a grill for medium-high direct cooking, about 400°F (200°C).
4. To prepare the sumac onions, finely slice the red onion (a mandolin works great to get paper-thin arches). Place into a bowl with all the remaining ingredients and toss with your hands to separate the onion strands, making sure they are well marinated. Set aside.
5. Remove the meat from the fridge. Working one metal skewer at a time, thread each piece of sirloin onto the skewer, repeating until they are all stacked with about 8–10 pieces each.
6. To prepare the flatbread dough, combine all the ingredients in a bowl. Mix everything together until a ball forms, then cover and rest for 15 minutes.
7. Place the skewers onto the hot grill and leave for 4–5 minutes. Flip the skewers over and cook for a further 4–5 minutes on the other side, or until the meat is nicely charred and browned. Remove the skewers from the grill and cover with foil.
8. Finish the flatbreads by dividing the dough into eight pieces, then roll out each piece to ¼ inch (6 mm) thick. Brush each side of the flatbreads with olive oil, then grill for 2–3 minutes per side.
9. Serve the skewers with sumac onions and flatbreads.

STRIP STEAK (US)

PORTERHOUSE/SIRLOIN (AUSTRALIA, NZ, UK)

TX STRIP AU POIVRE

SERVES 2

Ah, the steak with so many city-based names. NY strip. Kansas City strip. Considering how many ranchers and heads of cattle there are in Texas, it would make sense to have a more appropriate geographic reference in the name. So, for this recipe, let's call it the TX strip. This is my take on the classic 'au poivre' – perfect for all you black-pepper lovers.

- 2 x 14 oz (400 g) strip steaks
- 4 tablespoons black peppercorns
- 2 teaspoons salt
- 3 tablespoons neutral high-heat oil (e.g. avocado, rice bran, grapeseed), divided
- 1 small shallot, finely diced
- ¼ cup (60 ml) cognac (see Notes)
- 2 tablespoons brined and drained green peppercorns
- 1 teaspoon dijon mustard
- ½ cup (125 ml) beef or chicken stock
- 2 teaspoons balsamic vinegar
- ½ cup (125 ml) heavy (thickened) cream
- 2 tablespoons cold butter

1. Remove the steaks from the fridge.
2. Use a spice grinder to crush the black peppercorns to a very coarse consistency. Alternatively, roughly crack them by pressing on them with the bottom of a saucepan.
3. Season the steaks well with salt on both sides, then press the peppercorns into the surface to create a crust.
4. Place a cast-iron or stainless steel skillet over high heat. Add 2 tablespoons neutral oil.
5. Place the steaks into the hot skillet and cook undisturbed for 4–5 minutes. Flip and cook for a further 4–5 minutes on the other side. Remove the steaks from the skillet and loosely cover with foil while you prepare the sauce.
6. In the skillet, add the remaining oil and the shallot. Cook for 1–2 minutes, stirring often, until the shallot starts to brown slightly.
7. Add the cognac to deglaze the skillet. If you've got a gas stovetop – and you're feeling adventurous – you can tilt it forward slightly to flambé the cognac. This will ignite the alcohol with an impressive flame that lasts a few seconds.
8. Add the green peppercorns, dijon mustard, stock and balsamic vinegar, and scrape up all the browned bits from the bottom of the skillet. Simmer the sauce for 1–2 minutes to reduce.
9. Remove the skillet from the heat. Whisk in the cream, then the butter, until the sauce is smooth. Taste and add more salt if needed.
10. Plate the steaks and spoon generous amounts of the sauce over the top.

NOTES

Don't stress if you don't have a bottle of cognac on hand for this recipe. While the flavor won't be quite the same, you can always substitute with bourbon or whiskey.

Yes, this cooking method is the opposite of the JKF method I preach (page 100), but to get the pepper to stick, you have to leave it in the skillet until a crust forms.

• MEAT NERD FACT •

The main muscle in the strip steak is the *longissimus*, which is the same big, round muscle you find in the ribeye. The main difference? Strip comes from the hindquarter, and ribeyes from the forequarter!

TRIED 'N' TRUE TRI TIP WITH SALSA VERDE

SERVES 6–8

This is my go-to tri tip method, whether I'm cooking 350 of them for an event or just one for dinner at home. And you only need two ingredients! It also features my hallmark Hardcore Carnivore Black Rub – the first seasoning I ever concocted, and still a bestseller to this day. I pair it with a bright and fresh sauce: in this case, an Italian salsa verde, which is a cousin to the classic chimichurri.

1 x 3 lb (1.3 kg) whole tri tip steak

2–3 tablespoons Hardcore Carnivore Black Rub

½ cup (125 ml) water

2 tablespoons apple cider vinegar

2 tablespoons worcestershire sauce

SALSA VERDE

1 cup (30 g) roughly chopped flat-leaf parsley leaves

2 garlic cloves, roughly chopped

2 tablespoons capers

5 anchovies

¼ cup (7 g) oregano leaves

¼ cup (5 g) mint leaves

zest and juice of 1 lemon

½ teaspoon salt

½ teaspoon freshly ground pepper

¾ cup (185 ml) extra virgin olive oil

2 tablespoons white wine vinegar

1. Remove the tri tip from the fridge. If the meat has any silverskin, remove it with a boning knife.
2. Preheat a smoker or pellet grill to 275°F (140°C).
3. Season the tri tip on all sides with the rub, coating it thoroughly.
4. Place it into the smoker to cook for about 1 hour. Fill a spray bottle with the water, apple cider vinegar and worcestershire sauce. Spritz the tri tip every 15 minutes as it cooks. If using a pellet grill, rotate the tri tip once during cooking so it gets an even amount of radiant heat exposure.
5. Start checking the internal temperature with a meat thermometer around the 45-minute mark. When it reaches 135–138°F (57–58°C), wrap the tri tip in foil, rolling it up tightly to make a cylindrical shape (it makes a nicer shape when cut). Rest for 15 minutes.
6. While the tri tip rests, make the salsa verde. In a food processor, combine the parsley, garlic, capers, anchovies, oregano, mint, lemon zest and juice, salt and pepper. Pulse a few times until the ingredients are chopped. Stir in the olive oil and vinegar. Taste and add more salt if needed.
7. Slice the tri tip against the grain (see opposite) and drizzle with the salsa verde.

NOTE

Some may disagree, but I think tri tip is best when cooked to the medium side of medium-rare. The texture is more pleasant at this doneness, so I tend to pull it off the smoker at 138°F (58°C).

• BE THE BUTCHER •

HOW TO SLICE TRI TIP THE RIGHT WAY

The tri tip (*tensor fasciae latae*) is a sneaky one. While it is one whole muscle, the grain or direction of the muscle fibers shifts halfway along. (Remember, you learned all about the grain on page 41.)

The grain pattern on the tri tip fans out from one corner. To cut it properly, you need to start with the longer corner, cutting slices until you reach about halfway. Then, turn your knife about 150 degrees and continue the cuts. Honestly, it's easiest to visualize this one, so here's a handy diagram.

TENDERLOIN

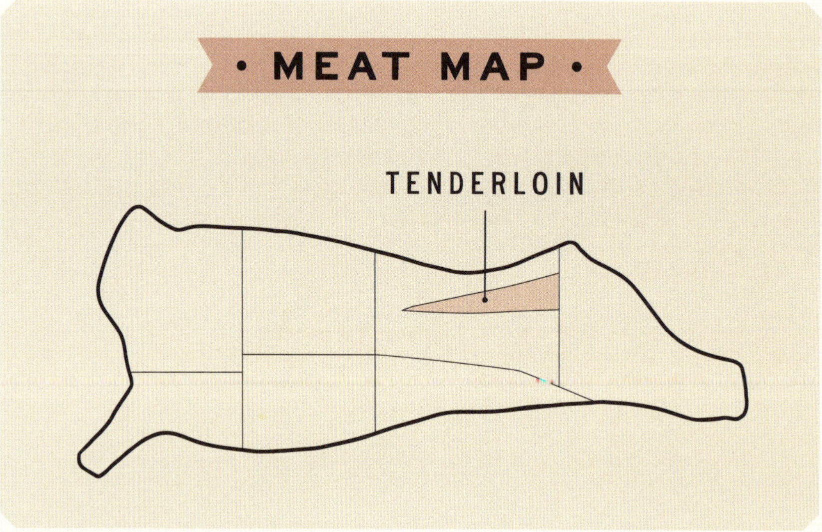

The most prized tenderloin muscle of all is the *psoas major*. Home of the filet mignon (or eye fillet, depending on where you're from), it deserves a chapter all its own. The *psoas* is part of the hip flexor group and is a skeletal, not locomotive, muscle. In other words, it gets very little use compared to other muscles, and that's exactly what makes it so tender.

I'm covering tenderloins from many different species in this section. Deer, pigs and sheep have tenderloins too, and because they're also four-legged animals, their tenderloins are just as tender as beef. Poultry also has a muscle we call 'tenderloin', but it's actually the *pectoralis minor*, a small flight muscle located under the breast. It too is tender, but not at all the same thing.

Tenderloins make up only about 1% of the meat on a steer, making them a rare commodity and part of why they're so prized. But here's the trade-off: that tenderness comes at the cost of flavor, with the tenderloin being far milder than a ribeye or picanha.

• BE THE BUTCHER •

HOW TO BUTCHER A TENDERLOIN

Every time you save the butcher from having to do extra work on the meat, you can save some bucks on your purchase. That includes knowing how to trim and prepare some of your own subprimals. With tenderloin being the most expensive muscle, it's a great one to clean yourself. Buying a whole tenderloin will always be cheaper per pound or kilo than buying pre-cut filet mignon (eye fillet) steaks.

You can buy whole tenderloin muscles in vacuum-sealed packs from some grocery stores, butchers and warehouses. The level of trimming varies: sometimes the side muscle (also called the chain or strap) is already removed, and the tenderloin may or may not have had the silverskin and *iliacus* muscle taken off. The iliacus is found at the thickest end of the tenderloin and is actually a separate muscle (sometimes called the heel).

1. Start by removing the chain (the thin muscle – *psoas minor* – that runs along the side). You can use your thumb to separate the main part of the tenderloin and the smaller side muscle, using a trimming knife to nick at any joins in the seam that won't pull away. The chain is not as tender as the true tenderloin, but it's a fantastic little morsel to throw onto the grill.
2. Trim away any exterior fat and as much silverskin as possible. Push a sharp, semi-flexible boning knife (page 26) directly underneath the silverskin. Angle the blade slightly up and away from the flesh and push the blade underneath to separate it. Continue trimming as much as you can, leaving the meat as intact as possible. Clearing all this away makes a significant difference to the final eating quality.

The next stage (see overleaf) is when you get to choose your own adventure.

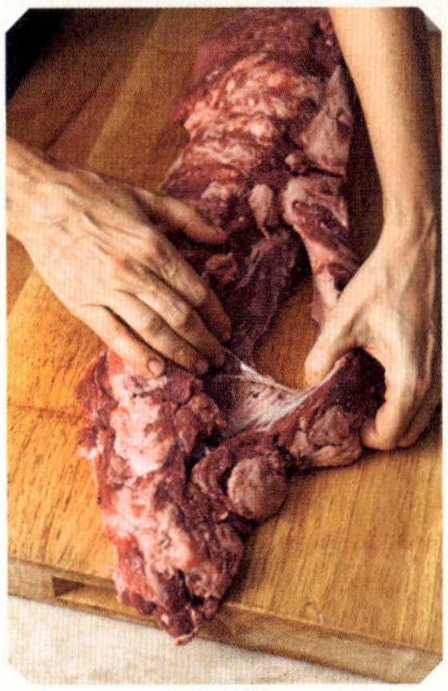
1

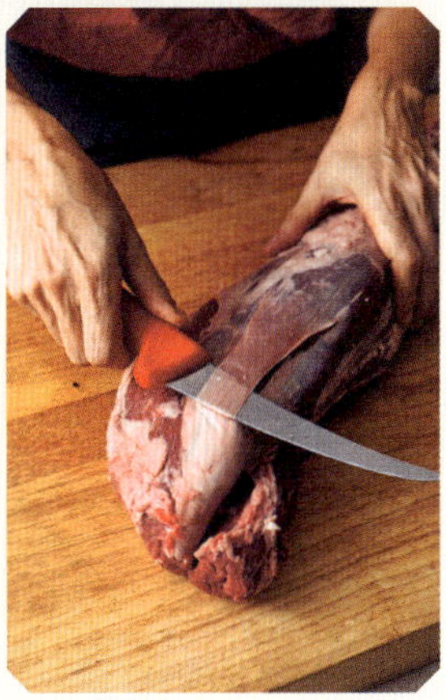
2

TENDERLOIN CUT OPTIONS

1

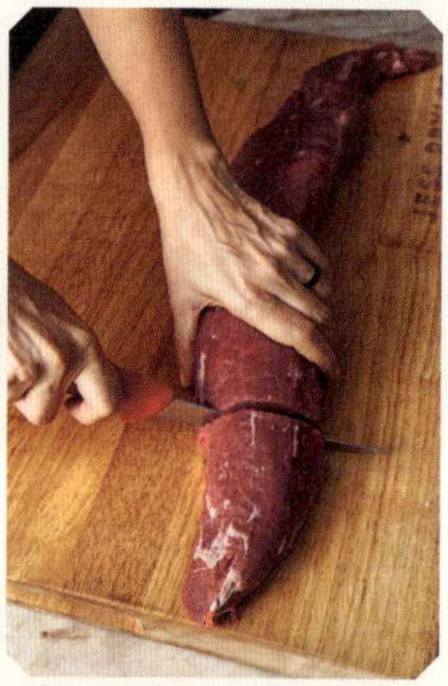

2

3

4

OPTION 1: CUT ONLY THE FINEST STEAKS

1. Cut away the heel (*iliacus*) muscle. When this is left on, there is some intermuscular membrane present in the steaks. You can either cut this heel into its own steaks or keep it whole for a mini tenderloin roast for two.
2. Once the heel is cut away, you will have only the tenderloin (*psoas major*) left. The muscle will taper off at either end into pieces that are too thin to cook as steaks. Cut a few inches in from each end to remove the tapered sections. These are the tenderloin tails, and I love to use them to make a luxe steak tartare (page 162).
3. The thick section in the middle of the tenderloin is the chateaubriand. Tie butcher's twine around the tenderloin every 1–2 inches (2.5–5 cm) to hold it in a neat cylinder.
4. Slice between the ties to create evenly sized steaks.

OPTION 2: GET AS MANY STEAKS AS POSSIBLE

- Leaving the thick end of the tenderloin (the heel) in place, remove the tapered end by cutting a few inches to cut it away completely. Trim back enough so the first steak you slice is reasonably sized.
- Tie butcher's twine around the tenderloin every 1 inch (2.5 cm) to hold it in a neat cylinder, then slice between the ties to create evenly sized steaks. The thinner you cut the steaks, the more you will get from a single tenderloin.

OPTION 3: LEAVE IT WHOLE

- Once trimmed, fold the thin, tapered end of the tenderloin back over itself to even it up with the thicker heel end. Secure the folded end in place by tying with butcher's twine. To maintain the cylindrical shape, tie twine every few inches along the tenderloin.
- I use this option whenever I am cooking a whole tenderloin (like my Reverse-Seared Tenderloin recipe on page 268). In this case, I prefer to leave the tapered tail in place to maximize the yield.

Note: You don't have to tie the steak with butcher's twine, but it is best practice and a great way to keep a lovely round shape.

PORK FILLET HEART (AUSTRALIA, NZ, UK)

PEACHY PORK TENDERLOIN WITH PROSECCO MUSTARD CAVIAR

SERVES 6

A soak in peach nectar brine leaves these 'tendies' perfectly seasoned, with a subtle peachy aroma. You can make the prosecco mustard a couple of days in advance. It tastes best when it's had some time to mellow.

MUSTARD CAVIAR

⅓ cup (55 g) yellow mustard seeds

½ cup (125 ml) prosecco vinegar (see Notes)

½ cup (110 g) brown sugar

1 teaspoon salt

¼ cup (60 ml) water

PORK

1½ cups (375 ml) peach nectar

1 cup (250 ml) water

1½ tablespoons salt, divided

2 tablespoons brown sugar

2 teaspoons ground cardamom

2 x 1 lb (450 g) pork tenderloins

2 tablespoons olive oil

1. Start by preparing the mustard caviar, which should be made at least a day in advance. Place the mustard seeds into a small saucepan and cover with water. Allow to soak for an hour to reduce the bitterness, changing the water once during the soak. Drain the seeds and discard the soaking water. Using the same saucepan, add the prosecco vinegar, brown sugar, salt and water, then simmer over medium heat for 20 minutes until the seeds are plump. Allow to cool, then pour into a clean jar or container and place in the fridge to allow the flavor to develop.
2. To prepare the pork, start by making the brine. Place the peach nectar, water, 1 tablespoon salt, brown sugar and cardamom into a small saucepan. Cook over medium heat, stirring regularly until everything is dissolved. Remove from the heat and allow to cool completely.
3. Place the pork into a container or resealable bag. Add the cooled brine and place in the fridge for 4–12 hours.
4. Preheat the oven to 350°F (175°C).
5. Remove the pork from the brine and pat it dry with a paper towel. Season with the remaining salt.
6. Place an oven-safe skillet over high heat and add the olive oil. Once the pan is hot, add the pork and sear for 4 minutes. Rotate by a third and sear for 4 minutes. Rotate a final time and sear for 4 minutes.
7. Place the skillet into the oven and cook for a further 10–20 minutes, or until the pork reads 140°F (60°C) on a thermometer inserted into the thickest part of the meat.
8. Remove the pork from the skillet and rest it loosely under foil for 5–10 minutes. Slice and serve with the mustard caviar.

NOTES

If you can't find prosecco vinegar, substitute with champagne vinegar or white wine vinegar.

The mustard caviar will keep for several weeks if you don't end up using it all.

While we traditionally sear meat on two sides, the cylindrical shape of pork tenderloins allows them to be rotated three times (think of it like searing a triangle), and more sear equals more flavor.

FILET MIGNON (US)

EYE FILLET (AUSTRALIA), FILLET (UK)

CLASSIC SURF AND TURF

SERVES 4

It's an oldie but a goodie, and with the classic pairing of steak and lobster tails, it just feels right to use filet. I wouldn't call this combo a powerhouse of flavor, but it does have a 'special occasion' vibe, with the air of upscale indulgence. I stuck to traditional flavors for this one, with lots of butter and a sprinkle of parsley to finish.

4 x 8 oz (225 g) filet mignon steaks

3 tablespoons salted butter

1 garlic clove, crushed

¼ teaspoons paprika

2 tablespoons lemon juice

¼ cup (7 g) finely chopped flat-leaf parsley leaves, divided

4 x 5–7 oz (150–200 g) lobster tails

¾ teaspoon salt, divided

½ teaspoon freshly cracked black pepper

1 tablespoon olive or neutral oil

1. Remove the steaks from the fridge.
2. Place the butter and garlic in a small saucepan and cook over medium heat for 2–3 minutes until the butter is melted and the garlic starts to soften slightly. Add the paprika, lemon juice and 1 tablespoon parsley. Stir to combine, then set aside.
3. Using a set of kitchen shears, cut the lobster shell. Start at the wide (open) end and cut a straight line down the top shell only, avoiding cutting into the meat. Gently pry the shell apart with your fingers to expose the meat, being careful not to snap it in two. Slide your thumb (or use a spoon) beneath the meat and the bottom shell to loosen and separate it, but make sure you leave the tail fan attached. Carefully lift the meat up and out of the shell, then lay it back down on the shell to create a butterflied appearance. Place the tails on a sheet pan (baking sheet) and season with ¼ teaspoon salt.
4. Place a skillet over high heat to preheat for 1–3 minutes.
5. Pat the steaks dry with a paper towel, then season generously on both sides with the remaining salt and the black pepper.
6. Add the olive oil to the hot skillet, then the steaks. Sear for 5 minutes, undisturbed, then flip and cook for a further 4 minutes. Remove the steaks from the skillet and loosely cover with foil to rest.
7. Brush some of the garlic butter over the lobster tails, then cook under a broiler (oven grill) for 8–10 minutes. Baste with butter once during cooking, and again when they come out.
8. Garnish the cooked steaks and lobster tails with the remaining parsley.

NOTES

If you want to keep the steaks perfectly round during cooking, tie a piece of butcher's twine around the outside to enhance the circular shape. After they're cooked, just snip, remove and discard.

Butterflying the lobster tails makes for the prettiest presentation, but if it seems too laborious, just split the shells in half.

T-BONES WITH BLAZIN' MEXICAN STREET CORN

SERVES 2–4

A big ol' T-bone is one of the most visually iconic steaks. It's even the steak emoji. I reckon it pairs beautifully with these Mexican elote-style grilled corn cobs, finished with crushed Flamin' Hot Cheetos. Trust me, it works. I also like to add a pinch of jalapeño powder to the T-bones just to give 'em a little extra kick.

- 2 x thick-cut T-bone or porterhouse steaks, about 1¼ –1½ inches (3–4 cm) thick
- 3 teaspoons salt, divided
- ½ teaspoon jalapeño powder (optional)
- ½ teaspoon garlic powder
- 4 corn cobs
- spray oil
- ¾ cup (185 g) mayonnaise
- ⅓ cup (50 g) finely crumbled queso fresco or feta cheese
- 2 cups (160 g) Flamin' Hot Cheetos
- 2 tablespoons finely chopped cilantro (coriander)
- lime wedges, to serve

1. Remove the steaks from the fridge.
2. Light a grill for medium-heat, two-zone cooking (page 36), about 400–500°F (200–260°C).
3. In a small bowl, combine 2 teaspoons salt with the jalapeño powder and garlic powder.
4. Season the T-bones well on both sides with the seasoning mixture, pressing it firmly into the meat.
5. Cook the steaks using the JKF method (page 100), flipping them every 1–2 minutes for 6–8 minutes, or until they form a great crust. Once they have a deep brown sear, move them to the indirect side of the grill to finish cooking. Orient them with the strip side closest to the hot zone, so the more delicate part of the steak is further away from the heat source.
6. Spray the corn lightly with oil, then grill on the hot zone for 3–4 minutes until evenly cooked, turning frequently so the kernels char but don't burn. They may pop slightly as they cook. Move the cobs to the indirect side to cook for a further 10 minutes. At this point, all your food should be on indirect heat.
7. Keep measuring the temperature of the T-bones while they're on the indirect side. Once the internal temperature reaches 130–135°F (54–57°C), remove them from the grill and rest under foil.
8. In a bowl, combine the mayonnaise, remaining salt and queso fresco. Stir to mix well.
9. Place the Cheetos into a food processor and pulse until a fine crumb has formed. You can also do this by placing them in a resealable bag and crushing them with a rolling pin or the bottom of a saucepan. Pour the crumbs onto a sheet pan (baking sheet) or large shallow container.
10. Slather the grilled corn with a generous amount of the mayonnaise mixture, then roll through the Cheetos crumbs to coat completely. Top with the cilantro.
11. Once the steak is rested, serve it alongside the corn with wedges of lime.

NOTE

If you want to add some wow factor, serve this bistecca alla fiorentina-style. The famous T-bones of Florence, Italy, are cut extra thick, so one steak feeds the whole table. It's a serious steak flex, but you need to find a butcher or meat market to cut it for you.

CHARGRILLED LAMB LOIN CHOPS WITH MINT CHIMICHURRI

SERVES 2

If you think lamb loin chops look like miniature T-bone steaks, you're not wrong – they're essentially the same cut, just on a smaller scale. The 'T' refers to the shape of the bone, which happens to be the transverse process bone separating the strip (backstrap) from the filet (eye fillet). I like to cook these over charcoal and serve them with a zingy, upgraded take on classic mint sauce.

- 6 x 2 lb (1 kg) lamb loin chops
- 1 cup (50 g) finely chopped mint leaves
- ½ cup (15 g) finely chopped flat-leaf parsley leaves
- 2–3 garlic cloves, finely diced
- 1 small shallot, finely chopped
- ⅓ cup (80 ml) red wine vinegar
- ¼ teaspoon red pepper flakes
- 1¼ teaspoon salt, divided
- ¼ cup (60 ml) extra virgin olive oil
- ¼ teaspoon ground pepper

1. Light a grill (preferably charcoal) for medium-heat cooking, about 350–450°F (180–235°C), and remove the lamb from the fridge.
2. Place the mint, parsley, garlic and shallot into a medium-sized bowl. Add the vinegar, red pepper flakes, ¼ teaspoon salt and olive oil. Stir until combined. Set aside.
3. Season the meat on both sides with the remaining salt and the pepper.
4. Place the meat onto the hot grill and cook for 3 minutes. Flip and cook for a further 3 minutes. Remove once the internal temperature reaches 120–130°F (48–54°C).
5. Rest the chops briefly, then serve with the mint chimichurri.

NOTES

You can also cook these in a hot pan on the stove, searing them for 3–4 minutes on each side.

I know it's unusual to give such a broad range for doneness, but these chops cook so quickly that they will carryover cook and be perfectly pink in the middle.

CLASSIC STEAK TARTARE

SERVES 2–4

Traditionally, steak tartare is made with tenderloin, but there's a smart workaround. If you trim your own tenderloin (page 154), save the tapered tails for tartare – it's a perfect way to use those awkward pieces. Otherwise, go with filet mignon, or for a more budget-friendly option, top sirloin (rump) or eye of round. Whatever cut you choose, it must be impeccably fresh. Eating raw beef, and raw yolks, always carries some risk, but the fresher the ingredients, the lower the risk.

- 8–10 oz (225–280 g) tenderloin tails
- 1 tablespoon finely diced shallot
- 1 tablespoon finely chopped flat-leaf parsley
- 1 tablespoon finely diced cornichon
- 1 tablespoon finely chopped capers
- 1 teaspoon dijon mustard
- 2 teaspoons worcestershire sauce
- 2 teaspoons olive oil
- ¼ teaspoon salt
- 4 slices grilled sourdough bread, cut into wedges
- 1 egg yolk

1. Using a very sharp knife, mince the tenderloin by hand. Slice it into thin strips, then cut across to make a small dice. If the pieces still feel too large, run your knife over them again, aiming for a texture that's fine but not paste-like.
2. Place the meat into a bowl, then add the shallot, parsley, cornichon, capers, dijon mustard, worcestershire sauce, olive oil and salt. Mix together with a spoon until everything is evenly distributed, taking care not to overwork the meat.
3. For presentation, set a 4-inch (10 cm) metal ring on a plate and spoon the mixture into it. Press lightly to fill and smooth the surface. Lift away the ring, then arrange the sourdough pieces alongside. If you don't have a ring, simply mound the tartare neatly on the plate.
4. Top the tartare with the raw egg yolk positioned in the middle and serve immediately.

NOTE

The easiest way to separate the delicate yolk is to crack the egg and let the white slip through your fingers. You'll be left holding only the yolk, ready to place on the tartare.

ROUND

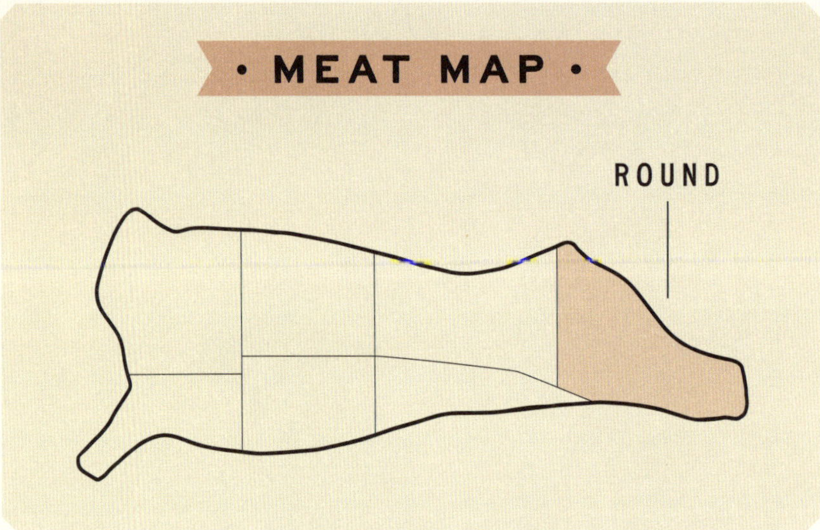

The round is the caboose of the primals. It's the bovine equivalent of the ham, and because it's the hind leg, it gets a serious workout. That makes it both lean and tough – not the most desirable combo when it comes to beef. The round still has plenty to offer. You just gotta know how to use it. It's perfect for lean roasts, stew meat, ground (minced) beef, jerky and deli roast beef.

A whole round primal, left bone-in with the rump and heel attached, is known as a steamship round. The name is said to come from the way it resembles a ship's hull when it stands upright. It became wildly popular at hotel and cruise buffets in the 1960s, where the whole primal was first roasted and then carved in front of guests for dramatic effect.

Let's take a look at the major muscle groups:

- **Top round** – known as inside round or topside (Australia, NZ, UK).
- **Eye of round** – sometimes called eye round.
- **Bottom round (outside round)** – known as silverside (Australia, NZ, UK) or gooseneck round when the heel is still attached. In the UK, steaks cut from this area are sometimes called salmon steaks.
- **Hind shank/shin** – the lower leg portion (also covered in the shank section on page 180).
- **Sirloin tip** – known as knuckle, ball of the round, round tip, tip center (or centre in the UK and Ireland), beef ball tip roast, sirloin tip roast, French roll roast and thick flank.

WHEN A STEAK ISN'T REALLY A STEAK

You'll often see sirloin tip steaks for sale, usually at an economical price. But here's the catch: you can slice any piece of beef into a 'steak,' but that doesn't mean it'll eat like one. Sirloin tip is the perfect example.

Buying something labeled 'steak' that turns out tough and chewy is exactly the kind of experience that dents people's confidence when choosing meat. But now you know that just because it says steak on the pack doesn't mean it's gonna be great for quick grilling. Sirloin tip is better suited to stews, or manually tenderize it for schnitzels, chicken-fried steaks or milanesa.

CROSS-SECTION OF THE ROUND PRIMAL

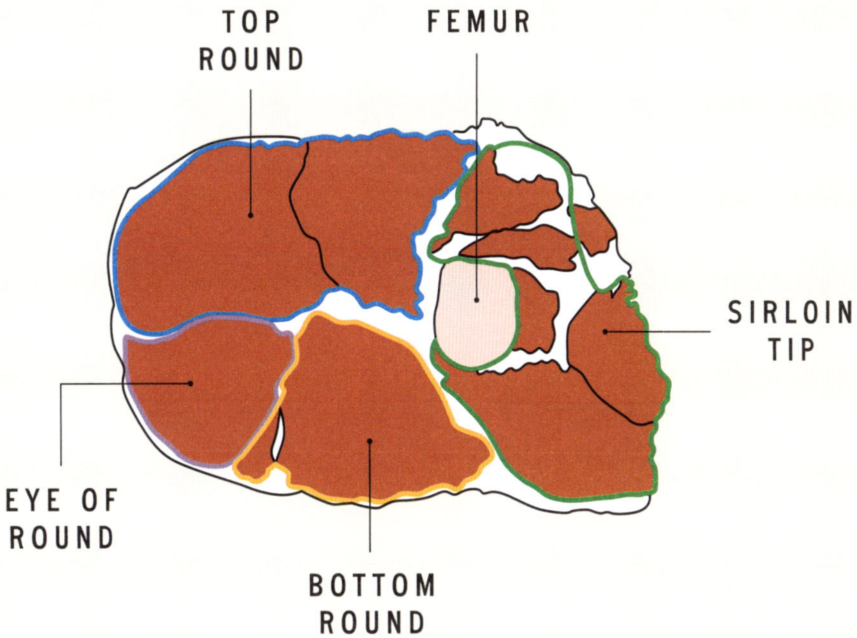

TOP ROUND (US)

TOPSIDE (AUSTRALIA, NZ, UK)

PASTRAMI-SPICED ROAST BEEF

SERVES 6–8

For all the steaks and roasts we get excited about, every carcass still yields some tougher cuts, and we need smart ways to use them. Thinly sliced deli meats are a perfect solution. Top round is the preferred cut for commercially produced roast beef, and you can use it at home to make your own. This is one of my favorite recipes – big flavor without the fuss of curing and steaming – and the classic pastrami spices create a deeply flavorful crust. Slice it thin and pile it onto rye bread slathered with mustard.

4 lb (2 kg) whole top round (see Notes)

1 tablespoon black peppercorns

1 tablespoon coriander seeds

½ teaspoon mustard seeds

3 allspice berries

1 teaspoon garlic powder

2 teaspoons paprika

1 teaspoon celery salt

1 tablespoon salt

1 tablespoon olive oil

1. Remove the beef from the fridge 20–30 minutes before cooking.
2. Preheat the oven to 450°F (230°C).
3. Place a small skillet over medium heat, then add the peppercorns, coriander seeds, mustard seeds and allspice berries. Toast for 1–2 minutes until fragrant, swirling the pan regularly to avoid burning.
4. Put the toasted spices in a spice grinder (or use a mortar and pestle) and grind until coarsely ground. You want them to have some texture – it's a great part of the crust. Add the garlic, paprika, celery salt and salt to the spice mix. Stir until combined.
5. Rub the olive oil over the beef, then coat with the spice mixture on all sides, concentrating on the top.
6. Place a rack inside a roasting pan and nestle the beef on top. Roast in the oven for 15 minutes.
7. Reduce the heat to 325°F (160°C) and cook until the internal temperature reaches 130°F (54°C). This may take 45–80 minutes, so start monitoring the temperature at the 45-minute mark.
8. Remove the beef from the oven, allow to cool, then refrigerate for easier slicing. Slice the beef thinly for use in sandwiches, charcuterie boards, etc.

NOTES

You can slice the roast by hand, but for the ultimate sandwich-style beef, a deli slicer is a must. It's the best way to get paper-thin slices that are meltingly tender.

Can't find top round? Use eye of round or bottom round (silverside).

RASPBERRY CHIPOTLE JERKY

MAKES ABOUT 1LB (450 G) OF JERKY

Eye of round is my favorite cut for jerky. It's extremely lean, which is essential, since fat can turn rancid as it spoils. I prefer using a dehydrator, but I'm including an oven/smoker/pellet grill method for y'all, too. No matter which method you choose, hit it with the last step to make sure it's safe to consume.

- 2 tablespoons olive oil
- 2 garlic cloves, crushed
- 1 teaspoon grated fresh ginger
- zest and juice of 1 lemon
- 3 cups (375 g) frozen raspberries
- ½ cup (110 g) granulated (white) sugar
- ¾ cup (185 ml) water or chicken stock
- 1 tablespoon salt
- 1 cup (7 oz/200 g) crushed canned chipotle peppers (see Note)
- 1 tablespoon ground black pepper
- 2.5 lb (1 kg) whole eye of round roast

1. Place the olive oil in a saucepan over medium heat. Add the garlic and ginger and cook until fragrant, about 2 minutes, stirring frequently. Add the lemon zest and juice, raspberries, sugar, water, salt and chipotle peppers.
2. Cook for 6–8 minutes, or until the raspberries soften. Use the back of a spoon to crush the raspberries as they cook.
3. Strain the mixture through a sieve into a storage container. Discard the seeds and contents of the sieve. Stir the black pepper into the remaining liquid. Allow to cool.
4. Place the whole eye of round into the freezer for 20–30 minutes to make it easier to cut. Slice the roast into long strips, or cut it in half and slice into smaller pieces. No matter what shape you choose, ensure the slices themselves are thin, no more than ¼ inch (6 mm). Also, try to slice them as evenly as possible.
5. Place the slices into the raspberry marinade, cover and refrigerate for 12–24 hours.
6. If using a dehydrator, lay the meat on the racks, discarding the marinade. Dehydrate at 145–155°F (62–68°C) for 6–8 hours, or until desired texture is reached.
7. If using an oven/smoker/pellet grill, discard the marinade, then lay the pieces of meat onto a wire rack. If using an oven, place the rack on top of a foil-lined sheet pan (baking sheet) for easy clean-up. Cook at 175°F (75°C) for 5–7 hours, or until desired texture is reached.

NOTE

If you cannot find crushed chipotle peppers, you can buy the whole ones (they usually come canned with adobo sauce) and just blend them in a food processor or blender.

CARNE GUISADA

SERVES 6–8

Guisada simply means 'stew' in Spanish, and there are countless variations. Some are chunky while others use shredded meat. Some include potatoes and carrots, and the consistency can range from brothy to almost curry-thick. The only real rule is that guisada should feature meat, slowly stewed until tender. This is my hearty take on a beloved Mexican classic.

- 1 teaspoon salt
- 1 teaspoon cracked pepper
- 1 teaspoon ground cumin
- 2 teaspoons dried Mexican oregano
- 1 teaspoon chipotle powder
- 2 lb (1 kg) bottom round roast
- 2 tablespoons tallow (page 244), lard or neutral oil
- 1 bunch cilantro (coriander)
- ½ onion
- 1 serrano pepper or other hot pepper
- 28 oz (800 g) canned diced tomatoes
- 3 garlic cloves
- 1 cup (250 ml) beef stock
- 2 tablespoons tomato paste
- 1 lb (450 g) yukon gold, kipfler or waxy yellow potatoes, cut into medium chunks

1. In a small bowl, combine the salt, pepper, cumin, oregano and chipotle powder to make the seasoning.
2. Pat the beef dry with paper towels, then cut into cubes, about 1½ inches (4 cm) wide. Generously season with the spice mixture, tossing well to make sure all pieces are coated.
3. Place a heavy-bottomed pan (or Dutch oven) over high heat and add the tallow.
4. Working in batches, brown the beef for about 15 minutes per batch, stirring once or twice to develop a crust. Transfer each batch to a plate before adding the next.
5. In a blender, combine the cilantro, onion, serrano pepper, canned tomatoes, garlic, beef stock and tomato paste. Blend until very smooth.
6. Return all the browned beef to the pot, then add the puréed mixture and potatoes.
7. Bring to a boil, then reduce the heat to a simmer. Cook for 1–2 hours until the beef is tender.

NOTES

Serve this with Beef Fat Tortillas (page 248) for the perfect combo.

Bottom round is a tough but lean cut. While it can dry out when used for shredded meat dishes, it's ideal for saucy, liquid-based stews. You don't need to buy a whole roast for this recipe – any stew meat will work, and you can even substitute with lamb or pork.

SKIRT
AND OTHER THINNISH STEAKS

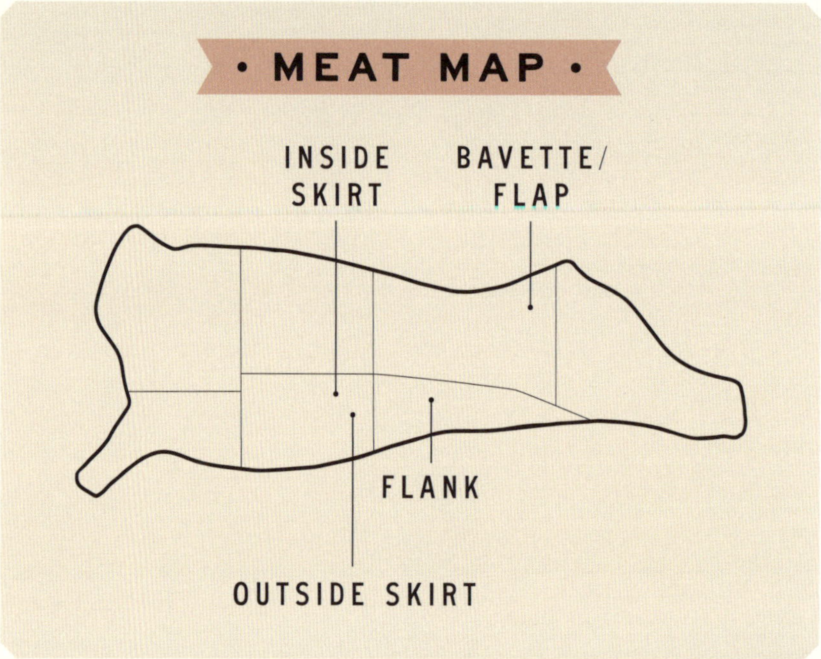

I have also included flap and flank steaks in this section, and while they aren't technically skirt steaks, they totally make sense here because they are fairly interchangeable in recipes, and they all have a very coarse and pronounced grain.

It's one of the most frequent questions I get asked: What's the difference between inside and outside skirt steaks? So, let's sort that out! Outside skirt comes from the diaphragm, so it's more tender and commands a higher price. It's rarely seen in grocery stores because it's so popular in countries like Mexico that processors can get a better price for exporting it. If you see steak simply labeled 'skirt', it's almost certainly inside skirt. While each skirt can be used interchangeably in recipes, inside skirt is definitely more chewy.

If you're looking for thick skirt (an Australian name for hanger steak), you'll find that over in the rare steaks section on page 224, because it's a little tougher to find.

IDENTIFICATION GUIDE

INSIDE SKIRT

Latin name: *transversus abdominis*

Appearance: wide and extremely long (when whole), with a prominent grain

Carcass location: from the plate subprimal, next to the tri tip

OUTSIDE SKIRT

Latin name: *diaphragma*

Other names: thin skirt

Appearance: narrow, half the width of the inside skirt

Carcass location: attached to the inside of the rib cage

FLAP

Latin name: *obliquus abdominis interni*

Other names: bavette steak

Appearance: pronounced deep ridges of grain, thicker in the middle

Carcass location: in the sirloin, supporting the abdomen

FLANK

Latin name: *rectus abdominis*

Appearance: oval shape, smooth surface, with a visible grain from one end to the other

Carcass location: flank primal (the only primal with a single steak)

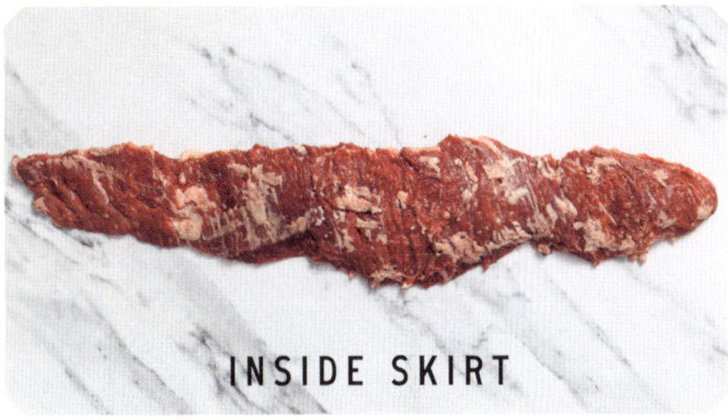

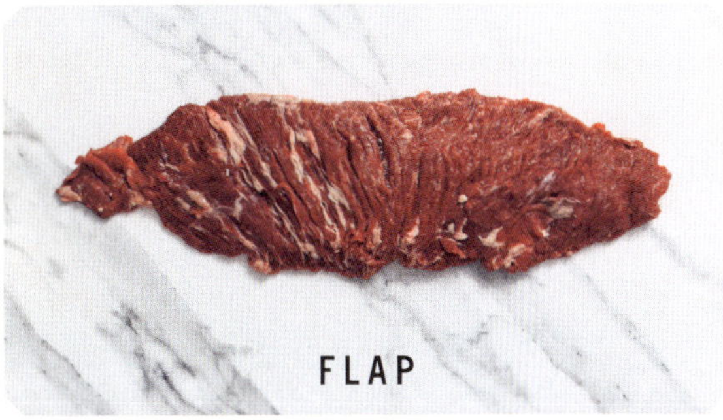

• MEAT NERD FACT •

Membrane on or off? Outside skirt has a thick piece of silverskin membrane covering one side. Sometimes it is trimmed away by the packing house, but occasionally you'll find it intact. I usually recommend removal since it can make things tougher. But if you like to grill over really hot heat, you can get the membrane to crisp up and be another textural element. So, try it both ways and find your personal preference.

OAXACAN MOLE NEGRO DRY-RUBBED SKIRT STEAK

SERVES 4

Skirt steak is a featured cut in Mexican cuisine, so it seemed fitting to pair it with a rub inspired by the rich and complex mole sauces of Oaxaca. I wanted this rub to capture the bitter chocolate, fragrant clove and earthy chili notes of traditional mole, and it really gets into all the crevices of the inside skirt for maximum distribution.

- 1.5 lb (700 g) inside skirt steak, cut into two pieces
- 4 tablespoons olive oil, divided

MOLE NEGRO RUB

- 1 tablespoon dark cocoa powder (see Notes)
- 1½ teaspoons salt
- ½ teaspoon cinnamon powder
- 1 teaspoon dried Mexican oregano (see Notes)
- 1 teaspoon ancho chili powder
- 1 teaspoon guajillo chili powder
- ½ teaspoon chipotle powder
- ¼ teaspoon ground cloves
- 1 teaspoon garlic powder
- ½ teaspoon granulated (white) sugar

1. Remove the steak from the fridge 15–20 minutes before you plan to cook it.
2. Combine all the rub ingredients in a small bowl and stir with a spoon to ensure they are combined.
3. Drizzle half the olive oil over the steaks, coating well on both sides. Apply 1–2 teaspoons of rub to each side, coating as evenly as possible.
4. Place a large, heavy-based skillet over high heat. Add the remaining olive oil to the skillet.
5. Lay the steaks in the hot pan and cook for 3–5 minutes, then flip and cook on the other side for a further 3–5 minutes.
6. Remove from the pan and rest briefly under foil for 5 minutes. Slice across the grain to serve.

NOTES

Make sure the skirt steak is in large pieces, not small strips (which would make it difficult to cook).

This recipe uses dark (sometimes called 'Dutch process') cocoa. It has a richer, more intense flavor, and a deeper color like dark soil. The more common cinnamon-colored cocoa will work if it's the only thing you can track down, but try to get the good stuff if you can!

If you can't find Mexican oregano, use regular dried oregano.

CARNE ASADA TACOS WITH SALSA MACHA

SERVES 4

The beauty of tacos lies in the simplicity of their ingredients: great meat, a fresh tortilla and a flavorful salsa. Carne asada (literally 'grilled meat' in Spanish) ups the ante by throwing the unmistakable edge of charred and grilled flavor compounds into the mix. Oh, and I should warn you that the salsa macha makes a fairly large batch, but that's intentional. Spoon it over your eggs in the morning and thank me later.

SALSA MACHA

2 ancho chilies

2 guajillo chilies

2 chile de árbol

2 pasilla chilies

2 cups (500 ml) olive oil

6 garlic cloves, roughly chopped

2 tablespoons sesame seeds

⅓ cup (55 g) pumpkin seeds (pepitas)

2 teaspoons apple cider vinegar or juice of half an orange

2 teaspoons dried oregano

1 teaspoon salt

CARNE ASADA

2 lb (1 kg) outside skirt steak (see Note)

1½ teaspoons salt

½ teaspoon chipotle powder

¼ teaspoon ground cumin

½ teaspoon garlic powder

½ teaspoon onion powder

1 teaspoon chili powder

½ teaspoon ground black pepper

1 tablespoon dried oregano

½ teaspoon paprika

½ teaspoon MSG (optional)

8 flour tortillas (try my Beef Fat Tortillas on page 248)

⅓ cup (20 g) finely chopped cilantro (coriander)

⅓ cup (50 g) finely chopped onion

1. Start by making the salsa macha (the longer it sits, the more time the flavors have to mingle and intensify). Prepare all the dried chilies by removing and discarding the seeds and stems, then roughly chop them.
2. Place the olive oil into a small saucepan over medium-high heat. Add the garlic, sesame seeds and pumpkin seeds. Stir regularly until the garlic turns a golden brown, about 3–5 minutes. Turn off the heat, then add the chopped chilies. Stir, then let the chilies steep for about 10 minutes. Pour the oil mixture into a blender and add the vinegar, oregano and salt. Pulse a few times. The mixture should still have a coarse texture. Pour into a clean jar and set aside.
3. Remove the skirt steak from the fridge.
4. Light a grill for direct high-heat cooking, about 450–550°F (230–285°C).
5. In a bowl, combine the salt and spices to create a seasoning rub.
6. Sprinkle the rub liberally over the skirt steak, pressing it firmly into the meat.
7. Cook the steak on the hot grill, flipping it every 1–2 minutes until the outside is seared, about 8–10 minutes. Remove the steak from the grill and rest under foil for a few minutes.
8. While the steak rests, warm the tortillas by grilling them for 30–60 seconds per side.
9. Slice the steak into strips, then assemble the tacos by piling the meat into the tortilla, spooning over some salsa macha and topping with cilantro and onion.

NOTE

If you can't find outside skirt for this recipe, you can substitute with flank, inside skirt or even butterflied bavette.

CERVEZA FAJITAS WITH FLAME-ROASTED VEG

SERVES 4

The mild acids in beer work as a tenderizer on the flap steak, but getting it 'drunk' in the marinade is what really gives it a bold and distinct flavor. While traditional fajitas are served sizzling on a screaming-hot pan, those theatrics can end up overcooking the meat. I prefer to let the flavor of the grill do its thing, even if it means less steam and smoke at the table.

- 2 lb (1 kg) flap/bavette steak
- 8 garlic cloves, crushed
- zest and juice of 4 limes
- 2 teaspoons salt, divided
- 12 fl oz (350 ml) beer (see Notes)
- 3 tablespoons neutral oil (e.g. avocado oil), divided
- 1 green bell pepper (capsicum), cut into strips
- 1 poblano pepper, sliced
- 1 onion, cut into strips

FAJITA RUB

- 1 teaspoon salt
- 2 teaspoons chili powder
- ½ teaspoon ground cumin
- 1 teaspoon garlic powder
- 1 teaspoon dried oregano (preferably Mexican)
- 2 teaspoons paprika
- 1 teaspoon onion powder
- ¼ teaspoon cayenne pepper
- ½ teaspoon MSG (optional)

1. Prepare the meat for the marinade. If it's about 1 inch (2.5 cm) or more thick, you'll need to butterfly it. To do this, lay the meat flat on a board and run a trimming or boning knife horizontally into the thickest part of the meat. Work carefully by making slow, controlled strokes with the knife to cut through. This will allow you to open the meat up like a book and create two even pieces. You can leave a slight join to create a larger connected piece or cut all the way through to separate them in two.
2. In a non-reactive container, combine the crushed garlic, lime zest and juice, 1 teaspoon salt and beer. Stir to combine and dissolve the salt. Add the meat, making sure it's fully immersed, then cover and place in the fridge for 1–2 hours.
3. Prepare the fajita rub by combining all the ingredients in a bowl.
4. Light a grill for medium-high heat direct cooking, about 450–500°F (230–260°C).
5. Drain and discard the marinade, then pat the meat dry with paper towels. Drizzle 2 tablespoons neutral oil over the meat, then massage to coat evenly. Next, distribute the seasoning mix over the steak pieces, pressing it in firmly.
6. Toss the peppers and onion in the remaining oil, then season with the remaining salt.
7. Place the meat on the hot grill and cook for 3 minutes, then flip and cook for a further 2–3 minutes. Flip once more and cook for a final 2 minutes. Remove from the heat and cover with foil to rest for 5–8 minutes.
8. Place a grill pan (see Notes) on the hot grill to heat up, about 1–2 minutes. Pour the oiled and seasoned veggies into the grill pan and cook for 3–5 minutes, tossing occasionally with the tongs so they soften and start to develop a bit of char.
9. Slice the meat across the grain and serve with the grilled veg.

NOTES

A whole flap steak is about 3–5 lb (1.3–2.25 kg), so you can easily scale up with this recipe. In its untrimmed form, it starts off quite thick, about 1¼ inches (3 cm), but tapers off at the end to a much thinner piece. To counteract the inconsistency, butterfly the steak so it's more even. Trimming this way also promotes faster and even cooking on the grill.

You can use any kind of beer you like for this recipe, but I often choose Lone Star or a Mexican-style lager.

For a complete fajita experience, I serve these with tortillas, guacamole, pico de gallo and some lime wedges.

A grill pan is preferred for this recipe. It's not the same thing as a griddle pan. Instead of having raised ridges to give grill marks, it has cutouts or holes, which allow the heat and flame of the grill to reach the food. Think of it this way: a grill pan is designed to go on the grill, whereas a griddle pan is designed to emulate a grill. If you don't have a grill pan, you can use a regular cast-iron skillet, though the flavor may be slightly different.

MISO FLANK STEAK RICE BOWLS WITH CURED EGG YOLK

SERVES 2

Curing egg yolks transforms them into rich, velvety gems that act like instant sauce once they meet warm rice and steak. Paired with miso-marinated flank, it's an effortless combination of deep flavor and lush texture that feels far more indulgent than the work it takes to make.

CURED EGG YOLK

½ cup (125 ml) soy sauce

3 tablespoons mirin

4 egg yolks

RICE BOWLS

8 oz (225 g) flank steak (preferably in one piece)

2 teaspoons mirin

2 teaspoons soy sauce

2 tablespoons dark or red miso paste

2 teaspoons toasted sesame oil

1 tablespoon neutral oil (e.g. peanut or vegetable oil)

1 bunch greens (e.g. Chinese broccoli or bok choy)

2 cups (370 g) cooked jasmine rice

2 scallions (spring onions), sliced

½ teaspoon sesame or nigella seeds

1. To make the cured egg yolk, combine the soy sauce and mirin in a small container. Gently lower in the egg yolks, then drape a folded paper towel on top so it soaks up the marinade and ensures the top of the yolk is cured too. Place a lid on the container and put it into the fridge. Leave it to cure for 7–8 hours for a runny texture, or 10–12 hours for a jammier consistency.
2. Place the steak in a container or resealable bag. In a bowl, combine the mirin, soy sauce, miso paste and sesame oil. Stir until combined. Pour over the meat, coating well, then place in the fridge to marinate for 1–2 hours.
3. Place a skillet over high heat and add the neutral oil. Remove the steak from the marinade and place it straight into the heated pan. Sear for 5 minutes, then flip and sear for a further 5 minutes on the other side. Remove the steak from the pan and place onto a board, loosely covered with foil, to rest.
4. Leaving the pan on the heat, throw in the greens to sear and wilt for 1–2 minutes, tossing frequently. They should get the perfect amount of seasoning from the marinade left in the pan.
5. To assemble the rice bowls, place a cup of cooked rice in the bottom of each bowl. Top with the greens, hot from the pan. Slice the flank steak across the grain into strips, then nestle on top of the rice. Gently lift the yolks from the curing liquid and place them on top. Finish with sliced scallion and sesame seeds.

NOTES

You can use any miso paste for this, but if you have a choice, the dark or red paste has a more intense flavor.

It's preferable to cook the steak as one large piece, then slice and portion. But if you can only find smaller portions, they will still do the job.

This recipe serves two but also makes four egg yolks. They're so tasty that you'll want an extra one. You're welcome.

SHANKS

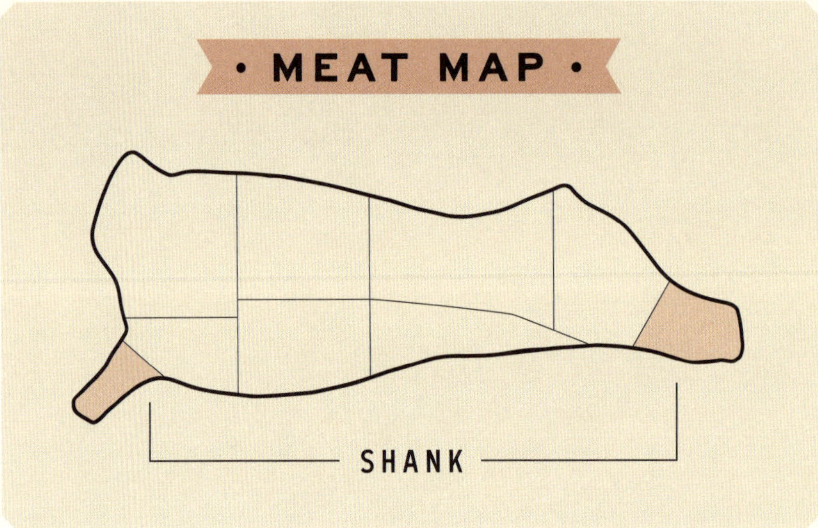

The shank (sometimes called the shin) comes from the animal's lower leg. It's one of the hardest-working muscles. Cattle spend at least eight hours a day standing, and that's a lot of weight to support! All that work makes the shank naturally lean, loaded with connective tissue, and tough if cooked quickly. But that very toughness is also its greatest strength: with time and gentle heat, the dense collagen breaks down into gelatin, transforming the shank into one of the most richly textured eating experiences.

I like to classify shanks in the same family of cuts as beef cheek and brisket – tough, sinewy pieces that, when treated the right way, collapse into tender, gelatinous splendor. Adding to their appeal is the marrow within the bones, enriching braising liquids and acting as a supporting star of the dish.

Both the foreshank (front leg, *humerus*) and the hind shank (back leg, *tibia* and *fibula*) are used, with the hind usually yielding a meatier portion. In general, shanks are considered a low-value cut, and most end up as ground (minced) meat. While lamb shanks are relatively easy to find, you may need to special-order a whole beef shank.

FRENCHED OR NOT?

Some shanks will come 'frenched', where the top section of meat is cut away to reveal the bone 'handle' that makes the whole thing look like a giant meat mallet. In reality, it just means you're missing out on extra meat, because the meat will shrink away naturally during cooking to reveal the hammer shape.

• MEAT NERD FACT •

The shank's firmness doesn't come from the muscle fibers themselves, but from the amount and distribution of connective tissue throughout the cut. These lower leg muscles work constantly to support the animal's weight, encouraging dense collagen networks. A cross cut shank slice makes this connective tissue matrix easy to see.

FRENCHED SHANK

CROSS CUT SHANK

OSSO BUCO

SERVES 4

The name of this classic Italian dish means 'bone with a hole', referring to the cross cut tibia right in the middle of each piece. When the shanks are cut this way, you get to enjoy the tender braised beef plus the bonus final bite of a mouthful of rich, fatty marrow plucked right from the center of the bone.

- 2 tablespoons olive oil
- 4 x 12 oz (325 g) cross cut veal or beef shanks (see Notes)
- 2 teaspoons salt
- 1 teaspoon cracked black pepper
- ⅓ cup (50 g) all-purpose (plain) flour
- 2 carrots, finely diced
- 1 small onion, finely diced
- 4 garlic cloves, crushed
- 1 teaspoon dried thyme
- 1 teaspoon dried rosemary
- 2 teaspoons tomato paste
- 2 cups (500 ml) white wine
- 1 cup (250 ml) beef stock
- 2 bay leaves

1. Place a braising pan (or Dutch oven) over high heat and add the olive oil.
2. Season the shanks with the salt and black pepper on both sides. Lightly dust each side of the meat with the flour, shaking off any excess.
3. Brown the meat in the pan, about 8–10 minutes per side, until deeply browned, then remove from the pan and set aside on a plate.
4. Add the carrot, onion and garlic to the pan and cook for about 5 minutes, or until softened.
5. Add the dried herbs and tomato paste and stir through, allowing the tomato paste to cook and darken slightly.
6. Pour in the wine and use a wooden spoon to scrape up any browned bits from the pan. Return the beef to the pan and add the beef stock and bay leaves.
7. Cover with a lid, turn the heat to medium-low and simmer for 2 hours until tender. Or finish in a 350°F (180°C) oven for 2 hours until tender.

NOTES

You can substitute the shanks in this recipe with ox tail or beef neck.

I recommend serving these over polenta or creamy mashed potatoes, spooning over lots of jus from the pan.

RED WINE BRAISED LAMB SHANKS

SERVES 4

Few dishes capture comfort quite like braised lamb shanks. They're slowly simmered in red wine and aromatics until the meat turns meltingly tender and the marrow enriches the sauce. This recipe is made for cold weather, and when you serve it over a big mound of creamy mashed potatoes, it's the sort of meal that warms you from the inside out.

- 2 tablespoons olive oil, divided
- 4 lamb shanks (see Note)
- 1½ teaspoons salt
- 1 teaspoon black pepper
- 1 onion, finely diced
- 2 carrots, finely diced
- 2 celery stalks, finely diced
- 6 garlic cloves, crushed
- 2 tablespoons tomato paste
- 1 tablespoon all-purpose (plain) flour
- 1½ cups (375 ml) red wine
- 2 cups (500 ml) beef stock or bone broth (page 256)
- 1 sprig rosemary
- 2 bay leaves
- 2 tablespoons salted butter

1. Preheat the oven to 325°F (165°C).
2. Place a large Dutch oven over high heat and add 1 tablespoon olive oil.
3. Season the lamb shanks on both sides with salt and pepper, then brown them for 5–7 minutes per side, or until they develop a golden brown color. Transfer the shanks to a plate and set aside.
4. Add the remaining olive oil to the pot, then add the onion, carrot, celery and garlic. Cook for about 5 minutes, stirring frequently, until the vegetables are softened. Add the tomato paste and flour and stir through.
5. Pour in the wine to deglaze the pan. Use your spoon to scrape up the browned bits on the bottom. Add the stock, then the rosemary and bay leaves.
6. Bring the mixture to a simmer, then cover with a lid and place in the oven to braise until tender, about 2–3 hours.
7. To serve, gently remove the shanks from the pot and spoon over some of the braising juices.
8. For a more refined finishing sauce, strain the braising liquid through a sieve and discard the veggies and herbs. Return the liquid to the pot and simmer over medium heat until it reduces to a glossy sauce that coats the back of a spoon. Remove from the heat and whisk through the cold butter. Spoon over the shanks just before serving.

NOTE

Since we're in the shank section, you can sub the lamb shanks with cross cut beef shanks (like the ones in osso buco) and it'll work like a dream. Veal shanks are another option.

WHOLE BARBECUED BEEF SHANK

SERVES 6

The sheer scale of barbecued items is part of what makes them so impressive. Huge briskets, monstrous racks of beef ribs, but none are quite as impressively primal as the smoked shank. A hulking swath of bone and muscle, it's tempting to plonk it down on the table and serve it whole, but I reckon it's best if you pull the meat before serving so you can remove any tougher bits of gristle and tendon.

- 1 x 7–10 lb (3–4.5 kg) whole beef shank
- 2–3 tablespoons hot sauce or mustard
- 2 teaspoons salt
- 1 teaspoon freshly ground black pepper
- ¼ cup (60 ml) worcestershire sauce
- ¼ cup (60 ml) water
- 1 onion, roughly sliced
- 4 cups (1 liter) beef stock

1. Remove the shank from the fridge and preheat a smoker to 300°F (150°C).
2. Coat the shank with hot sauce, then season generously with the salt and pepper.
3. Place into the smoker to cook for 3 hours.
4. In a spray bottle, combine the worcestershire sauce and water. Spritz the shank every 30 minutes as it smokes.
5. Place the shank into a large foil pan, scattering the onion slices around it. Add the beef stock and cover the pan with foil.
6. Return the pan to the smoker and braise for a further 5–6 hours until the meat is completely tender. Use a probe to check for tenderness by sticking it into several spots on the shank. If you prefer, you can finish cooking the shank in an oven at 300°F (150°C) since the smoke will not reach the meat anyway.
7. Remove the shank from the pan and allow to cool slightly.
8. Pull the meat, removing and discarding any tough tendon or silverskin pieces, leaving only tender bites. (To pull the meat, I prefer to use nitrile gloves over a layer of cotton gloves for heat protection. This allows you to feel for any 'unpleasant' bits much more easily.)
9. Ladle 1–2 spoons of braising liquid over the meat to moisten it, tossing it through with your gloved hands. Taste and add more salt if needed, then serve.

NOTES

Sometimes you'll see this sold as a 'Thor's hammer', another very creative use of meat-cut naming.

Not sure what to do with the meat? Treat it like any other pulled BBQ meat! Throw it in tacos, make sandwiches and add it to a pasta dish. Or eat it on its own for a full carnivore's feast.

I prefer to use a basic salt and pepper rub for this, but you can replace it with your preferred BBQ seasoning. Sometimes I use Hardcore Carnivore Camo seasoning, Black Rub or a combo.

CHICKEN

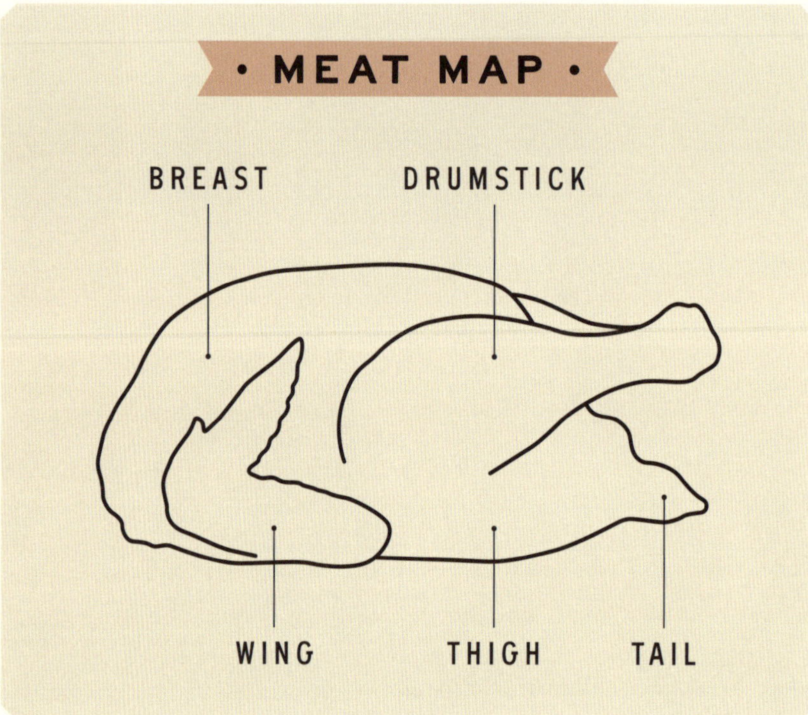

There's something to be said for the meat that comes from an animal that is the closest living relative to a T-rex dinosaur! Chicken is one of the most approachable proteins, with easily recognizable cuts and consistent cut names.

TEAM THIGH OR TEAM BREAST?

One of the first carnivorous food preferences we form is whether we prefer dark or light chicken meat. But have you ever stopped to think about what makes them different? Or why they are such different shades?

Color in chicken muscle is largely determined by how much activity the muscle gets. And remember, even though chickens have wings, they spend more time walking around than flying. Since white meat has less myoglobin, it appears paler in color, while dark meat has more myoglobin so the meat seems darker.

WHITE MEAT (WINGS, BREASTS)

- Short bursts of movement
- Less myoglobin
- Less fat
- Flight muscles

DARK MEAT (LEGS, THIGHS)

- Longer periods of continuous usage
- More myoglobin
- More fat
- Leg muscles

To learn more about myoglobin (the protein that gives meat color), check out page 44.

FEATHERED OMNIVORES

Sometimes you see 'fed vegetarian-only diet' as a marketing callout on some chicken packaging. The problem is, chickens are not natural vegetarians. When left in a free-range environment, they frequently eat insects, grubs, worms and even small animals like lizards and snakes.

THE CHICKEN GLOSSARY

• BROILER •

A chicken raised for meat

• COCKEREL •

A young rooster

• GIBLETS •

The edible organs, including heart, liver and gizzard

• HEN •

A mature female

• LAYER •

A chicken raised for egg production

• POULTRY •

Generally refers to any kind of domesticated bird, such as chickens, turkeys, quails, pigeons, ostriches, emus, game and waterfowl (ducks)

• PULLET •

A hen less than a year old

• ROOSTER •

A mature male

SMOKED CHICKEN DRUMS WITH HABANERO HOT HONEY

MAKES 8 DRUMSTICKS

It's hard to give a 'serving size' suggestion on this. Some people would be happy with a single drum, but I've seen grown men happily down at least three of these in a single sitting. I'll just tell you they're incredibly moreish, and that this recipe makes eight of them. And with that warning ... you decide how many mouths that might feed in your house.

- 8 cups (2 liters) water
- ½ cup (110 g) granulated (white) sugar
- ½ cup (125 g) salt
- 8 chicken drumsticks
- spray oil

SEASONING RUB

- 1 tablespoon light brown sugar
- 1 tablespoon paprika
- 1½ teaspoons salt
- ½ teaspoon chili powder
- ½ teaspoon ground black pepper
- ½ teaspoon onion powder
- ½ teaspoon garlic powder
- ⅛ teaspoon ground cumin

HOT HONEY

- ½ cup (175 g) honey
- 1 habanero pepper, deseeded and chopped (see Notes)
- 1 teaspoon apple cider vinegar

1. Pour the water into a large container and add the sugar and salt. Stir until everything is dissolved, then immerse the chicken drumsticks in the brine. Refrigerate for at least 4 hours, or overnight.
2. Preheat a smoker to 225°F (105°C).
3. Remove the chicken from the brine and pat well with paper towels.
4. Combine all the ingredients for the seasoning rub in a bowl and mix well. Season the chicken generously with the rub, then place into the smoker. Cook for 90 minutes.
5. While the chicken is cooking, make the hot honey by placing the honey in a small saucepan over low heat. Add the pepper and bring to a very low simmer, stirring a few times.
6. Remove the pan from the heat and allow to steep for 10–15 minutes until the flavors infuse.
7. Pour the honey through a sieve to remove the peppers, then pour into a clean jar. Stir through the apple cider vinegar and set aside.
8. After the chicken has been smoking for 90 minutes, increase the temperature of the smoker to 400°F (210°C). Spritz the chicken with a light coating of spray oil and cook for a further 15–20 minutes, or until the skin starts to bubble and become taut.
9. Remove the chicken from the smoker and drizzle with the hot honey.

NOTES

If you can't handle too much heat, replace the habanero with a milder chili like jalapeño. And if you can't find fresh peppers, use chili flakes.

If you're pressed for time, skip the brine. It definitely creates a juicier result, but it's more of a 'gold standard' than an 'essential step.'

I recommend apple, cherry, hickory, oak or maple woods for smoking chicken.

VIET-STYLE FISH SAUCE WINGS

SERVES 6–8 (MAKES ABOUT 15 WINGS)

Sweet, spicy, sour, crispy and fresh. The secret to these wings is to double-fry them, which locks in the crunch. Using two out of three joints of the whole chicken wing is key for this recipe. The smaller size allows the wings to cook to a safe temperature without burning, and favors the parts that can achieve maximum crispiness!

MARINADE

½ cup (140 g) granulated (white) sugar

½ cup (125 ml) water

½ cup (125 ml) fish sauce

zest and juice of 1 lime

1½ tablespoons sambal or chili and garlic paste

WINGS

3 lb (1.3 kg) whole chicken wings, cut into one-joint sections (see opposite)

6 cups (1.5 liters) peanut oil or any neutral oil

1 cup (125 g) cornstarch (cornflour)

¼ cup (5 g) mint leaves, to serve

¼ cup (7 g) cilantro (coriander) leaves, to serve

GLAZE

1 tablespoon water

1 teaspoon sambal

¼ cup (60 ml) fish sauce

½ cup (110 g) granulated (white) sugar

zest and juice of 1 lime

1. To make the marinade, place the sugar, water and fish sauce in a small saucepan. Cook over low heat, stirring frequently, until the sugar is just dissolved. Allow to cool, then add the lime zest and juice and the sambal.
2. Place the chicken wings in a non-reactive container and pour over the marinade. Place in the fridge for 2–4 hours, tossing regularly to distribute the marinade evenly.
3. Add the peanut oil to a deep, heavy-based pot and heat to 350°F (175°C).
4. Remove the wings from the marinade and dry each thoroughly with paper towels. Discard the remaining marinade.
5. Place the cornstarch in a bowl, then dip each wing into the cornstarch, shaking off any excess. Add to the hot oil, working in batches so as not to overcrowd the pot. Fry for 7 minutes, then use a mesh strainer or tongs to remove the wings from the oil. Place onto a rack or paper towels to drain. Repeat until all the wings are cooked, ensuring the oil returns to 350°F (175°C) between batches.
6. Place all the glaze ingredients, except the lime zest, into a small saucepan. Cook at a simmer over medium heat, stirring frequently, until the glaze is thickened and syrupy, about 8–10 minutes.
7. Add the wings back to the hot oil and cook for a further 3 minutes. Again, work in batches so as not to overcrowd the pot.
8. To serve, pile the wings onto a plate and drizzle with the reduced glaze. Top with the lime zest, mint leaves and cilantro leaves.

NOTE

Though it seems like you are creating the marinade all over again for the glaze, it's not advisable to reuse marinades from raw chicken. Even though you'd be heating it and killing off any harmful bacteria, it also contains proteins from soaking the chicken, so it ends up looking cloudy and unappealing.

• BE THE BUTCHER •

HOW TO CUT ONE-JOINT WINGS

To create these custom wing pieces, start with a whole chicken wing and make a cut between the drumette and the flat, pushing down firmly with a knife to separate them. This will leave you with the flat and wing tip as one piece, and the drumette as another.

Note: save the drumettes for Sticky Sesame Wings (page 198).

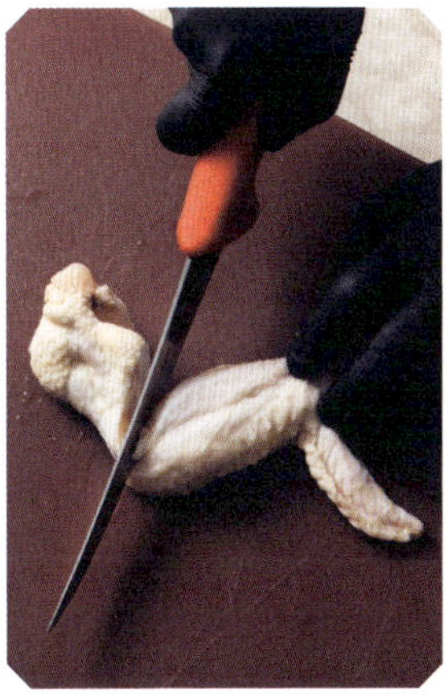

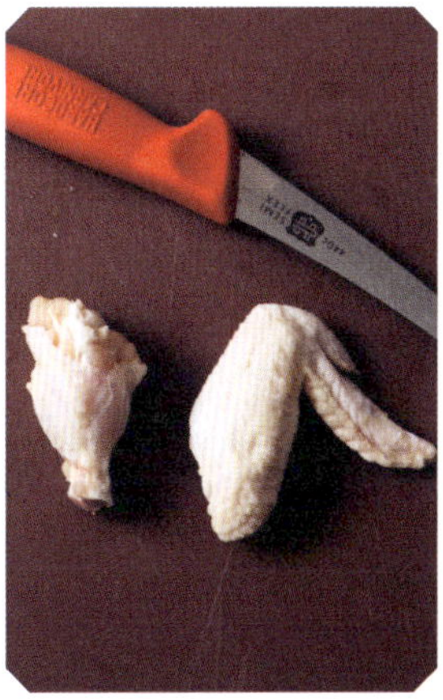

ULTRA-CRISPY ROAST CHICKEN

SERVES 4–6

One of the very best parts of an oven-roasted bird is the skin – and if you agree, you're going to absolutely love this version. With a traditional whole bird, only the skin on the top of the chicken gets crispy, while the skin on the underside is relegated to a still-tasty but soggy state. Spatchcocking puts all the skin at the top. Additionally, adding baking powder (which is alkaline) to the skin raises the pH level, which in turn promotes the Maillard reaction. Just make sure you use baking powder, not baking soda.

- 1 x 5 lb (2.25 kg) whole chicken
- 1–2 tablespoons olive oil
- 1 tablespoon salt
- 1 teaspoon baking powder

1. Preheat the oven to 450°F (230°C).
2. To spatchcock the chicken, remove and discard any giblets or internal organs remaining in the cavity. Using poultry shears, cut along either side of the spine and remove it completely. Make a cut through the cartilage at the top of the breast plate, being careful not to cut through to the skin. Flip the bird over and press down on the breast to crack the bone and make it flat. Tuck the wings under so the tips don't burn during cooking. For a detailed tutorial, see page 194.
3. Place a wire rack on a sheet pan (baking sheet) and arrange the chicken so it lays as flat as possible. Pat the skin dry using a paper towel.
4. Drizzle the olive oil over the chicken skin, using your hand to coat the skin well.
5. In a small bowl, combine the salt and baking powder, then sprinkle the mixture (as evenly as possible) across the top of the chicken. Lightly massage the salt mixture into the skin.
6. Place the chicken on the middle rack of the oven and roast for 50–60 minutes, or until the internal temperature reaches 165°F (73°C) at the thickest part of the breast.

NOTES

If you can't bear the idea of throwing out the giblets (and other bits and pieces), you can store them in your freezer and add them to the pot next time you make stock.

Technically, 165°F (73°C) is the safe temperature for cooked chicken, but due to carryover cooking and 'time at temperature', you can pull it out when it's a few degrees below and still have it reach a safe internal temperature.

• BE THE BUTCHER •

HOW TO SPATCHCOCK A CHICKEN

Spatchcocking (and yes, we all giggle at it) is a fancy term for butterflying a chicken and getting it to lay flat. It makes the bird physically more even, which means it also cooks more evenly, speeding up the cooking time.

You'll need: poultry shears or really robust scissors

1. Start with the bird breast side down, with the spine facing up towards you.
2. Cut along either side of the spine. It doesn't matter which end you start with. You can cut up from the tail or down from the neck cavity. You'll have to use a little more force when cutting through the ribs.
3. Once the backbone is loose, remove it completely and discard, or use it to make bone broth or chicken stock (page 257).
4. Using a sharp knife, make a nick right in the middle of the breastbone. This step is not essential, but it makes the next step much easier.
5. Flip the bird over so the breast is facing up, then press down firmly on the breast bone to break it. You should hear a little crunch when it gives.
6. Arrange the breasts and thighs so the bird lays as flat as possible.
7. If desired, tuck the wing tips under the breast to protect them (the tips are often the first to burn).

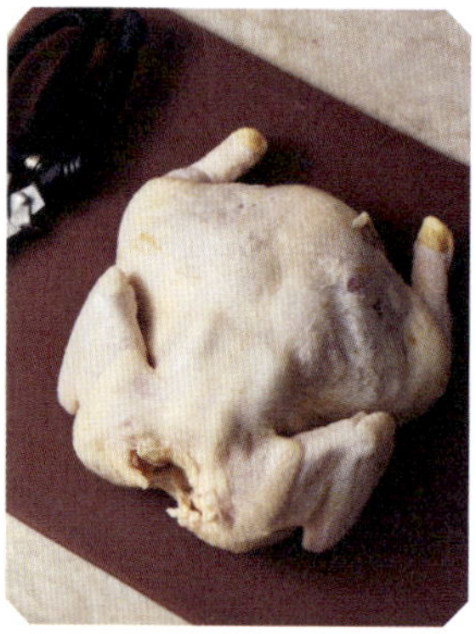

1

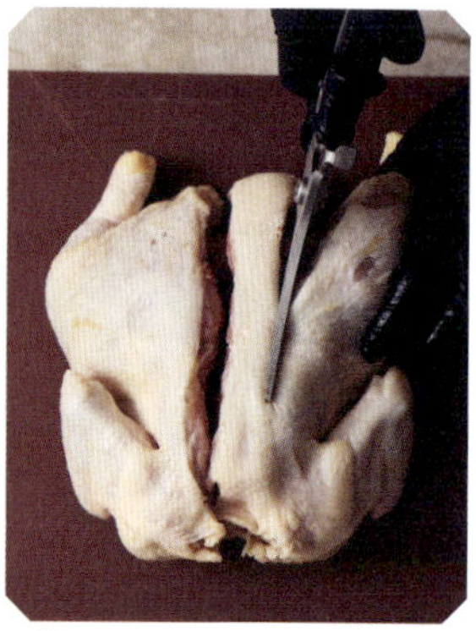

2

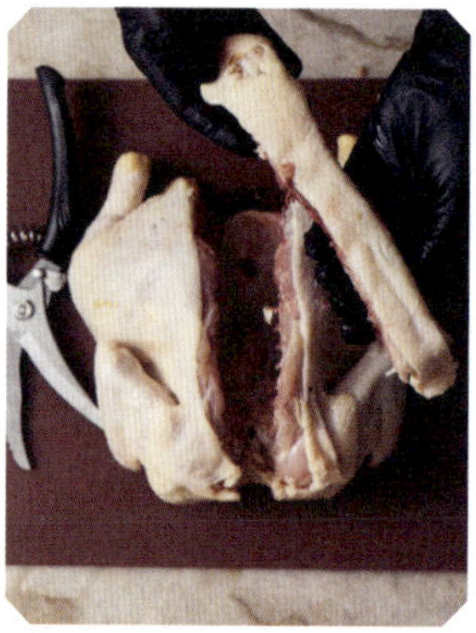

3

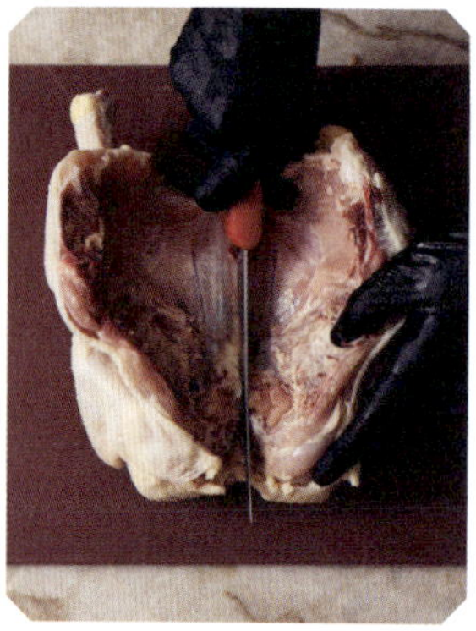

4

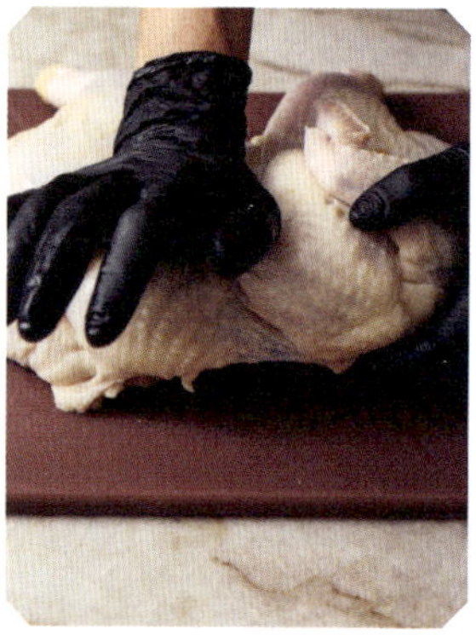

5

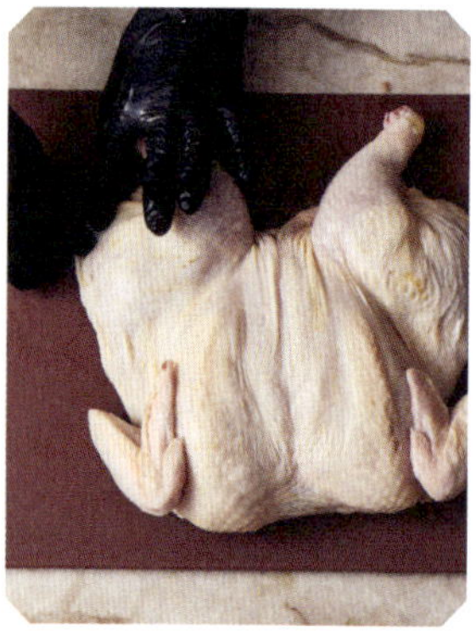

6

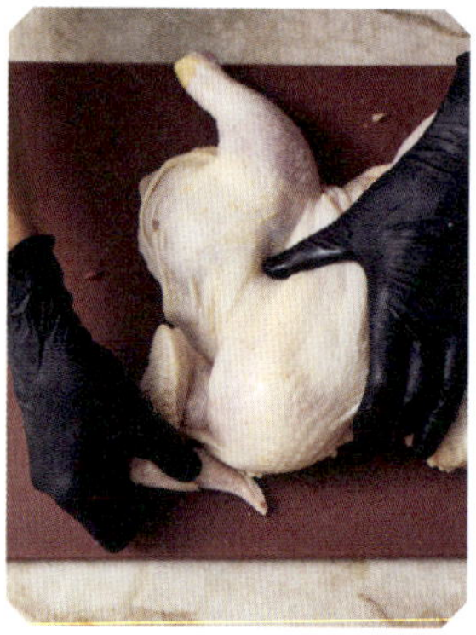

7

MEDITERRANEAN CHICKEN WITH LEMON AND OLIVES

SERVES 4–6

If you're looking for a great 'twofer', I've got you covered. Buying skin-on, bone-in chicken is always cheaper because the butcher has less work to do. So in this recipe, I wanted to give you some options and flexibility. You can make this recipe with boneless, skinless thighs. Or you can make it with regular bone-in and skin-on thighs. Better yet – and hear me out here – you can buy bone-in, skin-on thighs, peel the skins off and make my insanely good Salt and Vinegar Chicken Skin Chips (page 200), then use the remaining meat for this recipe.

- 8 chicken thighs
- 4 tablespoons olive oil, divided
- ¾ teaspoon salt
- 2 lemons
- 3 shallots, quartered
- 3 garlic cloves, crushed
- 1 cup (250 ml) chicken stock
- ¼ teaspoon ground turmeric
- ½ teaspoon dried thyme
- ½ teaspoon ground cumin
- ¼ teaspoon ground cinnamon
- 1 cup (160 g) whole Castelvetrano olives or green olives

1. Remove the thighs from the fridge. If using skin-on, pat the skins dry with a paper towel.
2. Place a large skillet over high heat and add 2 tablespoons olive oil.
3. Season the chicken with the salt, then place in the skillet (skin side down, if using) to sear for 5 minutes. The chicken should easily release from the skillet, otherwise just leave it another minute or two longer.
4. Use tongs to turn the thighs over and cook for a further 2 minutes on the other side, then remove to a plate.
5. Slice one of the lemons in half for squeezing and the other into 6–8 slices.
6. Add the remaining olive oil to the skillet and cook the lemon slices for about 2 minutes, or until caramelized. Remove the lemon and add to the plate with the chicken.
7. Add the shallot to the hot skillet. Cook, stirring frequently, for about 2–3 minutes. Stir in the garlic and cook for a further 1–2 minutes, keeping the garlic moving to ensure it doesn't burn.
8. Deglaze the skillet by adding the stock and the juice of the remaining lemon. Use a spoon to scrape up all the browned bits to create a sauce.
9. Stir in the turmeric, thyme, cumin and cinnamon.
10. Nestle the chicken thighs into the skillet, then scatter the lemon slices and olives between them. If you're using skin-on, take care not to wet the crisped skins.
11. Reduce the heat to a high simmer and cover the skillet with a lid.
12. Cook for 30–40 minutes until the chicken is cooked through and tender.

NOTE

I usually serve this with a side of basmati rice, spooning extra pan sauce over the rice to really capture the flavor.

BONE-IN QUARTER CHICKEN LEGS (US)

CHICKEN MARYLANDS (AUSTRALIA, NZ, UK)

SMOKY PASILLA AND ORANGE GRILLED MARYLANDS

SERVES 4

Fun fact: a 'chicken maryland' is just the name for a quarter chicken leg piece. That is, the thigh with the drumstick still attached. Continuing the great tradition of confusing meat-cut names, maryland is commonly used in the UK and Australia but not in the US, where the actual state of Maryland exists. Go figure! This marinade is all about flavor, not heat. Pasilla chilies are one of my favorites. They have a smoky and slightly sweet flavor, reminiscent of raisins and dark chocolate.

- 5 dried pasilla chilies
- 2 cups (500 ml) hot water
- 6 garlic cloves
- zest and juice of 2 oranges
- 2 teaspoons chicken bouillon (stock) powder
- 3 teaspoons salt
- 1 teaspoon ground cumin
- 3 tablespoons vegetable or olive oil
- 4 skin-on, bone-in quarter chicken legs

1. Place a comal (see Notes) or cast-iron skillet over medium heat and toast the pasilla chilies, moving them over the heat until fragrant, about 30–60 seconds.
2. Remove and discard the stems and seeds from the chilies, then place them into a small bowl or container. Cover with the hot water and leave them to soften for about 10 minutes.
3. In a blender or food processor, add the garlic, orange zest and juice, chicken bouillon, salt, cumin, vegetable oil and the softened chilies. Blend until smooth.
4. Prepare the chicken by using the tip of a sharp knife or specialty tool to pierce the skin with small dots all over.
5. Place the chicken into a resealable bag or container, then cover with the marinade. Place in the fridge and marinate for 12–24 hours.
6. Prepare a grill for low-medium-heat cooking, about 275–300°F (140–155°C). If using a charcoal grill, light the coals, then scatter across the grill, leaving ample space between each briquette.
7. Place the chicken skin side down over the grill and close the lid. Cook for 7–9 minutes. If you encounter flare-ups, move the chicken to a cooler part of the grill, but if you have your heat low enough, this should not be an issue.
8. Flip the chicken over and cook for a further 7 minutes on the other side. Flip the chicken one final time so the skin side is down, and cook for a further 2–4 minutes to crisp the skin. The internal temperature of the meat should reach 165°F (73°C) at the thickest point, so cook longer if necessary.

NOTES

Piercing the chicken skin using a knife or specialty tool creates little 'escape holes' for the fat to drain while the chicken is cooking, ensuring a crispier finish. You can buy specialty tools that have lots of little metal spikes (like nails) that are perfect for this job. They also work well on pork skin (page 72).

A comal is a flat metal pan used for toasting tortillas. You can easily use a cast-iron skillet or flat griddle to achieve the same cooking effect.

If you're looking for a great side dish pairing, I love serving these with Frijoles Refritos (page 249).

DRUMETTES

STICKY SESAME WINGS

SERVES 4–6

This recipe uses the drumette portions cut from the Viet-Style Fish Sauce Wings recipe (page 190), but you can use wing flats if you prefer. And sure, you could share these with four to six people as a little nibble, but if you're a serious wing fan, you may just wanna split 'em with one friend – and that friend may be you.

- ½ cup (125 ml) soy sauce
- 1 tablespoon granulated (white) sugar
- ¼ cup (60 ml) rice wine vinegar or mirin
- 2 tablespoons sesame oil
- 2 tablespoons grated fresh ginger
- 2 garlic cloves, crushed
- 2 lb (1 kg) chicken drumettes
- 1 tablespoon sesame seeds
- ¼ cup (15 g) sliced scallions (spring onions)

1. In a small bowl, combine the soy sauce, sugar, vinegar, sesame oil, ginger and garlic. Whisk or stir until the sugar is dissolved.
2. Place the drumettes into a resealable container or plastic storage bag, then cover with the marinade. Seal, then place in the fridge for 8–24 hours.
3. Preheat the oven to 425°F (215°C) and position a rack at the top.
4. Remove the wings from the fridge and discard the marinade.
5. Line a sheet pan (baking sheet) with parchment (baking) paper and position the wings on the pan, with space between each one. Place in the oven on the upper rack and bake for 30 minutes, turning the wings halfway through.
6. Place the sesame seeds in a small skillet and toast over medium heat for 1–2 minutes, or until they turn golden brown and fragrant.
7. Remove the wings from the oven and sprinkle with the toasted sesame seeds and scallions.

NOTES

I recommend marinating the wings overnight if you can. It really improves the flavor and texture of the chicken.

If you have hot spots in your oven, rotate the pan when you turn the wings over.

WHITE CHICKEN CHILI

SERVES 6–8

I would argue that white chili is not at all related to its beefier, crimson-hued cousin (aside from the fact that they are both cooked in a large pot). But if you take 'chili' to simply mean 'hearty stew', then you have a much better idea of what this warm bowl of comfort-eating will deliver. If you want to be a little extra, you can replace the canned corn with freshly charred kernels cut straight from the cob.

- 4 tablespoons salted butter
- 1 onion, finely chopped
- 3 garlic cloves, crushed
- ¼ cup (35 g) all-purpose (plain) flour
- 6 cups (1.5 liters) chicken stock
- 2 x 15 oz (425 g) cans white beans (see Notes)
- 2 teaspoons salt
- ¼ teaspoon ground black pepper
- ½ teaspoon chili powder
- 2 x 4 oz (115 g) cans diced green chilies, drained (see Notes)
- 3 chicken breasts
- 1 x 15 oz (425 g) can corn kernels, drained
- ½ cup (125 g) sour cream
- 8 oz (225 g) cream cheese, softened

1. Place a large, heavy-based pot over medium-high heat and add the butter. Once melted, cook the onion and garlic for about 3 minutes, stirring regularly, until the onion is softened.
2. Sprinkle the flour over the onion mixture and stir to make a loose paste. Cook, stirring constantly, for 1–2 minutes to cook out the raw flour taste.
3. Add the chicken stock a little at a time, stirring as you pour, until it is all incorporated. The flour mix will be thick and messy at first, but if you keep adding the stock slowly, it will eventually dissolve into the liquid.
4. Drain most (but not all) of the liquid from 1 can of white beans, then use a food processor, blender or immersion blender to blitz the beans and reserved liquid into a fine paste. Add this to the pot and stir through.
5. Add the salt, black pepper and chili powder, along with the green chilies.
6. Gently drop the chicken breasts into the liquid and simmer in the broth for 20 minutes. Make sure the broth does not boil or the meat will toughen.
7. Use tongs to remove the meat once cooked. Shred it with two forks and return it to the pot. Drain the remaining can of white beans and add it to the pot along with the corn kernels.
8. Place the sour cream and cream cheese into a small bowl. Add a ladle of the hot broth to the bowl and stir through. Repeat twice, stirring until the mixture is creamy. This should temper the sour cream and cheese so they don't curdle in the pot. Once tempered, add them to the pot and stir through.
9. Ladle the chili into bowls and serve.

NOTES

Any white beans will work for this chili – butter, cannellini, navy or great northern. For the can that gets blended up, I like to use butter beans.

Green chilies (sometimes called Hatch chilies) are New Mexico–style peppers available in both mild and hot varieties. The canned variety are soft, roasted diced pepper pieces with a slightly sweet and earthy flavor.

This recipe is great for using left-overs, too. If you have any left-over meat from Ultra-Crispy Roast Chicken (page 192) or Butter-Basted Roast Turkey (page 265), use that instead of the chicken breast.

SALT AND VINEGAR CHICKEN SKIN CHIPS

SERVES 4-6

When a recipe calls for skinless thighs, I often buy them with the skin on so I can save the skins and use them to make a bowl of these addictive 'meat chips'. Brimming with golden schmaltzy flavor, you can easily smash a whole bowl without sharing, though your cardiologist may be less impressed.

8-12 chicken thigh skins

½ teaspoon fine sea salt

1½ teaspoon vinegar powder

METHOD #1: AIR FRYER

1. Working in batches, stretch the skins out across the bottom of the air fryer basket.
2. Cook at 400°F (200°C) for 12 minutes, turning halfway during the cook.
3. Combine the sea salt and vinegar powder in a bowl.
4. Remove the skins from the fryer and place on a paper towel to drain. Sprinkle the vinegar mixture on the skins while they're still warm.

METHOD #2: OVEN

1. Preheat the oven to 375°F (185°C).
2. Line a large sheet pan (baking sheet) with parchment (baking) paper. Lay the chicken skins on the paper, stretching them out and leaving space between each one.
3. Cover with another layer of parchment paper, then place another sheet pan on top so the skins are sandwiched in the middle and pressed flat.
4. Place the pans in the oven and cook for 45–55 minutes until the skins are golden and crispy.
5. Combine the sea salt and vinegar powder in a bowl.
6. Remove the top sheet pan and piece of parchment paper. Sprinkle the vinegar mixture on the skins while they're still warm.

NOTE

To make a batch that's worth your while, save the skins in a baggie in the freezer until you've collected enough to cook up as chips.

LAMB

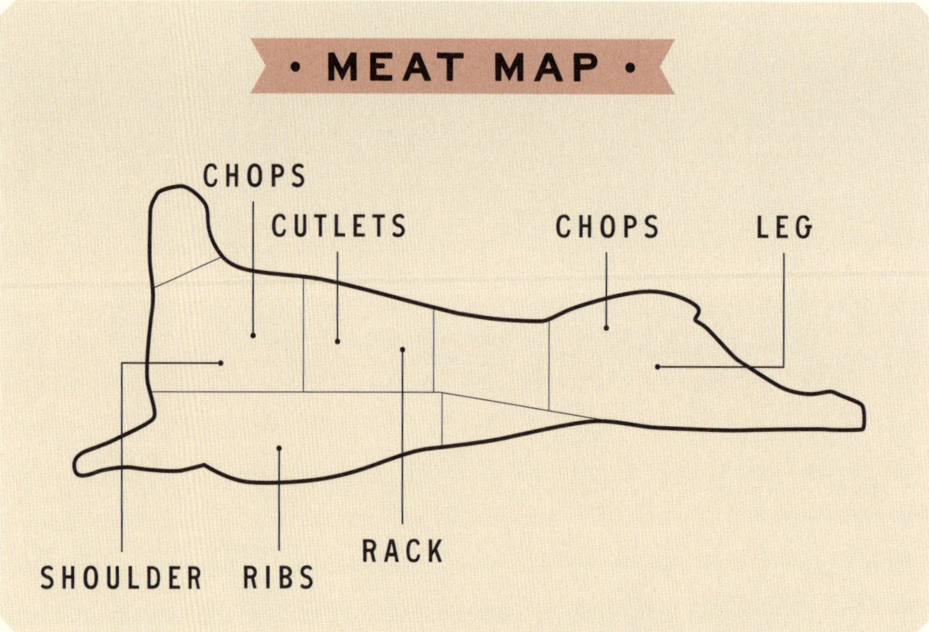

Lamb is one of the most underrated proteins in the butcher's case. It's often reduced to a repetitive set of familiar dishes or written off as 'too strong', which has done it a real disservice. In reality, lamb is deeply flavorful, with a wide range of cuts that respond beautifully to quick, high-heat cooking, as well as others that are perfectly suited to long, slow methods.

I grew up eating plenty of lamb. With Australia's ovine flock sitting at around 70 million head, one of the largest in the world, Aussies take lamb pretty seriously.

When I moved to the US, one of the hardest culinary adjustments to get used to was how little lamb featured on menus, and how few lamb cuts appeared in grocery stores. I was shocked at how uncommon it was, but eventually learned the roots of this shortage went back to World War II. Back then, it wasn't lamb at all – it was mutton: the older, gamier, greasier version. It was canned, boiled and packed into military rations for durability, which left it with an unmistakably gamey (and slightly rancid) funk. Soldiers came home vowing never to eat anything sheep-related again, and subsequent generations of Americans grew up missing out on the joy of lamb.

I'm on a personal mission to turn that around. Every American I've cooked lamb for who had never tried it before became an instant convert. So, if you haven't had it yet … what on earth are you waiting for?

I've eaten lamb around the globe, and to this day, I still think Australia produces the best. It's worth seeking out the good stuff. And don't worry, it's exported everywhere.

You can find more lamb recipes on pages 183, 218 and 225.

• MEAT NERD FACT •

For meat to qualify as **lamb**, the animal must be under 12 months old and have no permanent incisor teeth. Teeth are an indicator of age. Hunters often use them to age deer, and in the meat industry, this process is called dentition. Sheep between 1 and 2 years old, with some permanent incisors, are classified as **hoggets**, while **mutton** comes from animals over 2 years old. As sheep age, their flavor grows stronger and the meat becomes tougher, which is why mutton is typically reserved for bold, slow-cooked dishes like curries and stews.

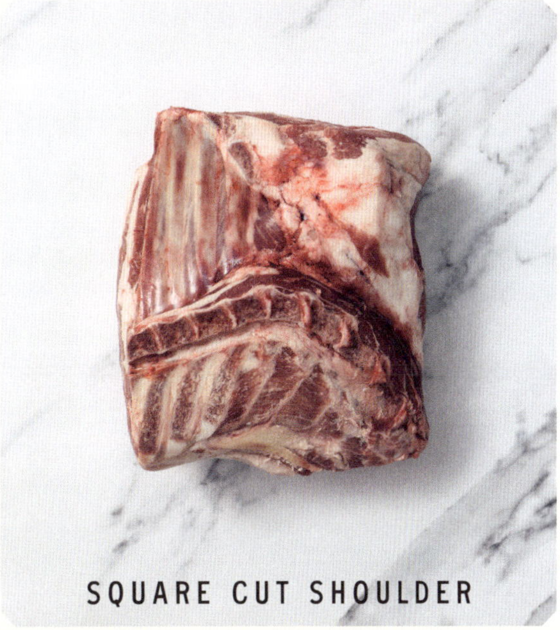

SQUARE CUT SHOULDER

MEET THE SQUARE CUT SHOULDER

Square cut lamb shoulder is one of those 'secret' cuts many home cooks never encounter. It's far more common in food service and whole-animal butcher shops than in supermarket cases, which is a shame, because it's a phenomenal piece of meat. Taken from a hard-working part of the animal, it's packed with connective tissue and fat, which means big flavor and incredible results with low-and-slow cooking.

For BBQ enthusiasts, this is a cut worth seeking out. I reckon it was built for the smoker. It can handle a long cook, soaks up smoke beautifully, thrives with a chunky bark and turns into incredible pulled lamb. If you ever spot one at a butcher shop or restaurant supply, grab it – you'll see why it deserves a place in every pitmaster's rotation.

CHARCOAL LAMB RIBS WITH VINEGARY GOCHUGARU CUCUMBERS

SERVES 2–4

People always ask me what my favorite cut of meat is, and though I can never pick just one, lamb ribs are up there with the best of them. I feel quite strongly that there is no better way to cook them than over charcoal (trust me, I've experimented!). There's a kind of magical alchemy that happens when the sizzling lamb fat meets those coals.

4 x 1.5 lb (700 g) sections of lamb ribs or riblets

2 tablespoons olive oil

SPICE RUB

1 tablespoon coriander seeds

¾ tablespoon salt

½ teaspoon ground black pepper

½ teaspoon ground allspice

¼ teaspoon onion powder

½ teaspoon garlic powder

¼ teaspoon granulated (white) sugar

CUCUMBER SALAD

6 mini (Lebanese) cucumbers, roughly chopped

1 tablespoon soy sauce

2 teaspoons sesame oil

1½ teaspoons gochugaru chili flakes

2 teaspoons toasted sesame seeds

2 tablespoons rice vinegar

¼ teaspoon salt

1 teaspoon granulated (white) sugar

1. Prepare a grill for two-zone grilling (page 36) at medium-high heat, about 400–500°F (210–260°C). Remove the lamb from the fridge 20–30 minutes prior to cooking.
2. Combine all the ingredients for the spice rub in a bowl, then coat the lamb with the olive oil and season generously with the spice rub on all sides (yes, even the backs of the ribs).
3. Place the seasoned ribs directly over the heat, meat side down, and sear for 1–2 minutes. The lamb is fatty, so this process will happen quickly. Flip the ribs bone side down, and cook for a further 1–2 minutes. If you start seeing flare-ups, just flip them over sooner.
4. Once the ribs have been seared over high heat, move them to the indirect side and close the lid. Allow to cook with gentle indirect heat for a further 10–15 minutes. The lamb meat should be pulled back to expose some of the bone, and the fat should be rendered.
5. While the ribs finish cooking, combine the salad ingredients in a bowl, stirring well so the dressing is evenly distributed.
6. Remove the ribs from the grill and rest briefly for 5 minutes under foil, then slice between the bones. Give the salad another stir and serve with the ribs.

NOTE

I'm not gonna lie to you: sometimes lamb ribs aren't what you expect them to be. Much like beef ribs, they can be cut in a variety of different ways, but they're all still 'ribs.' So, if you end up with ones that have been cut down near the breast, there's usually a pretty gnarly piece of cartilage running through there. The recipe will still work (and they'll still taste great), but ideally ribs come from a little higher on the ribcage, and are often sold in little 'sections' of three ribs. Sometimes they are even called 'riblets.'

ROSEMARY-AND-GARLIC-CRUSTED LAMB ROAST

SERVES 6–8

I think a beautifully browned and perfectly pink-in-the-middle lamb roast is just about one of the best ways you can welcome someone to your table. The smell of the roasting garlic and sizzling lamb fat perfumes your kitchen like an appetizing sneak preview of what's to come. And like many large roasts that seem intimidating, it's actually really easy to execute.

- 1 x 5 lb (2.25 kg) boneless lamb leg
- 10 garlic cloves
- 2 tablespoons olive oil
- 3–4 large sprigs rosemary
- 2 teaspoons salt
- 1½ teaspoons ground black pepper
- 3 tablespoons dijon mustard

1. Preheat the oven to 450°F (235°C).
2. If your lamb is tied with twine or in a net, remove it so you can season more thoroughly.
3. Place the garlic and olive oil in a food processor. Remove the leaves from the rosemary and add them to the processor, discarding the woody stems. Pulse to blend until a rough paste forms. Set aside.
4. Season the lamb with the salt and pepper. Lift the pieces where the bone was removed and season the cavity too. Slather the dijon mustard all over the lamb.
5. Place a rack inside a deep roasting pan (there will be a lot of fat rendering out during the cooking process).
6. Place the lamb leg on the rack, with the 'smooth' fat cap facing up (i.e. the side where the bone was removed should be on the rack).
7. Spread the garlic and rosemary paste over the top of the lamb, then place in the oven. Roast for 15–20 minutes to give the meat some color, then reduce the heat to 325°F (160°C).
8. Once the heat is turned down, the roast will take 60–90 minutes to cook, so start monitoring the internal temperature around the 30-minute mark. You can also cover the roast with foil if the crust is getting too dark. The final internal temperature should be 135–140F° (57–60°C) at the thickest part, which I describe as the 'medium' side of medium-rare.
9. Remove the lamb from the oven and let rest for 15–20 minutes under foil before carving.

GRILLED ZA'ATAR LAMB CUTLETS WITH CHARRED LEMON LABNEH

SERVES 2–4

This is one of those cuts that confusingly has a lot of different names. Lamb lollipop, cutlet, lamb chop, rib chop, lamb tomahawk and loin chop. The word 'cutlet' is derived from the French term côtelette, which means 'rib'. Since this cut has the rib attached, I like to call it a cutlet. The cut itself is the same as a beef tomahawk – just on a very miniature scale! You can actually cut your own cutlets very easily from a rack of lamb; just slice between the bones.

1½ cups (360 g) plain Greek-style yogurt
1½ teaspoon salt, divided
8 lamb cutlets
2 tablespoons olive oil
1–2 tablespoons za'atar seasoning
2 lemons
½ tablespoon honey

1. Start by making the labneh the day before. You can also make it up to a week in advance. Mix the Greek yogurt with ½ teaspoon salt. Scoop the mixture onto a piece of cheesecloth and bring all four corners of the cheesecloth together, tying it around a wooden spoon. Lay the spoon across the top of a deep container so the cheesecloth pouch hangs inside it. There should be ample space between the bottom of the container and the cheesecloth where the liquid can collect.
2. Place in the fridge overnight and let the yogurt strain for 12–18 hours. Discard the liquid and remove the labneh from the cheesecloth. Store in a sealed container and place back in the fridge until ready to use.
3. Put the lamb cutlets on a sheet pan (baking sheet). Drizzle with the olive oil over both sides to coat well. Mix the za'atar with the remaining salt and season the lamb generously on both sides. Cut one of the lemons in half and squeeze the juice over the lamb, catching and discarding any seeds. Place the pan in the fridge and let the lamb marinate for 30–60 minutes.
4. Light a grill for medium-heat cooking, about 300–350°F (155–175°C).
5. Place the lamb cutlets on the grill and cook them for 8–10 minutes in total, flipping them over every 2 minutes.
6. Cut the remaining lemon in half lengthways and place on the grill for 3 minutes per side (ensuring you char/blacken both sides).
7. Once cooked, remove the lamb from the grill and cover loosely with foil. Rest for 5 minutes before serving.
8. While the lamb rests, finish the labneh by zesting the charred lemon, then add the zest and juice, along with the honey. Mix well to combine.
9. Serve the lamb with a generous scoop of labneh. I like to 'swipe' the labneh across the plate, then nestle the lamb on top.

TRIPLE 8 AIR FRYER LAMB RACK

SERVES 2

When I started writing this book, I knew I wanted it to offer in-depth info for meat nerds to sink their teeth into, while also helping home cooks build confidence with meat. So, this is one of those ridiculously easy recipes that I hope gets people eating more lamb (I think it's a seriously underrated protein). The name comes from the method – 8 minutes on each side, followed by an 8-minute rest. And it doesn't get much easier than an air fryer!

- 2 lb (1 kg) rack of lamb, preferably frenched
- 1½ teaspoons dried chives
- 1 teaspoon dried thyme
- 1 teaspoon dried mint
- 1 teaspoon salt
- ¼ teaspoon garlic powder
- ¼ teaspoon onion powder
- ¼ teaspoon ground white pepper
- 1½ tablespoons olive or avocado oil

1. Remove the lamb from the fridge.
2. Prepare the spice blend by placing the chives, thyme, mint, salt, garlic powder, onion powder and white pepper into a spice grinder (or use a mortar and pestle). Grind to a fine powder (see Notes).
3. Pour the powder into a small bowl, then stir through the olive oil to form a paste.
4. Preheat an air fryer for 2–3 minutes at 375°F (190°C).
5. Slather the paste all over the lamb rack, massaging it in with your hands.
6. Place the rack into the hot air fryer with the bones facing up (so the meatier side has as much contact as possible with the hot metal). Cook for 8 minutes at 400°F (200°C).
7. Flip the rack over and cook for a further 8 minutes.
8. Remove the rack from the fryer and wrap tightly with foil to rest for 8 minutes.
9. Slice between the bones and serve.

NOTES

'Frenched' just means that the bones have been scraped clean, which is mainly for appearance. Most lamb racks will come this way. The variable is where the frenching starts (i.e. how much bone is exposed).

Though fresh herbs are much more fragrant, I use dried herbs in this recipe, and I like to grind them really finely in a spice grinder. I reckon there's less tendency for the spices to burn in the air fryer when the particles are really small and dry. If you don't have a spice/coffee grinder or a mortar and pestle, this step is not essential, but it is recommended.

6-HOUR ROASTED LAMB SHOULDER

SERVES 8

Memories of great meals are incredibly powerful. I vividly remember the best bite of lamb shoulder I've ever experienced, served by friend and chef Rachel Hannaford more than 15 years ago – and I've been chasing down that flavor ever since. I'm not sure anything could live up to the lofty heights of that taste-memory, but this recipe is damn close.

- 3 lemons
- 3 large onions, quartered
- 6 sprigs rosemary, divided
- ¼ cup (7 g) oregano leaves
- 1 teaspoon ground black pepper
- 6 garlic cloves
- 1 x 6.5 lb (3 kg) lamb shoulder (square cut or banjo cut)
- 3 teaspoons salt, divided
- 2 tablespoons olive oil
- 2 cups (500 ml) water
- 2 tablespoons all-purpose (plain) flour
- ½–¾ cup (125–185 ml) beef or chicken stock

1. Preheat the oven to 425°F (215°C).
2. Cut the lemons in half, then squeeze the juice into a bowl and set aside. Arrange the squeezed lemons and onions at the bottom of a large roasting pan.
3. Using a food processor or immersion blender, combine the leaves from 2 rosemary sprigs (discarding the stems), along with the oregano, black pepper, garlic and lemon juice. Blend until a paste is formed.
4. Score the top of the lamb by making shallow cuts diagonally across the top of the fat cap.
5. Turn the lamb over and season the bottom (rib bone) side with 1 teaspoon salt.
6. Returning the lamb meat side up, slather the herb and garlic mixture across the meat, massaging it into the scores and across the sides. Add the olive oil and continue to massage into all the nooks and crannies.
7. Season the top liberally with the remaining salt, then roast in the oven for 45 minutes.
8. Add the water to the roasting pan (taking care not to pour it onto the meat itself), then cover the pan tightly with foil. Lower the oven temperature to 325°F (165°C) and roast for 5 hours.
9. Uncover the lamb, baste with the juices from the pan and cook uncovered for a further 15–20 minutes to finish browning the top.
10. Remove the lamb from the pan and cover loosely with foil.
11. To prepare the gravy, strain the contents of the roasting pan through a sieve, collecting the pan juices into a saucepan. Place the saucepan over medium heat and whisk in the flour. Slowly add the stock a little at a time until desired consistency is reached. Add more stock if you prefer a runnier gravy.
12. To serve, pull pieces of the lamb away with a pair of tongs and pour the gravy on top.

made in

GRILLED GREEN CURRY LAMB WITH COCONUT AND HERBS

SERVES 4

Smoky from the grill and slathered with a green curry and coconut milk marinade, these Thai-inspired lamb chops bring big, bold flavor with minimal effort. They char beautifully over the fire, while a tangle of fresh mint, cilantro and holy basil keeps every bite bright and fragrant.

4 lamb shoulder (forequarter) chops, leg chops or leg steaks

¼ cup (55 g) green curry paste

13.5 fl oz (400 ml) canned coconut milk

juice of 1 large lime, divided

2½ teaspoons fish sauce, divided

1 tablespoon brown sugar, plus 1 teaspoon

1 cup (20 g) mint leaves

1 cup (30 g) cilantro (coriander) leaves

1 cup (30 g) Thai basil leaves

2 Thai bird's eye chilies, thinly sliced

2 teaspoons neutral oil (e.g. canola or vegetable oil)

¼ teaspoon salt

1. Place the lamb into a resealable bag.
2. In a bowl, mix the curry paste with the coconut milk, half the lime juice, 2 teaspoons fish sauce and 1 tablespoon brown sugar. Stir to blend the ingredients together, then pour over the lamb. Seal the bag and massage so the lamb is well coated. Place in the fridge to marinate for at least 8 hours, or overnight.
3. Prepare a grill for medium-heat direct cooking, about 375–400°F (185–210°C).
4. Remove the lamb from the bag and place onto the hot grill. Close the lid and cook for 7 minutes. Use tongs to turn the lamb over and cook for a further 6–7 minutes on the other side.
5. While the lamb cooks, place the mint, cilantro, basil and chili into a bowl. In a small jar (I love using small Mason jars to make dressing!), combine the neutral oil with the salt, remaining lime juice, fish sauce and brown sugar. Shake vigorously to emulsify the dressing, then pour over the herbs. Use your hands to toss and coat everything in the dressing.
6. To serve, place the lamb on a plate and top with a generous handful of the fresh herb mixture.

NOTES

You can use three different lamb cuts in this recipe – shoulder chops (also called forequarter chops), leg chops and leg steaks (which are pretty much leg chops, just boneless). These cuts can be swapped in most recipes because they're similar in size, thickness and cooking time. But if I had to choose, I'd probably lean towards shoulder chops. They're less lean, with some lovely fat seams that crisp up beautifully on the grill.

Yes, I am a fan of the #JKF method (page 100), but in this recipe, the meat is literally dripping in marinade, so it's easier to leave it and turn it just once.

Make sure you use Thai-style canned coconut milk, not the dairy alternative you get in cartons.

GROUND MEAT

Ground (minced) meat is the most frequently purchased meat. It's the backbone of the beloved hamburger and a staple of busy weeknight dinners. Used across cuisines worldwide, it's versatile and adaptable to a wide range of cooking methods. It's also one of the most effective ways to use the whole animal, minimizing waste in the process.

GROUND MEAT? OR MINCED MEAT?

Whether you call it 'minced' or 'ground' depends on where you are in the world – it's the same thing, just with different regional names. Even in other languages, it varies by region: most of Latin America calls it *carne molida* (ground meat), while Argentinians prefer *carne picada* (chopped beef). The terminology may hint at hand-minced origins before grinders were common, but today, ground meat is a global staple with a reliably consistent texture.

NO LIPS, DEFINITELY NO ASSHOLES

What started as a punchline in the legendary Ackroyd/Candy movie *The Great Outdoors* has become a case of life imitating art. The famous line about hot dogs being made from 'lips and assholes' has caused a lot of people to assume that ground meat is of questionable origins. The truth is that regulatory bodies governing meat processing have strict rules regarding what can and cannot go into ground meat.

In the US, UK and Australia, none of the following items are allowed in the processing of ground meat: bones, organs (offal), ligaments or tendons, brains and spinal cords. What is allowed is skeletal muscle and fat. There are also some exceptions, like cheek meat and heart, but they have to be clearly disclosed on the label.

IS MEAT FROM MORE THAN ONE ANIMAL USED?

Yes, but it's not actually a bad thing. When meat is produced commercially, the trim from many carcasses might be combined (for efficiency) and your ground meat can reasonably come from more than one source. While traceability can be a selling point, it's more about marketing than measurable quality or safety improvements. For the average consumer, there's no practical benefit to a single-carcass grind, because robust food safety controls offset any cross-contamination concerns.

In fact, combining meat from several animals improves efficiency and reduces waste. Fatty trim from one carcass can be blended with leaner meat from another to create the ideal fat-to-lean ratio and produce a more consistent, saleable product.

That's not to say that there's anything wrong with buying from small ranchers and farmers who can guarantee ground meat of 'single origin'. It's just that one is not actually better than the other.

FAT PERCENTAGES OF GROUND MEAT

Most packages of ground meat (primarily beef) display a lean-to-fat ratio, like 80/20. You'll see this referenced often in burger recipes. While some people choose based on nutrition, from a culinary perspective, a decent amount of fat is preferred.

If you've ever wondered why your burger or meatballs turn out dry and tough, it's likely because the blend is too lean. Fat functions as both a binder and a lubricant, helping the meat hold together while contributing to a juicy mouthfeel. There's no getting around it – fat is what keeps meat moist.

If the fat percentage isn't listed, here's a simple trick: check the color. Leaner ground meat looks darker red or pink because it's mostly muscle, while higher-fat blends appear lighter thanks to the white fat mixed in.

BEST PRACTICES FOR GRINDING YOUR OWN MEAT

It's actually pretty easy to grind your own meat at home, and you can store and freeze it in vacuum-sealed portions. Here are some tips if you wanna give it a try.

- **Cold is key.** Put the grinding components of your machine in the freezer for 20 minutes before you are ready to go. Keeping the equipment and the meat cold will reduce the fat-smearing and give better texture.
- **Use a double grind.** For the best consistency, start with a coarse 10 mm plate (great for chili), then finish with a finer 4–5 mm plate.
- **Try a range of cuts.** Great options for a fattier beef blend are brisket and chuck. For a leaner option, try sirloin/rump. You can also experiment with blending different cuts and extras, like bacon (which is great for adding smokiness and extra fat).
- **Store to grind later.** When you trim things like brisket or pork butt, you can save the fat in a bag in the freezer and use it to add more oomph the next time you're grinding your own blend. This is also a great option for hunters who want to add some juiciness to their wild game.

HUNTER'S PIE WITH MUSHROOMS AND THYME

SERVES 6–8

I named this 'hunter's pie' because of the venison and beef meat blend, but if you're feeling less 'hunty', then by all means substitute the venison for all beef, or even pork. Traditionally, you'd find mashed potatoes on a hunter's or shepherd's pie, but I prefer an uber-crunchy topping made from buttery sheets of phyllo pastry.

- 2 tablespoons olive oil
- 1 onion, finely diced
- 4 cups (8 oz/225 g) sliced baby bella (Swiss brown) mushrooms
- 2 garlic cloves, crushed
- 2 tablespoons thyme leaves
- 1 lb (500 g) ground (minced) beef
- 1 lb (500 g) ground (minced) venison
- 1½ teaspoons salt
- 1 teaspoon ground black pepper
- 1 teaspoon ground nutmeg
- 2 tablespoons worcestershire sauce
- ⅓ cup (50 g) all-purpose (plain) flour
- 1 cup (250 ml) red wine
- 1½ cups (375 ml) beef stock
- 12 oz (350 g) phyllo (filo) pastry sheets, thawed
- ½ cup (125 ml) melted salted butter

1. Preheat the oven to 375°F (190°C).
2. Place a large, deep, oven-safe skillet over high heat and add the olive oil. Once hot, add the onion, mushrooms, garlic and thyme. Cook for 5–7 minutes until the onion is soft and the mushrooms have developed some color. Use a slotted spoon to remove them from the pan and place into a bowl.
3. Add the meat to the pan and brown for 6–8 minutes, stirring occasionally. Add the salt, black pepper and nutmeg, along with the worcestershire sauce. Use a wooden spoon to break up any larger chunks of meat as it cooks.
4. Sprinkle the flour over the meat and stir to combine. It will thicken up and absorb any moisture in the pan immediately. Cook for 1–2 minutes, then add the wine to deglaze the pan, scraping any browned bits from the bottom. Stir in the stock and reduce the heat to medium. Add the mushroom mixture back into the pan and stir through. Simmer for an additional 5–7 minutes, stirring frequently, until the broth thickens into a gravy, then remove from the heat.
5. Brush one sheet of phyllo pastry with melted butter, then scrunch it into a loose ball and arrange on top of the meat filling. Repeat with the remaining phyllo and butter until the top of the pie is covered.
6. Bake for 20–25 minutes until the top is golden brown.

NOTE

If you don't have an oven-safe skillet, transfer the mixture to a baking dish or deep pie dish for the final step.

LEVANTINE LAMB AND RICE

SERVES 6–8

What I like most about this dish is watching the grains of rice soak up the precious lamb fat, swelling up with flavor and doubling down on delicious lamb-y goodness. This Lebanese-inspired dish balances the bolder lamb flavor with fragrant spices like cinnamon and allspice, and a punch of citrusy sumac at the end.

- ⅓ cup (50 g) pinenuts
- 2 cups (400 g) basmati rice
- 2 tablespoons olive oil
- 1 tablespoon salted butter or ghee
- ½ onion, finely diced
- 2 garlic cloves, crushed
- 1 lb (500 g) ground (minced) lamb
- 2 teaspoons ground cinnamon
- 1 teaspoon ground cumin
- 1 teaspoon ground allspice
- 2 teaspoons salt
- 3 cups (750 ml) chicken stock
- ⅓ cup (6.5 g) mint leaves, torn
- ⅓ cup (60 g) pomegranate seeds
- ⅓ cup (90 g) tahini
- 1 teaspoon ground sumac

1. Place a small skillet over medium heat and add the pinenuts to the dry pan. Cook, tossing/stirring frequently, for about 3–5 minutes, or until they are golden and fragrant. Set aside.
2. Place the rice into a bowl, cover with water and agitate with your hands to rinse the grains. Drain the cloudy water out through a sieve, then repeat once or twice until the water is clear.
3. Place a large sauté pan over medium-high heat and add the olive oil and butter. Once foaming, add the onion and cook for 5 minutes until softened, stirring frequently. Add the garlic and cook for another 2–3 minutes.
4. Next, add the ground lamb, cinnamon, cumin, allspice and salt. Cook until the lamb is slightly browned, about 5 minutes. Stir regularly to break up the lamb into smaller pieces.
5. Add the drained rice to the pan and stir for a minute to lightly toast and allow the grains to soak up the lamb fat in the pan.
6. Pour in the stock, then allow the mixture to come to a boil before reducing the heat to a simmer. Place the lid on and cook for 15 minutes until the rice has absorbed the liquid. Turn the heat off and leave to rest for 5–7 minutes.
7. Remove the lid and dress the pan with the mint leaves and pomegranate seeds. Drizzle with tahini, then scatter the toasted pinenuts on top. Sprinkle with the sumac to finish.

PORK 'MONEY BAGS' WITH GINGER AND SCALLION

MAKES ABOUT 35 PIECES

The epitome of 'good things come in small packages', these crunchy, bite-sized morsels have a savory pork filling, with extra crunch from the water chestnuts.

- 1 lb (500 g) ground (minced) pork
- 2–3-inch piece fresh ginger, peeled and grated
- 4 garlic cloves, crushed
- 3 scallions (spring onions), green parts only, finely sliced
- 1 x 8 oz (225 g) can water chestnuts, drained and finely diced
- 1 tablespoon soy sauce
- ½ teaspoon salt
- 2 teaspoons shaoxing wine or rice wine vinegar
- 1 teaspoon toasted sesame oil
- 1 teaspoon MSG (optional)
- 2 tablespoons cornstarch (cornflour)
- 35–40 wonton wrappers
- 4 cups (1 liter) peanut oil, for frying
- sweet chili sauce, for dipping

1. Place the ground pork into a large bowl. Add the ginger, garlic, scallions, water chestnuts, soy sauce, salt, shaoxing wine, sesame oil and MSG (if using). Mix until everything is combined, trying not to overwork the meat. I find it easiest to use my hands for this.
2. Sprinkle the cornstarch over the top and work it in until just combined.
3. Start assembling the money bags. Take a wonton wrapper and scoop about 2 teaspoons of the filling inside. Dip your finger in a little water, then wet the edges of the wrapper. Bring the corners together to form a pouch, pressing tightly at the top to seal. Repeat with the remaining wrappers until all the filling has been used.
4. Heat the peanut oil in a nonstick or stainless steel pot. Once it reaches 350–375°F (170–190°C), gently lower the first batch of money bags into the oil. Fry for 3–4 minutes until light golden brown. Remove with a slotted spoon and place on paper towels to drain. Allow the oil to come back up to temperature before frying the next batch.
5. Serve immediately with a generous ramekin of sweet chili sauce for dipping.

NOTE

Frying wonton wrappers can be a bit tricky. While we usually look for a deep golden brown for most fried foods, these wrappers can easily overcook and become tough, so I recommend snatching them out of the oil when they're a pale golden color. They tend to firm and crisp up as they drain and cool.

CLASSIC AMERICAN CHEESEBURGER

SERVES 2

My buddy Adam Biderman owns The Company Burger in New Orleans, and he's a total burger zealot. Though there are lots of opinions on what constitutes a classic American burger, I've seen the way he obsesses over everything, from texture and size of buns to grinding his own meat from scratch daily. So, I trust his research completely and present to you Adam's version of a classic cheeseburger. You'll notice there's no call for condiments, and to quote Adam: 'I'm a mayo ketchup man, but apparently people like mustard also, so I take no stance on sauce.' Basically, he's telling you to put whatever you like on there. But I'm telling you to add pickles.

- 1 lb (500 g) ground (minced) beef (about 80/20 lean-to-fat ratio)
- ½ teaspoon salt
- 4 slices American cheese
- 1–2 tablespoons salted butter
- 2 burger buns
- mayo, ketchup (tomato sauce) and mustard (optional)
- ⅓ cup (50 g) diced onion
- 6 pickle slices

1. Heat a large skillet or griddle over very high heat.
2. Form the meat into four balls and use a burger smasher or wide, firm spatula to press them down to make burgers. Alternatively, form four patties by hand, taking care not to overwork the meat. The patties should be about ¼ inch (6 mm) thick, and no thicker than ½ inch (1 cm).
3. Press or place the patties into the pan and turn the heat down to medium-high. Season the patties with the salt, then cook for 3 minutes. Use a firm spatula to flip them over. Immediately top them with the slice of cheese and cook for a further 3 minutes. The cheese should melt from the heat of the pan, but if it's being stubborn, cover it briefly to encourage a full melt.
4. Spread the butter on both cut sides of the bun. Place cut side down into the skillet and toast for 30–60 seconds, or until lightly golden brown. If you're using a large griddle, toast the buns at the same time as the burgers cook, but if you're short on space, toast them before cooking the beef and set them aside. Or skip the butter and toast them directly in the remaining beef fat once the patties are removed.
5. Assemble the burgers by adding your condiments of choice to the buns, then stack two patties on top of the bottom bun. Top with the diced onion and pickle slices, then set the top bun in place.

NOTES

For the record, Adam loves a classic soft burger bun, but potato buns are an incredible substitution.

I always buy my American cheese from the deli and have them slice it fresh (instead of buying the stuff that comes individually wrapped). That's the trick to getting that restaurant-style melt.

BURGER BLUEPRINT: THE GOLDEN GROUND RULES

Here are some basic tenets to follow when you're seeking burger perfection.

- Never pre-season your burger patties. Adding salt too early alters the texture, making them dry and tough. Instead, season while cooking.
- You simply have to use a fattier beef blend if you want your burgers to be juicy and bursting with flavor. The fat is crucial to the taste and sear you will achieve, and lean won't give you the same results.
- The only ingredient you should use in your patty is meat. If you add binders like egg or breadcrumbs, you're making a meatball, not a burger.
- For thick burgers, make a little divot in the patty to stop it from puffing in the middle and to promote even cooking.
- Use a burger press to force the burger into full contact with the pan or griddle. Maximum contact = maximum crust. This doesn't mean you need to squish it down – just enough weight to make sure all the surface is getting a nice pan tan.
- Burgers shrink when they cook, so when you form a burger patty, make it slightly larger (20% or so) than the bun you're using.
- Freshly ground meat performs better than beef you purchase in a chub or roll. Often, the more 'economical' stuff is very finely ground, which affects the texture and water-holding capacity. The extended shelf life of the vacuum-sealed packages can also mean the meat loses more water as it sits. You're less likely to see a watery consistency with freshly ground beef, especially when packed on foam trays, which have absorbing pads to soak up excess moisture. And less moisture = better browning.
- Don't overwork the meat when forming your patty. Functional proteins like myosin can form gel-ish structures and become sticky. These act like meat glue and bind proteins together, making for a tougher bite.

WOOD-PLANKED MEATLOAF

SERVES 4–6

You might not usually associate plank cooking with beef, but this version (which is cooked over indirect heat on the grill) tastes so much more complex and intense than regular ol' baked loaf. Grilling planks are untreated, food-safe boards usually made from cedar, which impart a subtle smoke perfume into the meat.

MEATLOAF

- 1 tablespoon olive oil
- ½ onion, diced
- ½ cup (55 g) dry breadcrumbs
- ⅓ cup (80 ml) milk
- 1 teaspoon dried oregano
- 1 teaspoon dried parsley
- 2 garlic cloves, crushed
- 2 tablespoons worcestershire sauce
- 2 teaspoons salt
- 1 teaspoon Aleppo pepper flakes or ½ teaspoon red pepper flakes
- 2 tablespoons tomato paste
- 2 eggs, beaten
- 2 lb (1 kg) ground (minced) beef (about 80/20 lean-to-fat ratio)

GLAZE

- ½ cup (125 ml) ketchup (tomato sauce)
- ½ cup (125 ml) sweet BBQ sauce
- ⅓ cup (75 g) brown sugar
- 1 tablespoon apple cider vinegar

1. To make the meatloaf, place a small saucepan over medium heat. Add the olive oil, then cook the onion until soft and translucent, about 5–7 minutes.
2. In a large bowl, add the breadcrumbs and milk. Allow the crumbs to soak up the milk and soften.
3. Add the oregano, parsley, garlic, worcestershire sauce, salt, pepper flakes, tomato paste and eggs. Stir until all the ingredients are combined.
4. Add the ground beef and combine with your hands. Try to incorporate it as quickly as possible so as not to overwork the meat and make it tough.
5. Line a loaf pan with parchment (baking) paper and stuff the meatloaf mixture into the loaf pan. Place in the fridge to set for 15 minutes.
6. Heat a grill for two-zone cooking (page 36) at medium-high heat, about 375–400°F (190–210°C).
7. Remove the meatloaf mixture from the fridge and turn the loaf pan over, meat side down, onto the middle of the wooden grilling plank (see Notes). Remove the loaf pan, then peel back the parchment paper. The meat should be in the shape of a loaf.
8. Place the plank onto the indirect side of the grill and close the lid.
9. In the meantime, place the glaze ingredients in a saucepan over low heat and stir until the sugar dissolves.
10. Once the meatloaf has been cooking for 15 minutes, brush the glaze over the top using a basting brush. Continue to glaze every 15 minutes until the meatloaf is done.
11. Rotate the meatloaf occasionally during cooking so each side is evenly exposed to the heat. Cook for 60–75 minutes, or until the internal temperature measures at least 160°F (70°C) on a meat thermometer.

NOTES

Wooden grilling planks for cooking are readily available in grocery and specialty stores. Cedar is the most common variety, though you can use any wood-species you find.

Soaking breadcrumbs in milk is known as a 'panade', which helps to both bind the meatloaf mixture and keep it moist.

Technically, ground beef should be cooked to an internal temperature of 165°F (73°C) to be considered food safe. But the longer cooking time and thickness here mean that the temperature will continue to climb after you take it off the grill, which is why you can remove it a little earlier.

Chuds
Chuds

RARE STEAKS

Not every great steak is sitting front and center in the meat case. Beyond the familiar ribeyes and filets are the 'rare' steaks – cuts you may see less frequently, but they're absolutely worth grabbing when you do.

Each of the cuts here has its own reason for being harder to find: some only appear once per animal, like hanger steak or tongue. Others, like quail or duck, are simply less common because they're not as widely consumed. And then there are steaks like the Denver, which are part of every carcass but often not separated out as a distinct cut. Whatever the reason, when these cuts turn up at the butcher or market, snatch 'em up and give them a shot. They might not be everyday purchases, but they deliver big flavor and a sense of discovery that keeps cooking exciting.

TIGER CRY LAMB

SERVES 4

Each lamb produces only two small striploins, a highly prized cut known for its tenderness and clean, delicate lamb flavor. This is the same muscle as the loin or backstrap in other animals, and the same one that forms lamb racks and cutlets. That's why striploins are harder to come by, since they're more often sold as part of racks rather than being boned out individually. You are more likely to find beef or pork served with Thai-style tiger cry sauce, but I reckon its bold, bright, sweet-and-sour flavors are an ideal match for the richness of lamb.

4 x 12 oz (325 g) lamb striploins

MARINADE

1 tablespoon dark soy sauce

1 tablespoon oyster sauce

½ tablespoon brown sugar

1 tablespoon neutral oil (e.g. canola or avocado oil)

1 tablespoon grated fresh ginger

1 tablespoon crushed garlic

½ teaspoon ground white pepper

TIGER CRY SAUCE

1 tablespoon fish sauce

2 tablespoons lime juice

1 tablespoon khao khua (see Note)

1 tablespoon tamarind paste

1 tablespoon Thai chili flakes

1 tablespoon brown sugar

2 tablespoons finely chopped cilantro (coriander)

2 tablespoons water

2 tablespoons finely diced shallots

1. Place the striploins into a non-reactive container or a large resealable bag. In a bowl, combine all the marinade ingredients, then pour them onto the lamb. Seal or cover, then place in the refrigerator for 1–3 hours.
2. Make the tiger cry sauce by mixing all the ingredients in a bowl, then set aside.
3. Place a skillet over medium-high heat. Once hot, place the striploins into the hot pan and cook for 4–5 minutes. Flip over and cook for 4–5 minutes more, then remove to a board and cover loosely with foil to rest for 3–5 minutes.
4. Slice the striploins across the grain and serve arranged on a plate next to the sauce. Dunk each piece into the sauce and enjoy.

NOTE

Khao khua is a Thai ingredient made from sticky rice that has been toasted and then ground. It lends a distinct nutty flavor and textural oomph when added to dishes, but it can be omitted if you can't find it.

DUCK BREAST WITH ROASTED BALSAMIC FIGS

SERVES 2

In my opinion, perfectly cooked duck has three major features: rosy meat, crispy skin and rendered fat. There's no point in nailing the first two only to have an unpleasant thick band of fat right under the superficially crisp skin. This stove-to-oven method is quite foolproof, and the jammy figs are the perfect sweet pairing, with a built-in pan sauce.

2 duck breasts

1 teaspoon salt, divided

½ teaspoon five-spice powder

ROASTED FIGS

8 oz (225 g) fresh, ripe figs

1 tablespoon olive oil

1½ tablespoons balsamic vinegar

3 sprigs thyme

¼ teaspoon salt

2 teaspoons honey

1. Preheat the oven to 400°F (200°C).
2. Remove the duck breasts from the fridge and pat dry with paper towels on both sides.
3. Make shallow cuts across the top of the duck breasts, slicing through the fat but stopping before you cut the meat.
4. Season the skin with ½ teaspoon salt, then place the breasts skin side down into a cold stainless steel or cast-iron pan. Place the pan over low heat.
5. With the meat side up, you can now season with the remaining salt and five-spice powder. If you have one, place a steak weight on the breasts to force the skin to have complete contact with the pan. Starting the pan cold over low heat will allow the fat to render slowly and more completely. Cook for about 15 minutes, occasionally pouring off the excess fat into a heatproof container.
6. As the fat begins to render, cut the stems off the figs and slice in half lengthways. Nestle them cut side up in a small skillet or oven-safe dish. Drizzle the olive oil over the top, then pour over the vinegar. Throw in the thyme and season with the salt. Place in the oven and roast for 15 minutes. Once roasted, drizzle with the honey and finish under the broiler (oven grill) for 1 minute to caramelize the tops. Set aside.
7. When the duck breasts have cooked for 15 minutes, turn them over and cook meat side down for 1–2 minutes.
8. Flip the breasts and cook skin side down again, then place them in the oven to cook for a further 6 minutes.
9. Remove the breasts from the oven and rest them on a board for a few minutes before slicing.
10. Serve the duck with a generous helping of roasted figs, and spoon the sauce from the bottom of the fig pan over the sliced breast.

NOTE

The excess fat in the pan can actually prevent the skin from crisping (and make a huge spluttery mess), so it helps to remove it. Once it cools, pour through a strainer into a clean jar and save in the fridge. You can use it to make White Bean Dip with Duck Fat–Roasted Garlic (page 246).

• MEAT NERD FACT •

We expect our duck to be served pink in the middle, but why is that okay when we're supposed to cook chicken all the way through? It's an interesting technicality that has a lot to do with how chickens and ducks are commercially raised. In short, chickens tend to have more exposure to their own feces (I know, ewww) than ducks do, so their risk of contamination with bacteria is higher. The official answer is this: from a safety perspective, your duck should be cooked until well done, but from a risk-versus-juicy-reward angle, the probability of getting sick is lower.

GRILLED QUAIL WITH MANGO-CHILI GLAZE

SERVES 4–6

I couldn't possibly write a meat book without including one of my favorite game birds: quail. Part of the pheasant family, the meat has a flavor I would describe as a cross between chicken and very lean duck. You can find the birds butterflied with most of the bones removed (except the legs and wings), which makes them perfectly flat for even grilling.

- 1 cup (250 ml) mango nectar
- 1 tablespoon achiote sauce (see Note)
- ¼ teaspoon guajillo chili powder
- ¼ teaspoon chipotle chili powder
- 2 teaspoons tamarind paste
- ½ teaspoon paprika
- 2 tablespoons granulated (white) sugar
- 1 tablespoon olive or neutral oil
- 8 whole semi-boneless quail
- ½ teaspoon salt

1. In a small saucepan over medium heat, combine the mango nectar, achiote sauce, chili powders, tamarind paste, paprika and sugar. Stir until everything is dissolved, then reduce the heat to a simmer and cook for about 15 minutes. Stir occasionally until the mixture reduces by half and thickens to a syrupy consistency.
2. Preheat a grill for low-medium direct heat, about 300–350°F (150–175°C).
3. Drizzle the olive oil over the quail, coating well on both sides, then season with the salt.
4. Place the quail onto the hot grill and cook for 1–2 minutes. Flip and cook on the other side for another 1–2 minutes. While the second side is cooking, start basting the quail with the mango glaze. Flip again, cooking for another minute, and glaze the side now facing up. Repeat another 2–3 times until the total cook time is 10 minutes and the glaze has developed a lovely char.
5. Serve immediately.

NOTE

Achiote sauce is made from annatto seeds, which have a naturally vivid orange-red color. It's often found as a paste, but I find the premade sauces easier to work with. It doesn't lend much extra flavor to the dish, so if you can't find it, just omit it.

COFFEE-RUBBED HANGER STEAK WITH BLISTERED SHISHITOS

SERVES 2

Hanger steak has a really pronounced grain – thick, visible bundles of muscle fibers with deep crevices between them, perfect for holding on to the chunky pepper and coffee grounds in this fragrant spice rub.

- 1 whole hanger steak, butchered into two pieces (see opposite)
- 8 oz (225 g) shishito or padrón peppers
- 4 teaspoons freshly ground coffee
- 1 teaspoon garlic powder
- ½ teaspoon onion powder
- 2 teaspoons paprika
- 2 teaspoons salt
- 1 teaspoon freshly ground black pepper
- ½ teaspoon chili powder
- 1 teaspoon granulated (white) sugar
- 1 tablespoon olive oil
- spray oil
- sea salt flakes, to serve

1. Remove the hanger steaks from the fridge.
2. Light a grill for medium-high heat searing, about 450°F (230°C).
3. Thread the shishito peppers onto long metal skewers, jamming them up against each other to form 'keyboard' rows of peppers. This makes it easier to flip them while grilling.
4. In a bowl, combine the coffee, garlic powder, onion powder, paprika, black pepper, chili powder and sugar.
5. Coat the hanger steaks in olive oil, then sprinkle over the coffee seasoning, pressing and massaging it into the meat.
6. Spritz the peppers with a little spray oil on both sides.
7. Place the hanger steaks onto the grill, turning every 2 minutes until they reach an internal temperature of around 135°F (57°C), about 8–10 minutes all up.
8. Remove the steaks from the grill and loosely cover with foil so they can rest.
9. In the meantime, increase the grill temperature (or stoke the coals), then place the shishito peppers over the heat for 2–3 minutes on each side, or until they blister and soften slightly. Remove the skewers.
10. Cut the steaks into slices and serve with the peppers. Top with a good pinch of sea salt flakes.

• BE THE BUTCHER •

HOW TO CUT A HANGER STEAK

Sometimes referred to as a 'hanging tender' or 'thick skirt', or by its French name 'onglet', the hanger steak has long held another moniker – 'the butcher's secret steak.' But the secret is most certainly out.

The hanger is one of the only steaks that comes from inside the ribcage, along with the outside skirt (page 171), and it's one of the few cuts where there is only one per animal (along with the tongue, brain, etc.).

The hanger is the lumbar portion of the diaphragm, and it has a seam of heavy connective tissue running right through the middle. For best results, I like to separate the two 'pillars' of hanger meat, removing the seam completely. A boning knife (page 26) is perfect for this.

1. The whole hanger steak is rectangular in appearance.
2. Make a cut as close to the connective seam as possible to separate one side.
3. On the remaining piece, position the knife between the seam and the meat, cutting the seam away.
4. You are now left with two 'pillars' of steak, shaped like square tubes.

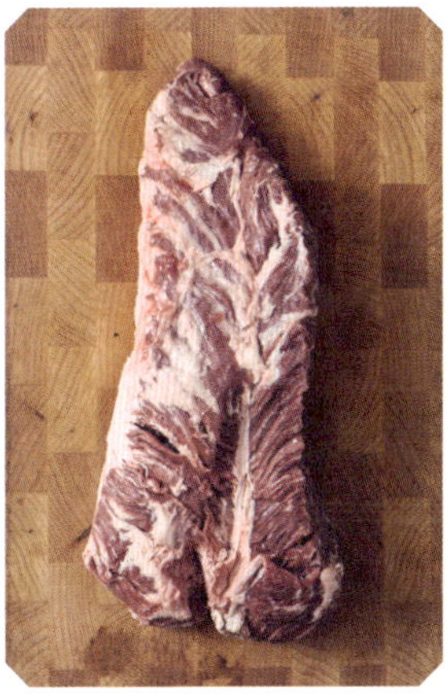

1

2

3

4

DENVER BUTTER BOARD STEAK WITH CHARRED SCALLION BUTTER

SERVES 2

Denver is what I would classify as a 'modern' steak, having been introduced to the world in 2009. It's one of those great 'meat science' discoveries, just like flat iron, where research was done on how to cut and butcher differently to yield alternate and improved options. The Denver is a cut from the chuck area and is actually the start of the *serratus ventralis* muscle, the same muscle that goes on to become beef ribs. It's a great little cut that hits all the major pillars – value, marbling and flavor.

½ tablespoon neutral oil (e.g. vegetable or canola oil)

3 scallions (spring onions)

2 Denver steaks

2 teaspoons salt, divided

2 oz (55 g) salted butter, softened

1. Remove the steaks from the fridge.
2. Place a stainless steel or cast-iron skillet over medium-high heat.
3. Add the neutral oil to the pan, then lay the scallions on top. You can use a weight (like a burger press) to encourage pan contact.
4. Cook the scallions for 8–10 minutes, turning them occasionally. They should be wilted, with some patches that are dark and charred. Once the color is deep enough, remove from the pan.
5. Season the steaks with 1½ teaspoons salt on both sides and place into the hot pan. Cook for 4 minutes, then flip and cook for a further 5 minutes on the other side.
6. In the meantime, mince or finely slice the scallions and add to the softened butter. Season with the remaining salt. Stir to combine everything together.
7. Remove the steaks from the pan and place on a plate. Loosely cover with foil to rest.
8. Prepare a wooden board (a cutting board is perfect) and use a knife or spoon to spread the charred scallion butter directly onto the board. Slice the steaks and arrange them on the butter. Serve immediately.

HOW TO MAKE A STEAK BUTTER BOARD

I'm on a mission to make butter boards the preferred way to serve a steak.

Traditionally, a single pat of compound butter is served sitting on top of the steak. It often doesn't melt properly and there's never enough to cover the whole steak. So why put it on the steak when you can put it under?

The butter board method lets the heat of the steak gently melt the spread butter beneath it, and every piece can be dragged through the melted butter for perfect coverage on every bite.

Here's how to make a butter board:

1. Prepare your softened compound butter of choice.
2. Spread the butter onto a clean wooden board.
3. Slice your cooked steak.
4. Nestle the sliced steak into the butter and let it rest for a minute or two to encourage melting.
5. Drag a slice through the butter and enjoy the perfect bite.

HARDCORE
CARNIVORE

STEAK WITH TALLOW FRITES

SERVES 2

Though hard to find, *teres major* is one of my favorite cuts, so I had to include it to give it the spotlight it deserves. As for the fries, I knew I had to track down the chef behind the best I've ever had – ultra-crispy, even after they cooled, and fried in rich beef tallow. I took a chance and reached out to Chef Marc Marrone, who generously shared his recipe. And thankfully so – because they truly don't get better than this. Fair warning: it's a bit involved and packed with steps, but absolutely worth the effort.

FRITES

1.5 lb (700 g) russet burbank potatoes (see Notes)

¾ oz (20 g) salt

4 cups (1 liter) water

4 cups (1 liter) beef tallow (page 244)

STEAK

2 x 1 lb (500 g) whole *teres major* steaks

2 teaspoons avocado or other high-smoke-point oil

1½ teaspoons salt

TARRAGON MAYO

1 large egg

1 tablespoon dijon mustard

1 tablespoon white wine vinegar

¾ cup (185 ml) neutral oil (e.g. canola oil)

1 tablespoon finely chopped tarragon leaves

¼ teaspoon salt

¼ teaspoon black pepper

1. The night before serving, peel the potatoes, then julienne them about ¼ inch (5–6 cm) thick. You can also use a fry cutter to speed up the process.
2. Whisk the salt into the water to dissolve, then add the potatoes. Allow to soak overnight to remove excess starch.
3. The next day, drain and discard the water. Lay the potatoes out in a single layer on paper towels. Press with more paper towels to get rid of as much water as possible.
4. Place a large Dutch oven over medium heat and add the tallow. When it reaches 250°F (115°C), blanch the potatoes by lowering them into the tallow. Fry for 5–7 minutes until they turn opaque and develop a leathery exterior. If you have a deep fryer, Chef Marrone recommends packing the fries tightly into the basket to encourage them to steam.
5. Using a skimmer, remove the fries and allow them to drain. Spread them out in a single layer on a sheet pan (baking sheet) to cool, then place them into the freezer, uncovered, for at least 2 hours. This will help them dehydrate further. Keep them in the freezer until you're ready to cook the steaks.

6. Remove the steaks from the fridge.
7. Prepare the tarragon mayo by adding the egg, dijon mustard and vinegar to an immersion blender cup. Blend for a few seconds, then slowly drizzle in the neutral oil in a continuous stream while blending. It will start to thicken, but if it gets too thick, add a touch of water while the blender is still running. Add the chopped tarragon, salt and pepper. Blitz for a few more seconds to incorporate. Scrape the mixture into a bowl, then cover and store in the fridge until ready to use.
8. Place a cast-iron skillet over high heat and add the avocado oil and a spoonful of the reserved melted tallow from the frying pot.
9. Season the steaks on all sides with the salt, then place them into the skillet to sear. After 2–3 minutes, turn them a third of the way over and sear for another 2–3 minutes. (They're cylindrical, so rather than turning twice, we're doing it three times.) Turn the steaks another third and cook for a further 3 minutes. Use a meat thermometer to check the internal temperature of the steaks, aiming for a final temp of 130°F (54°C). If they are not ready yet, continue to turn the steaks every 2 minutes until they reach the right temperature. Remove the steaks from the pan and cover with foil to rest.
10. While the steaks are resting, heat the tallow to 375°F (185°C). Remove the blanched fries from the freezer, then lower them into the tallow and fry for 3–5 minutes until golden brown. Remove them with a skimmer and drain on paper towels. Season with salt and pepper to taste.
11. Slice the steaks across the grain, then arrange on a plate and serve with the fries and tarragon mayo.

NOTES

If you want to take the fries to a more intense level, Chef Marrone sometimes adds skin-on garlic cloves and fresh thyme to the tallow about a minute before the fries have finished their second cook.

Chef Marrone also insists that using the right potato is essential for optimal results. His favorite potato for fries is the kennebec, but a russet (specifically, a burbank russet) will also do a great job.

THIS STEAK IS A 'MAJOR' HIDDEN GEM

Teres major is definitely a 'rare' steak. I mean, every steer has two of them, but they are really hard to find at retail stores. The *teres major* is a small cylindrical muscle cut from the shoulder/chuck, but it's a hidden gem because it's extremely tender, great value for money and a perfect serving for one.

The problem is, *teres major* is known by a few different names and often confused with a muscle called the *supraspinatus*. That leaves people unsure of which muscle is actually the teres, so I'm going to solve that for y'all!

CROSS-SECTION OF THE CHUCK PRIMAL

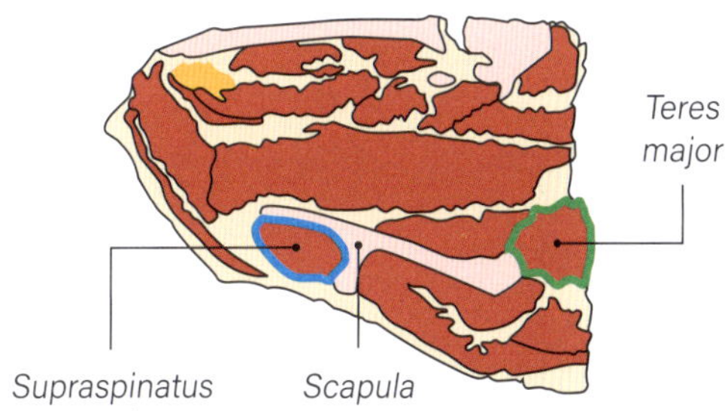

TERES MAJOR

- Rated as TENDER in Warner-Bratzler shear force tests.
- Also known as petite tender and bistro filet.

SUPRASPINATUS

- Rated as TOUGH in Warner-Bratzler shear force tests.
- Also known as the mock tender, chuck tender, scotch tender and chuck fillet.

You can imagine how generic terms like 'petite tender' and 'chuck tender' are subjective, which has contributed to the confusion with this cut!

TEX-MEX BARBACOA AND CHEESY GRITS

SERVES 8

Beef cheeks are one of the hardest-working muscles on the animal – and they're packed with flavor. The meat is laced with collagen, which breaks down into silky gelatin as it cooks, just like brisket. And, like brisket, cheeks need long, slow cooking to become tender. Once they do, the meat is so yielding you can shred it apart with just the gentle squeeze of your hand. Traditional Mexican barbacoa uses an entire cow's head, but this version leans Tex-Mex, pairing the cheeks with cheesy grits and a guajillo chili braise.

- 6 dried guajillo chilies
- 4–5 lb (2–2.5 kg) beef cheek meat
- ½ tablespoon salt
- ½ tablespoon coarse black pepper
- 6 garlic cloves
- 1 onion, quartered
- 2 bay leaves
- 4 cups (1 liter) beef stock

GRITS

- 1 cup (250 ml) water
- 2 cups (500 ml) milk
- 1½ cups (195 g) grits (not instant)
- 1 teaspoon salt
- 1 tablespoon salted butter
- 2 cups (190 g) shredded (grated) cheddar cheese

1. Place a large, heavy-based pot (I use a cast-iron Dutch oven) over medium heat.
2. Remove the stems and seeds from the guajillos and place them into the pot to toast for 1–2 minutes until fragrant, turning them halfway through toasting.
3. In the same pot, add the beef cheek meat, salt, pepper, garlic, onion, bay leaves and stock. Briefly stir the ingredients, then bring the mixture to a boil before reducing to a simmer and covering the pot. The cheeks will take anywhere between 4 and 5 hours to tenderize. At the 4-hour mark, they should be 'acceptably' tender, but if you let them cook even further, they will be fall-apart tender, which is preferable for this recipe.
4. When the beef cheeks are nearing the end of their cooking time, prepare the grits. In a saucepan, bring the water and milk to a simmer, then slowly whisk in the grits. Add the salt, then turn the heat to low for a super-gentle simmer. Stir every few minutes to avoid them sticking to the bottom of the saucepan. After 25–35 minutes, once the liquid is absorbed and the grits are tender, stir in the butter and cheese.
5. When the beef cheeks are tender, remove them from the liquid and place them in a large bowl. Remove and discard the bay leaves.
6. Shred the beef cheek meat, removing any tougher silverskin or unpleasant bits that haven't softened. I do this with heatproof gloves so the barbacoa remains hot, but you can wait until it cools a little before you shred. Taste and add more salt to taste, if needed.
7. Use an immersion blender to blend the liquid that remains in the pot.
8. To serve, spoon some grits into the bottom of a shallow bowl. Top with a generous amount of beef cheek meat, then spoon some of the pot sauce over the top. Serve immediately.

NOTES

There can be quite a bit of variation in how beef cheek meat is cut and packaged. Some are neatly trimmed, containing mostly the cheek muscle, while others include sections of lip meat. Lip meat is perfectly edible, but the texture isn't as desirable. It can also catch people off guard – the *buccal papillae* (small nodules that help move feed around in the animal's mouth) can look unsettling, almost like tiny pointed teeth.

I like to use stone-ground grits for the best texture, though you may need to follow the directions on the box if they vary from the method here. You may also need to add more liquid if they are too thick. The key points: cook them with milk for richness, and don't skip the cheese. If you can't find grits, soft polenta works in a pinch, though it's not quite the same, and you can always serve the beef cheek meat over rice instead.

LENGUA TOSTADAS

SERVES 6

Tongue might make some folks squeamish – after all, it's the food that tastes you back. But it's time to get over that. When cooked properly, beef tongue (or lengua in Spanish) is tender, juicy and surprisingly rich. Piled into tostadas with salsa and avocado, it's proof that the best flavors often come from the cuts we overlook.

1 beef tongue
1 onion, quartered (with half reserved for the salsa)
6 garlic cloves
3 bay leaves
6 cloves
2 tablespoons salt
12 tostadas (see Notes)
2 cups (460 g) refried beans, warmed
1 cup (75 g) finely shredded green cabbage
2 avocados, sliced
1 bunch cilantro (coriander), finely chopped
½ cup (50 g) finely grated cotija or parmesan cheese
2 limes, cut into wedges

SALSA

6 chile de árbol or 1–2 bird's eye chilies (see Notes)
2 tablespoons olive oil
1 lb (450 g) fresh tomatillos, husks removed
4 garlic cloves
½ teaspoon salt
½ teaspoon chicken bouillon (stock) powder
⅓ cup (80 ml) water

1. Slice the tongue into 4–6 large pieces and place in a large stockpot. Cover with water, then place on the stove over high heat.
2. Add two onion quarters, the garlic, bay leaves, cloves and salt. Bring to a boil, then reduce the heat and simmer for 3 hours until the meat is tender.
3. While the meat is cooking, make the salsa. Place the árbol chilies in a bowl, cover with water and allow to soften and rehydrate for 10–15 minutes.
4. Place a skillet over medium-high heat and add the olive oil. Add the fresh tomatillos and remaining onion to the pan. Cook for 5–8 minutes, turning occasionally, until they are charred and have begun to soften. Add the garlic and cook for a further 2–3 minutes, stirring occasionally.
5. In a blender, add the contents of the skillet, along with the drained, softened chilies, salt, chicken bouillon and water. Blend until smooth, then set aside.
6. Once the tongue is tender, remove from the pot and discard the rest of the contents. Peel and discard the tough outer layer of the tongue, then use cleavers or your hands to break apart and shred the meat.
7. To assemble the tostadas, spread 2–3 tablespoons of refried beans across one tostada. Top with the shredded meat and a generous spoonful of salsa.
8. Garnish with the shredded cabbage, avocado, cilantro and cheese. Repeat with the remaining tostadas.
9. Serve with lime wedges on the side.

NOTES

If you can't find tostadas, make your own by frying corn tortillas in a little oil for 2–3 minutes until crispy.

Chile de árbol are fiery little chilies. If you prefer less heat, reduce the quantity.

SEARED VENISON WITH BROWN BUTTER PISTACHIO DUKKAH

SERVES 4

I learned to hunt when I moved to Texas. It's just a core part of life there, and a classic tradition when the weather gets cold. The venison backstrap (boneless loin) is among the prized cuts, though as a lean meat it benefits from a little extra fatty richness – and that's where the browned butter comes in. The size of backstrap can be quite variable (especially if you're hunting, not buying the meat), so cooking times may differ. Just focus on the finishing temperature.

- 2 x 1 lb (500 g) venison backstrap, about 8 inches (20 cm)
- 1 cup (260 g) plain Greek-style yogurt
- 1 tablespoon lemon juice
- 2 tablespoons honey
- 3 garlic cloves, crushed
- 1 teaspoon salt
- 1–2 tablespoons neutral oil (e.g. canola or avocado oil), divided
- 8 tablespoons salted butter

DUKKAH

- ½ cup (70 g) raw pistachio kernels
- ¼ cup (40 g) raw hazelnuts
- 3 tablespoons sesame seeds
- 1 teaspoon fennel seeds
- 1 tablespoon coriander seeds
- ½ teaspoon cumin seeds or ground cumin
- 1 teaspoon ground cinnamon
- ¼ teaspoon salt

1. Place the venison in a resealable bag.
2. In a bowl, stir together the Greek yogurt, lemon juice, honey, garlic and salt. Pour the marinade over the venison, then seal the bag. Massage the bag gently so the meat is evenly coated, then refrigerate for 2–3 hours to marinate.
3. In the meantime, make the dukkah. Place the nuts, sesame seeds, fennel seeds, coriander seeds and cumin seeds in a dry skillet. Toast over high heat for about 2 minutes, swirling the pan regularly, until fragrant and lightly golden.
4. Allow to cool, then place into a food processor along with the cinnamon and salt. Pulse in very short bursts until the mixture resembles coarse crumbs (or you can put all the ingredients in a resealable bag and smash them with a rolling pin). Set aside.
5. Remove the venison from the fridge and wipe off any excess marinade, patting the backstraps dry with paper towels.
6. Place a cast-iron or metal skillet over high heat. Once hot, add 1 tablespoon neutral oil. Place the venison in the skillet and cook for 4 minutes. Turn with tongs and cook another 4 minutes.
7. Continue flipping every 2 minutes until the internal temperature reaches 130°F (54°C). If the pan appears dry, add the remaining oil.
8. Transfer the venison to a cutting board, cover loosely with foil and leave to rest.
9. In the meantime, make the browned butter. Place a small saucepan over medium heat and add the butter. Swirl occasionally as it melts and foams.
10. After 5–7 minutes, the milk solids will sink and turn golden brown. Remove from the heat and stir in the dukkah.
11. To serve, slice the venison and spoon the brown butter dukkah mixture over the top.

NOTE

Wanna try this recipe but can't find venison? You can substitute with lamb backstraps (reduce the cook time) or a couple of thicker-cut beef steaks.

MEAT FAT

No book on meat could truly be complete without a section on fat. So, these are a collection of recipes that use rendered fat (not just large chunks of raw fat) as a key flavor ingredient. But first, a word on what makes fat so important.

FAT IS FLAVOR

This phrase should probably be on a T-shirt or bumper sticker somewhere. But it's not just a cry from meat lovers across the globe; it's actually proven by science.

Studies on the flavor profile of fat have been carried out for years, and we know that fat influences tenderness and juiciness. Fat-soluble compounds also contribute to the distinct flavor in different species, which means that fat differentiates the taste between beef, pork, lamb and other meats. Wanna test it for yourself? Try grabbing a super-lean piece of beef, like eye of round (page 165), and grinding it with some lamb fat or pork fat. You'll find the patties will taste strongly of the fat-contributing animal more than the beef!

Interestingly, what the animal eats can really influence the flavor and aroma of the fat. Remember, smell is part of taste. If you want to check that on your own, try blocking your nose the next time you eat something and you'll be shocked at how muted the flavor is! A great example of this is jamón ibérico – one of the most famous meats in the world. Jamón ibérico is made using a particular breed of black-footed pig that is fed a diet of acorns, which plays a huge role in its unique and prized flavor.

If you're as old as I am, you may remember that McDonald's fries tasted better when we were kids. For over 40 years (the 'golden fry' era, if you will), right up until the '90s, McDonald's fries were cooked in beef tallow, and they were delicious! Even after this period, they added beef-based flavor into their cooking oil to get close to that unmistakable taste … until they got sued by some vegetarians who ruined the fun for all of us. But the point is, fat really is flavor!

There's an important nose-to-tail and economical aspect to using all the fat. Both ethically and financially, it's best to use as much of the animal as possible. Finding a way to use extra brisket trimmings can make you feel like you've maximized your bang for buck. But even if you don't do a lot of home butchery, you can always buy fat trimmings from the butcher or grocer (it's cheap) and follow my guide for how to render it yourself (page 244). And if that's still too much effort, you can buy most animal fats in the grocery store these days.

One thing to note: many commercially produced fats (especially pork lard) have additives in them to prolong shelf life and preserve flavor. Sometimes, these additives can create a different texture and result when the fat is used in things like baked goods and tortillas.

• MEAT NERD FACT •

Not all animal fat behaves the same. Differences in fat composition affect how fat melts and solidifies, a property commonly described by titer. Higher-titer fats are firmer and melt at higher temperatures, while lower-titer fats feel softer and more fluid when cooked. Fat associated with heavily worked cuts like brisket and shank tends to be higher-titer and holds its structure longer during cooking. By contrast, fat found along the back and rib section, such as ribeye or strip loin, is typically lower-titer and melts more easily.

BEEF OR PORK FAT

HOW TO MAKE YOUR OWN TALLOW OR LARD

MAKES ABOUT 2 CUPS (500 ML)

Making your own tallow (beef fat) and lard (pork fat) is easy – and a wonderful way to get the most out of your meat purchases. I save the fat offcuts when I'm trimming bigger cuts like brisket and store them in a freezer bag until I've collected enough to make a batch of tallow. This rendering process gently melts the fat and separates it from the meat, connective tissue and other impurities, so you can use it as a cooking ingredient.

2–3 lb (1–1.3 kg) beef or pork fat

⅓ cup (80 ml) water

1. Cut the fat into medium-sized chunks, no larger than about 2 inches (5 cm). Trim and discard any visible pieces of meat.
2. Place a heavy-based pot (like a Dutch oven) over low heat. Add the fat and water.
3. Cook for 4–6 hours, stirring occasionally. It is normal for larger chunks of fat to remain in the pot even after 4 hours. Not all of it will melt and render.
4. Carefully strain the rendered fat through a sieve to remove most of the large pieces.
5. Prepare a clean glass jar (the fat will be hot!). Place a funnel or small strainer lined with cheesecloth over the jar, then strain the fat a second time.
6. Allow to cool and store in the fridge.

NOTES

The key to this method (and achieving snow-white fat) is a low and gentle heat. If you end up with a light brown tallow or lard, you may have allowed the fat to fry and cook, but it's still safe to use.

Tallow/lard will keep for 6–12 months and must be stored in a fridge.

You can also use a slow cooker set to low instead of the stovetop method.

WHITE BEAN DIP WITH DUCK FAT–ROASTED GARLIC

SERVES 4–6

Duck fat is one of the most revered animal fats to cook with. It has an incredibly silky mouthfeel, but it's actually quite neutral in flavor (meaning, you won't actually taste duck). Here it does double duty, roasting the garlic cloves to a golden brown and creating a velvety-soft texture in the finished dip.

- 2 tablespoons duck fat, divided
- 12 large garlic cloves
- 1 x 15 oz (425 g) can cannellini beans
- juice of 1 small lemon
- ¼ teaspoon salt
- ¼ teaspoon sumac
- ½ teaspoon thyme leaves

1. Preheat the oven to 375°F (190°C).
2. Melt 1 tablespoon duck fat in the microwave or a small saucepan.
3. Place a piece of parchment paper (baking paper) on a small sheet pan (baking sheet), then spread the garlic cloves on top. Drizzle the melted duck fat over the garlic cloves, tossing to coat them. Spread into a single layer and roast in the oven for 20–25 minutes until golden and fragrant. Move the garlic occasionally to ensure it roasts evenly.
4. Drain the cannellini beans, reserving the liquid. Place the beans in a food processor or blender, along with the remaining duck fat, roasted garlic, lemon juice, salt, sumac and thyme.
5. Blend to a smooth paste, adding the reserved bean liquid a little at a time until the desired consistency is achieved.

NOTE

You can find duck fat in a jar in most grocery stores. In my first cookbook, I have a recipe for fat-roasted potatoes and it works well with duck fat, too.

COUNTRY-STYLE WHITE GRAVY

MAKES ABOUT 2 CUPS (500 ML)

Who woulda thought gravy could cause such a cultural divide? In my home country of Australia, gravy is pretty much consistently brown and always made from the pan drippings of something that was roasted to a golden-brown color. But in the United States, if you ask for 'gravy', you'll most likely get country gravy, a snow-white sauce flecked with lots of black pepper. White gravy is commonly served over chicken-fried steak or fluffy, buttery biscuits.

- 4 tablespoons pork lard or bacon grease
- ¼ cup (35 g) all-purpose (plain) flour
- 1 cup (250 ml) warm chicken stock (see Notes)
- 1 cup (250 ml) milk
- ½ teaspoon salt
- ½ teaspoon freshly ground black pepper
- ¼ teaspoon dried thyme (optional)

1. Place the lard in a skillet over medium-high heat.
2. Once melted, sprinkle over the flour and whisk continuously to form a roux. Cook the roux for about 3–5 minutes, still whisking, until it develops a slight color.
3. Add in the stock a little at a time, whisking constantly. It will initially seize up and become a clumpy mess, but it will eventually smooth out.
4. Once all the stock has been incorporated, add the milk, pouring ¼ cup (60 ml) at a time until the desired consistency is reached. If you prefer a thicker gravy, use less liquid. If you prefer it thinner, use additional milk or stock.
5. Add the salt, pepper and thyme (if using), and stir through. Add more salt and pepper to taste. Serve immediately.

NOTES

Typically, only milk is used for the liquid, but I like to include some stock to boost the meaty flavor and keep the gravy a little runnier in consistency.

For a fun variation, substitute the milk with fresh black coffee for a take on 'red eye gravy.' This is traditionally made with the drippings from cooked country hams and doesn't use any flour.

BEEF FAT FLOUR TORTILLAS

MAKES 12 TORTILLAS

These Sonoran-style tortillas come with a little history lesson. Sonora is a state in the north of Mexico (right on the border) and is known for cattle ranching, so the tallow is plentiful. Once the Spanish introduced wheat, the northern states found it easier to cultivate than corn, so the fat-laden flour tortilla became synonymous with the region. The tortillas themselves are slightly translucent, soft and malleable, and have the most subtly delicious beef flavor. Use them for the Carne Asada Skirt Steak Tacos on page 174.

- 2 cups (300 g) all-purpose (plain) flour
- ⅔ cup (170 ml) hot water
- ⅓ cup (80 ml) beef tallow (page 244)
- 1½ teaspoons salt

1. Combine all the ingredients in a bowl and mix together with your hands, allowing the hot water to soften the tallow.
2. Place the dough onto a mat or counter and knead for 3–5 minutes. Cover with plastic wrap and allow to rest for 10 minutes.
3. Knead the dough for a further 2–3 minutes. Divide into 12 portions and roll each into a ball. Cover with plastic wrap and rest for 20–30 minutes.
4. Heat a comal (a flat metal pan used for toasting tortillas), a dry griddle or a dry cast-iron skillet over medium-high heat.
5. Working one ball at a time, roll out the dough with a rolling pin as thin as you can make it without tearing.
6. Place the tortilla into the hot comal and cook for 30 seconds. Flip and cook another 30 seconds on the other side. Flip back to the first side for a final 15–20 seconds.
7. Remove from the heat and place in a tortilla warmer until ready to use.
8. Repeat until all tortillas have been cooked.

NOTES

Feel like mixing it up? Substitute the beef tallow with either pork lard or duck fat. You could even use vegetable shortening for a non-meat version.

I like to use silicone baking mats for kneading and rolling. They're nonstick, easy to work with and a breeze to clean.

You can use a tortilla press if you prefer, but I think a rolling pin achieves thinner results.

If you don't have a tortilla warmer (an insulated container for tortillas), make a pouch out of foil to keep them warm.

FRIJOLES REFRITOS

SERVES 4–6

If you go to any Tex-Mex restaurant in Texas (or arguably, the world), you can bet your food is going to come with a side of frijoles (refried beans). Now, you might assume that a humble side of beans is a strictly vegetarian affair – not so. The secret to truly incredible flavor comes from a generous helping of rich, savory pork fat.

2 cups (400 g) dried pinto beans (see Notes)

½ onion

1 teaspoon salt

3 tablespoons pork lard (see Notes)

3 garlic cloves, crushed

½ teaspoon dried Mexican oregano

¼ teaspoon ground cumin

½ teaspoon chili powder

GARNISHES

1 tablespoon crumbled queso fresco or any crumbly fresh cheese

1 tablespoon finely chopped cilantro (coriander) leaves

1 fresh jalapeño, sliced

1. Place the beans in a large bowl and cover with water. Discard any stones, debris or wonky beans that float to the surface. Soak for 30–60 minutes.
2. Drain the beans, then place into a large pot. Fill with fresh water so the beans are covered by at least 2 inches (5 cm) of water. Add the onion and salt.
3. Bring to a boil, then reduce to a simmer and cook for 60–90 minutes until the beans are completely tender. If the water level gets too low (at bean level or lower), top up with additional hot/boiling water.
4. Strain the beans and set aside, saving the cooking liquid.
5. Place the fat into the empty pot over medium heat. Add the crushed garlic, stirring regularly, and cook for about 1–2 minutes, or until fragrant. Add the oregano, cumin and chili powder. Stir for 1 minute to lightly fry the spices.
6. Add the beans, plus ¼ cup (60 ml) reserved cooking liquid. Using a potato masher, mash the beans into a soft paste, adding more cooking liquid a little at a time as needed. You can also do this with the back of a wooden spoon, but I find it easier to use a masher.
7. Add salt to taste and more cooking liquid to reach the desired consistency.
8. Garnish with queso, cilantro and jalapeño.

NOTES

Lard is rendered, soft pork fat that is like a thick paste. It cannot be substituted for chunks of fresh pork fat.

If you're not up for making your own, you can buy pork lard in most grocery stores. For a smokier finish, use bacon fat.

Dried beans lose flavor as they age and sit, so find the freshest dried ones possible. Often, small local producers or brands have fresher beans than the ones that sit on the shelf at the grocery store.

The consistency of the beans is personal preference. Some folks prefer a drier, denser texture, while others love a silkier, smoother finish You can also use canned beans in place of dried; just skip the soaking and simmering.

CRISPY SMASHED ROAST POTATOES

SERVES 4

When it comes to side dishes, there is no greater pairing than potato and beef fat. It's a symbiotic relationship where the best crisping abilities of the tater are unleashed, while the full flavor of the fat is allowed to be the star of the show. In short, if you love fries, you're gonna lose your mind over these. The hyperbole is real.

- 2 lb (1 kg) baby yukon gold potatoes
- ½ cup (125 ml) beef tallow (page 244) or duck fat
- 1 teaspoon salt
- ¼ teaspoon ground black pepper
- ¼ teaspoon garlic powder
- 1 teaspoon paprika

1. Preheat the oven to 450°F (230°C).
2. Bring a pot of water to the boil, then add the potatoes. Boil for 10–20 minutes until the potatoes are tender.
3. Drain into a colander and let them sit for 5 minutes to release some steam.
4. Brush the bottom of a metal sheet pan (baking sheet) with 2 tablespoons melted beef fat.
5. Place the potatoes in the pan. Working one at a time, use the bottom of a flat glass or jar to press and smash the potatoes down with gentle, firm pressure. They should be about ½-inch (1 cm) high. Leave space between each potato on the tray.
6. Brush the tops with ¼ cup (60 ml) fat.
7. Combine the salt, pepper, garlic powder and paprika in a small bowl. Sprinkle evenly on each potato, then place in the oven. Roast for 35–45 minutes until crispy (the undersides touching the tray will be very crispy, while the tops may not be as brown). Baste the potatoes with the remaining fat once more during cooking. The fat should always be sizzling on top of the potatoes while they cook. If you don't see a sizzle, they're too dry and need more fat.
8. Serve immediately!

NOTE

Small baby potatoes are the way to go here. They crisp up better than a larger spud and cook faster, too.

BONES

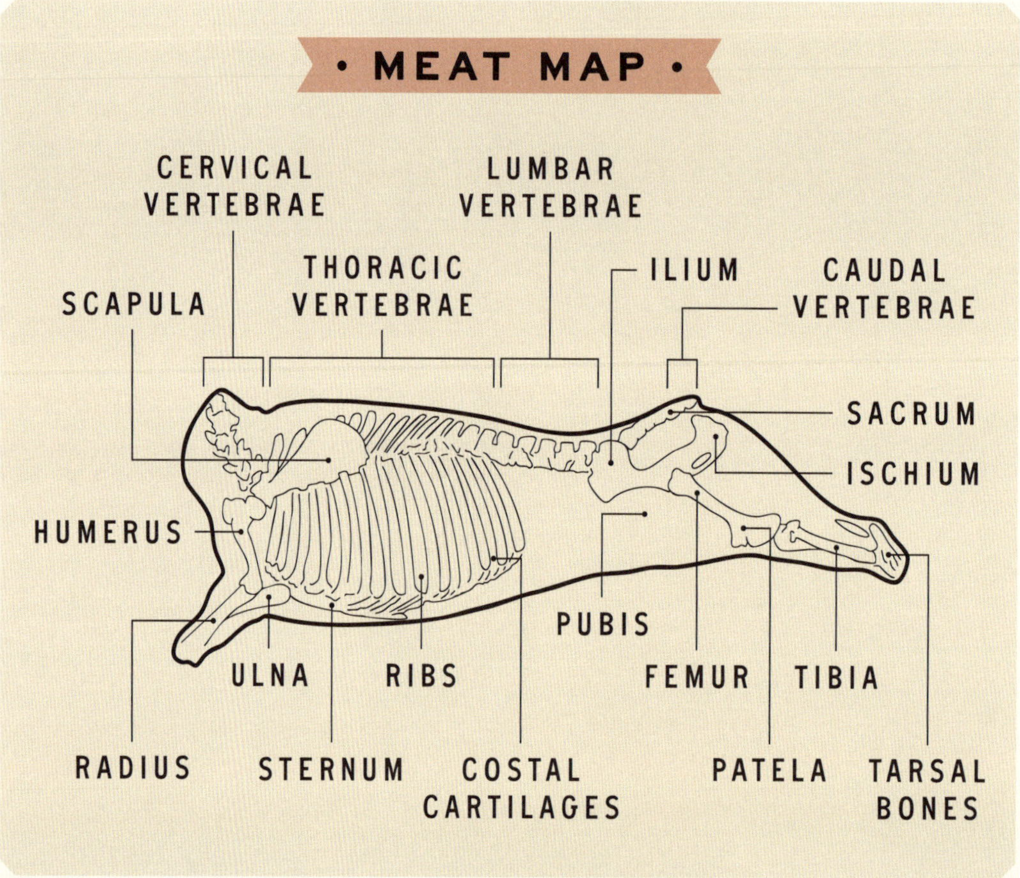

It wouldn't feel right to explore so many meat cuts without also highlighting the value and versatility of bones. I've shared a few recipes here, including for bone marrow and bone broth, but bones are used in many more ways than you might expect.

Rich in collagen (which becomes gelatin when processed) and packed with protein, bones are used in a surprising variety of edible and non-edible products. Here are some examples:

- marshmallows
- crochet hooks/needles
- glue
- fine china (yes, literal bone china)
- fertilizer
- charcoal pencils
- sandpaper
- shampoos and conditioners
- medication gel caps
- granulated (white) sugar.

But if we're talkin' about bones, we have to address one of the biggest meat debates of all.

BONE-IN OR BONELESS STEAK?

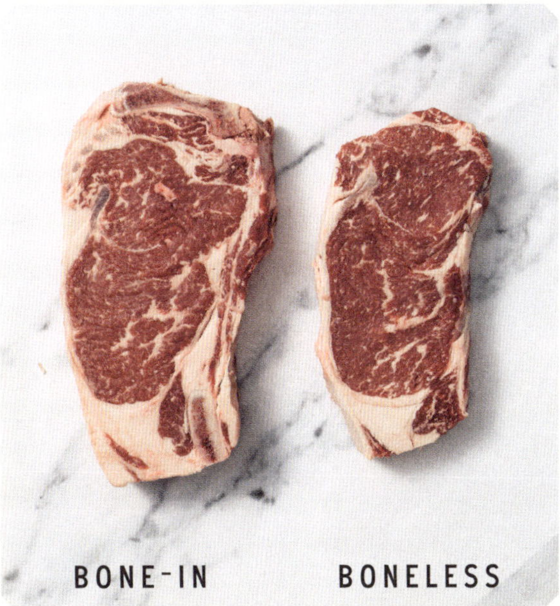

So let's settle the age-old question. Does steak on the bone actually have more flavor? The short answer is no. And here's why.

The science behind it isn't as straightforward as we'd like it to be. There are some studies where taste-testers preferred bone-in cuts, but there are even more peer-reviewed journal articles (read: legit, verified meat science research) which show that cooking a steak with the bone still attached has little to no flavor benefit. There's just not enough consistent evidence to support the argument that

bones make steak taste better. Lots of opinions, yes. But no real evidence.

The only time you may actually get some flavor out of bones is during long, slow cooking, where the bones are immersed and simmered in liquid, such as broths, stews and soups. In these cases, the bones can contribute amino acids from gelatin, marrow, lipids and even some minerals into the broth. And even then, we're talking about hours of simmering, not just 10 minutes of searing.

So, what about all those folks who swear a bone-in steak just tastes better?

Well, the bone can definitely affect how heat reaches the meat during cooking. It acts like a little insulator or shield, slowing down the heat transfer and protecting the meat around it. That, in turn, can lead to a more gentle cook overall, which might contribute to juiciness and tenderness. But that's still not going to influence flavor.

A steak on the bone also offers a sort of primal appeal. There's something satisfying about grabbing a steak by the bone and gnawing on it like a caveman. For some folks, it's the best part of the experience. But that's a matter of texture, not flavor.

For the record, I usually prefer boneless steaks. My biggest gripe with bone-in? The height difference. The bone raises part of the meat off the cooking surface, which means you get little gaps that don't sear properly. And as we all know, real flavor lies in a hard, crusty Maillard sear!

ROASTED BONE MARROW WITH MALT VINEGAR MIGNONETTE

SERVES 4–8

Rich and fatty, with a texture similar to meat jelly, bone marrow tastes like pure, unadulterated beef essence. The mignonette is traditionally served as an accompaniment for raw oysters, but I think the fresh, bright pop of vinegar and shallot is perfect for cutting through the intense richness of the marrow.

- 3 lb (1.3 kg) canoe cut marrow bones
- ½ cup (125 ml) malt vinegar
- 2 tablespoons finely minced shallot
- ¼ teaspoon freshly ground black pepper
- ¼ teaspoon honey
- 1 teaspoon salt
- 1 tablespoon finely chopped flat-leaf parsley
- fresh baguette slices, to serve

1. Preheat the oven to 450°F (230°C).
2. Place the marrow bones cut side up on a sheet pan (baking sheet) or roasting dish. Roast for 20–25 minutes until the marrow fat is bubbling and brown.
3. In the meantime, prepare the mignonette by combining the vinegar, shallot, black pepper and honey in a bowl. Stir and add salt to taste.
4. Once the marrow is roasted, remove from the oven and sprinkle with the salt and parsley.
5. Serve with the mignonette and baguette slices.

NOTES

Canoe cut bones (as the name suggests) are bones that are cut lengthways. Cooking them on their backs holds all the marrow in place as it renders and melts. I prefer these to the cross cut marrow bones (which look like small circles of bones), because it's much easier to scrape out the marrow and spread it across the baguette.

Often you'll find cut marrow bones in the frozen foods section of the grocery store.

SLOW COOKER BONE BROTH

MAKES ABOUT 9 CUPS (2.25 LITERS)

I use beef back ribs for this bone broth so I can get a 'twofer' deal. The bones make a solid base for the broth, and the meat is then repurposed for my Red Wine Ragù with Pappardelle on page 108. If you prefer a more classic option, bones like pork knuckles, beef necks, chicken feet and turkey necks can yield a more gelatinous result, and it's completely fine to mix different species.

- 1 x 3.5 lb (1.5 kg) rack of beef back ribs
- 1 teaspoon salt
- 2 carrots, roughly chopped
- 1 onion, cut in half
- 2 tablespoons apple cider vinegar

1. Preheat the oven to 450°F (230°C).
2. Place the back ribs on a sheet pan (baking sheet) and season with the salt. Roast for 20 minutes until brown.
3. Remove the back ribs from the oven and slice between each bone. Add to the slow cooker, along with the carrots and onion.
4. Cover with water and add the apple cider vinegar, then turn the heat to low and cook for 18–22 hours.
5. Remove from the oven and discard the carrots and onion.
6. Carefully remove the ribs and let cool. The meat should be extremely tender and may fall away from the bone.
7. Pull the meat away from the bones and shred it. Take care to remove and discard any membrane, bone fragments or hard bits. You should get about 4 cups (500 g) shredded meat. Place in a container to use for another recipe.
8. Pour the broth through a cheesecloth or strainer into a large container. Place in the fridge to allow the fat layer on top to harden. Remove and discard the fat. Your bone broth is now ready to enjoy.

NOTES

If you're using other bones and don't plan to keep the meat, discard the bones in step 6 and skip step 7.

I like to freeze the broth in two-cup portions so it can be used in other recipes.

CHICKEN STOCK

MAKES ABOUT 8 CUPS (2 LITERS)

This is a great way to reuse the bones from the Ultra-crispy Roasted Chicken recipe (page 192), or even a rotisserie chicken you pick up from the store. My grandmother also used one or two pieces of flanken cut beef ribs in her chicken stock, just to give it a flavor punch. Of course, quite a few variables can affect the final volume, so the yield of each batch may vary slightly. Once made, I freeze mine into two-cup portions to use as needed.

- 1 chicken carcass or roughly 2 lb (1 kg) chicken bones
- 4 chicken drumsticks
- 2 parsnips
- 2 large carrots, scrubbed
- 3 celery stalks
- 1 onion, skin on

1. Place the chicken carcass and drumsticks into a large stockpot. Cut the parsnips, carrots and celery into 2–3 large pieces and add to the pot. Cut the onion into quarters (slice through just to the root to hold everything together).
2. Pour in enough cold water to cover the meat and vegetables by about 2 inches (5 cm).
3. Slowly bring the pot to a boil over medium-high heat, then reduce to a simmer and cook for 3–4 hours. Use a spoon to skim off and discard the 'scum' that bubbles to the surface.
4. Pour the stock through a cheesecloth or strainer into a large container. Place in the fridge overnight to allow the fat layer on top to harden. Remove and discard the fat. Your chicken stock is now ready to enjoy.

NOTES

The stock is unseasoned to give it more flexibility in future dishes. The salt can concentrate during the simmering process, so if you want to add some, I recommend doing it at the end before straining.

To avoid wastage, sort through the strained remnants and pick out any meat from the thighs. It should be nice and tender.

CELEBRATION MEATS

Celebration meats are the centerpieces that anchor our most memorable meals – the juicy roasts reserved for holidays, feasts and special gatherings. Whether it's a bronzed turkey, a glistening ham or a perfectly rosy prime rib, these large-format cuts are international classics. They require more time, care and often a bit of planning, but the payoff is a showstopping main that feeds a crowd and sets the tone for the occasion. It's time to cook these festive classics with confidence!

PRIME RIB PRIMER

Prime rib, also known as standing rib roast, is a block of ribeye steaks that hasn't been sliced. It can include as many as seven bones, though there are lots of ways in which it may be trimmed or sold.

TYPES OF PRIME RIB

BONELESS: A rib primal section with all the bones removed, commonly called a ribeye roll.

BONE-IN: The same cut as boneless prime rib, but with a portion of rib bone left attached across the back. The bones are cut flush with a bandsaw so they don't extend beyond the meat.

BONE-IN, FRENCHED: A variation where the rib bones extend out past the meat. The bones have also been frenched, with all surface fat, muscle and sinew removed for a dramatic presentation.

COOK TO TEMP, NOT TIME

Prime rib is a roast that cooks at its own pace. You always cook it to temperature and not according to a specific time. You may need to make some time adjustments for size (shorter cook time for smaller roasts, longer for larger). Because of the size of the roast, I recommend taking it out of the oven a full 10°F/5°C *under* your target temperature to account for carryover cooking.

FYI, it's pretty common for the end pieces to cook more than the middle, so serve those to guests who prefer their roast more well done.

HOW TO HOLD PRIME RIB

Cooking to time and not temperature can be pretty challenging when you've invited guests over to eat at a certain time. But the beauty of a piece of meat this big is that you have more flexibility in holding it until it's ready. My advice is to give yourself an extra hour of cooking time and hold the meat at temperature until you're ready to serve. The easiest way to hold at temperature is to put it into a small cooler (un-iced), which will insulate it like a hot box.

BONELESS

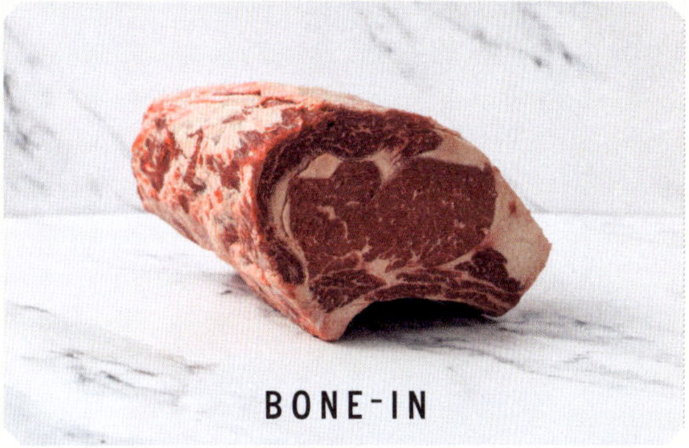

BONE-IN

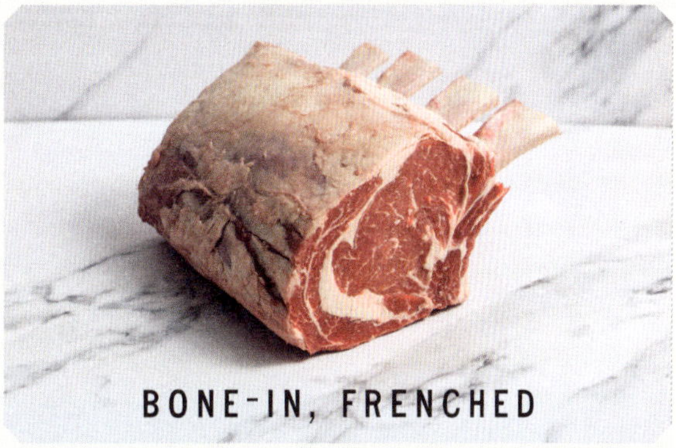

BONE-IN, FRENCHED

SHOWSTOPPER PRIME RIB

SERVES 8

A hallmark of classic steakhouses and special-occasion dining, prime rib carries a reputation for being both indulgent and intimidating. The sheer size (and price tag) can make people hesitant to cook it at home, but it's surprisingly easy to achieve a rich, mahogany crust and a tender, perfectly medium-rare interior. So go ahead, treat yourself! The recipe below is for classic oven-roasted prime rib, but if you prefer to barbecue it, you can follow this exact method and cook it in a smoker instead.

- 1 x 8–10 lb (3.5–4.5 kg) four-bone frenched prime rib roast
- 1–2 tablespoons salt
- 1 cup (8 oz/250 g) softened salted butter
- ½ cup (15 g) finely chopped flat-leaf parsley
- ⅓ cup (10 g) finely chopped oregano
- 2 tablespoons thyme leaves
- salt flakes

1. Remove the prime rib from the fridge 20–30 minutes prior to cooking.
2. Preheat the oven to 450°F (170°C).
3. Pat the prime rib with a paper towel to dry the surface, then season all over with the salt, including the sides.
4. Place the butter in a bowl along with the parsley, oregano and thyme. Stir to blend into compound butter.
5. Place the prime rib onto a rack within a roasting pan. Ensure the prime rib has airflow all around it and that the pan can catch the juices.
6. Spread the butter over the top and sides of the prime rib. Do not apply to the bones.
7. Place in the oven and roast for 30 minutes.
8. Using a turkey baster or spoon, scoop up the melted butter from the pan and baste the roast all over.
9. Decrease the heat to 275°F (135°C) and roast for a further 2½–3½ hours, basting every 30 minutes.
10. The prime rib is ready when the internal temperature reaches 120–125°F (48–51°C). Start monitoring the temperature after the first 60 minutes at the lower heat. Meat is variable, so the cooking time is too.
11. Remove from the oven and cover with foil to rest for at least 20 minutes before slicing.

NOTES

Feel free to freestyle on the herbs. You don't have to use the combo I've provided. Omit any you don't like and add others you love (marjoram, chives and rosemary would all be great too).

An offset spatula (often used for cake decorating) is the easiest tool for spreading the herb butter.

If you don't have a roasting pan, use a heatproof pan/tray with lower sides, but make sure it's not completely flat. You want to capture the butter as it melts.

If your prime rib hasn't been frenched, the recipe is still the same. It will also work on boneless prime rib (though the cook time may be shorter).

Don't put the roast straight from the oven into the cooler (if holding). You risk overcooking it. Always let it drop a little in temperature.

DOUBLE-SMOKED HAM WITH CHILI CARAMEL GLAZE

SERVES 8–10

Most commercially available hams are already cured and smoked, so all you need to do is reheat them. But that's also a golden opportunity to layer in your own signature flavors. Here, the ham goes back into the smoker for a second round, building an even deeper, richer smokiness, before getting drenched in an insanely moreish chili caramel. If you happen to have any caramel left over, it's phenomenal on ice cream, too.

- 1 x 6.5 lb (3 kg) smoked ham (see Notes)
- 1¼ cups (275 g) granulated (white) sugar
- ¼ cup (60 ml) water
- 3 tablespoons rice wine vinegar
- 1½ tablespoons soy sauce
- 1 tablespoon fish sauce
- 3 tablespoons sriracha
- 1 tablespoon miso paste
- ¼ teaspoon red pepper flakes
- 2 drops red food coloring (optional; see Notes)

1. Preheat a smoker to 225°F (105°C). Hickory and fruit woods like apple or cherry pair well with ham.
2. Prepare the ham by removing it from the packaging. Discard any netting, plastic pieces or rind.
3. Fill an aluminum pan with 2–4 cups (500 ml–1 liter) water. This will provide extra moisture to support the ham as it reheats. Place a rack over the top of the pan, then set the ham on the rack.
4. Gently place the water pan and ham into the smoker and begin cooking. It will take 2–3 hours to heat all the way through to 140°F (60°C).
5. In the meantime, prepare the chili caramel glaze. Place the sugar and water in a heavy-based saucepan over medium heat. Stir briefly until the sugar dissolves, then stop stirring. Cook until the mixture starts to develop color, swirling the pan occasionally. Do not walk away, as the browning process happens quickly and the caramel can burn fast.
6. Once the sugar is a deep amber color, pour in the rice wine vinegar and whisk vigorously, taking care as the mixture will splutter. Add the soy sauce, fish sauce, sriracha, miso paste, red pepper flakes and red food coloring (if using), then whisk again to combine. Reduce the heat and continue cooking, stirring regularly, until the glaze reaches 205–210°F (96–98°C). It may foam and bubble, so keep a close eye on it.
7. When the ham has about 20–30 minutes of heating left, start painting it with the chili caramel using a pastry brush or silicone basting brush. Repeat 2–3 times, allowing 5–10 minutes between coats for the glaze to set.
8. Remove the ham from the smoker and serve.

NOTES

Spiral cut, bone-in, boneless, whole or half leg ham – the choice is yours. They will all work with this recipe. Just make sure it's not a fresh/raw ham, which requires different cooking methods.

If your ham has a rind on it (that's the skin, which will feel like a thick, rubbery sleeve on the outside), be sure to remove it completely before you begin reheating.

The red food dye is, of course, optional, but it does make the glaze look extra vibrant.

Here's a quick 'ham-culator': prepare for a cooking time of 15–20 minutes per pound (or 33–44 minutes per kilo). It's better to have your ham completely warmed and holding than keeping your hungry guests waiting, so when in doubt, start it a little earlier.

Do not sleep on this glaze recipe. I've used it to make the most insanely moreish chili caramel chicken wings, and drizzled it on pan-seared dove/duck breast and even brussels sprouts. It's a winner.

PORK CROWN ROAST WITH WARM APPLE MOSTARDA

SERVES 8–10

This old-school roast is a more cost-effective choice for celebrations, with plenty of wow factor when it hits the table. Crown roast is made from two pork loins that have the baby back ribs attached, cinched and tied together to form the crown effect. Most butchers will prepare one for you by special request; just make sure to order in advance.

- 1 x 8–10lb/3.5–4.5 kg pork crown roast
- 1 tablespoon smoked paprika
- 1 tablespoon sweet paprika
- 1 teaspoon garlic powder
- ½ teaspoon onion powder
- 1 teaspoon dried thyme
- 3 teaspoons salt
- ½ cup (125 ml) water

APPLE MOSTARDA

- 4 pink lady apples
- 1 cup (170 g) golden raisins (sultanas)
- ⅓ cup (80 ml) red wine vinegar
- ¼ cup (60 ml) apple cider vinegar
- 1 cup (250 ml) water
- ¾ cup (165 g) brown sugar
- ½ teaspoon salt
- 2 teaspoons dijon mustard
- 2 tablespoons wholegrain mustard
- 4 tablespoons salted butter

1. Preheat the oven to 300°F (145°C) and remove the pork from the fridge.
2. In a small bowl, combine both paprikas, garlic powder, onion powder, thyme and salt to make the dry rub.
3. Place a rack inside a large roasting pan. Coat the crown roast generously with the rub, then set it on the rack. Pour the water into the bottom of the pan (without touching the meat). Roast for 2–3 hours, or until the internal temperature reaches 135°F (57°C).
4. Remove the pan from the oven and increase the heat to 500°F (260°C). Return the roast for 10–15 minutes to brown the exterior. Remove again, tent loosely with foil, and rest for 10 minutes.
5. To make the apple mostarda, peel, core and dice the apples. Place them in a saucepan along with the golden raisins, both vinegars, water, sugar and salt. Bring to a simmer over medium heat and cook for 20–30 minutes, stirring occasionally, until the apples are tender. Remove from the heat, then stir through both mustards and the butter before serving.
6. Carve the roast between each bone and serve with a generous spoonful of warm apple mostarda.

NOTE

Pork crown roasts can be tied in a few ways. Some have a gap in the center, while others are trussed tightly with no space at all. The closed versions cook more slowly since hot air can't circulate through the middle, so add up to an extra hour of cooking. Some roasts are also partially cut between the bones like an accordion, so they can fan open into a circle and cook a little faster.

BUTTER-BASTED ROAST TURKEY

SERVES 8–10

While a jolly, rotund turkey may be more traditional, I'm here to tell you that you should be spatchcocking your turkeys. Splaying them open will not only let them cook faster, but it also helps them cook more evenly. What's more, you should definitely brine your bird – it makes a huge difference to juiciness, and it's your best defense against dry meat. Use the master brine guide on page 29 and start brining the day before you plan to cook. That said, many commercial turkeys are already pre-brined. Always check the packaging for terms like 'self-basting', 'enhanced', 'solution added' or 'contains added water' (see page 16 for more on this). If you spot any of those, skip the brine. Double-brining can leave the meat overly salty and with a mushy texture.

- 1 x 12–15 lb (5–6 kg) whole turkey
- 1 cup (8 oz/250 g) softened salted butter
- 1 teaspoon garlic powder
- 1 teaspoon onion powder
- ½ teaspoon ground sage
- 1 teaspoon salt
- 2 teaspoons soy sauce
- 2 teaspoons worcestershire sauce
- ¼ cup (85 g) apricot, apple or orange preserves (jam), without fruit pieces

1. If you brined your turkey, remove the bird from the brine and discard the mixture. Rinse the turkey under cold running water, being careful to minimize water splashing.
2. If your turkey isn't brined, pat the entire turkey dry with paper towels, soaking up as much moisture as possible. Yes, even under the wing in the turkey's armpit.
3. Place the turkey on a sheet pan (baking sheet), then refrigerate overnight (uncovered) to dry the skin.
4. Spatchcock the turkey by cutting along either side of the backbone and removing it completely. Use a knife to make a nick in the breastbone/sternum, then flip the bird over and press firmly on the breast to crack the bone. Arrange the thighs so the bird lays flat, and tuck the wings under the breast. For more detailed instructions, see page 194.
5. Preheat the oven to 450°F (230°C) and position a rack in the center of the oven. Place the turkey on a wire rack set into a sheet pan (baking sheet). Pour about half a cup of water into the bottom of the pan to prevent burning, but make sure the water doesn't make contact with the bird.
6. In a medium bowl, combine the butter, garlic powder, onion powder, sage, salt, soy sauce and worcestershire sauce. Stir to combine. Reserve a quarter of the mixture and set aside.
7. Using your fingers, gently loosen the skin away from the flesh. Create pockets over each half of the breast and each of the thighs. Scoop some of the seasoned butter into your hands and gently push it into the skin pocket, spreading the butter evenly between the four pockets.
8. Roast the turkey for 15 minutes, then lower the temperature to 325°F (160°C).
9. Rotate the pan every 30 minutes to promote even cooking (most ovens have hot spots).
10. Roast for 12 minutes per pound (or 23 minutes per kilo). Around the halfway mark, start checking the internal temperature near the thickest part of the thigh.
11. Once the internal temperature reaches 160°F (71°C), prepare the glaze. ›

12. In a small saucepan, combine the reserved butter with the preserves. Warm gently over low heat, stirring often, until the butter melts and the preserves loosen into a smooth, brushable glaze. (Alternatively, microwave in 20-second bursts, stirring in between.)
13. Brush a thin coat of the glaze over the turkey skin using a basting or pastry brush.
14. Return the bird to the oven and continue roasting until the breast reaches 165°F (73°C) and the thigh around 170–175°F (76–79°C). For a deeper color, brush on a second light coat of glaze in the last 5–10 minutes of cooking.

NOTES

Many store-bought turkeys come with the giblets and neck tucked into the cavity or under the neck skin. Remove these before cooking and save them to make gravy. You may also find a plastic truss or a pop-up thermometer. Both should be discarded. Since the turkey is being spatchcocked, the truss isn't needed, and you'll get far more accurate results by using a probe thermometer.

The preserves glaze won't make the meat taste sweet, but it will give the turkey a beautifully shiny, lacquered finish.

BEWARE THE CURSE OF THE FROZEN TURKEY

While no one wants a Griswold-style disaster with a hollow, overcooked bird, the opposite can be just as devastating. One of the most common mistakes is underestimating how long it takes to thaw a turkey. People forget just how solidly frozen that 'meatsicle' really is. And that usually leaves guests hungry for hours while the bird takes even longer to cook – or worse still, being served a turkey that's raw in the middle.

And trust me, holiday food poisoning isn't the kind of memory you want to send people home with. So, to avoid devastating consequences, follow this handy thawing guide and plan ahead.

BIRD WEIGHT (POUNDS)	BIRD WEIGHT (KILOS)	THAWING TIME IN FRIDGE
4–12	1–5	1–3 days
12–16	6–7	3–4 days
16–20	8–9	4–5 days
20–24	9–10	5–6 days

REVERSE-SEARED BEEF TENDERLOIN

SERVES 8–10

Nothing says 'luxe' like whole tenderloin. It's an elegant and impressive choice. You can buy it pre-trimmed and tied, or take on the task yourself (page 153). Tenderloin is a perfect candidate for reverse searing: a gentle heat to bring it to temperature, then a hard sear on the grill to nail the crust.

1 x 4.5 lb (2 kg) whole trimmed and trussed beef tenderloin (see page 154)

1½ tablespoons dijon mustard

1–1½ tablespoons salt

3 teaspoons freshly ground black pepper

¼ cup (60 ml) worcestershire sauce

spray oil or melted beef tallow (page 244)

1. Prepare a grill for two-zone cooking (page 36) at low-medium temperature, around 275–300°F (140–155°C).
2. Remove the tenderloin from the fridge and pat dry with paper towels.
3. Smear the mustard in a thin coating over the whole tenderloin, then season evenly with the salt and pepper.
4. Place the tenderloin on the indirect side of the grill, as far away from the heat as possible. Cook until the internal temperature reaches 125°F (51°C), which will take about 1 hour, refilling your fuel to maintain temperature as needed.
5. Pour the worcestershire sauce into a spray bottle and spritz the tenderloin every 15–20 minutes.
6. Remove the tenderloin from the grill and rest under foil for 10–15 minutes.
7. While it rests, prepare the grill for a high-heat sear by increasing the temperature to 450–500°F (230–260°C) or stoking the coals as necessary.
8. Spritz the outside of the tenderloin with some spray oil, or brush with a thin layer of melted tallow.
9. Place the tenderloin over the hot side of the grill and sear one surface for 1 minute. Roll it a quarter turn and sear the next side for 1 minute. Continue rolling and searing until all sides are evenly browned.
10. Remove from the grill and wrap tightly in foil. Rest for another 10–20 minutes.
11. Remove and discard the twine, then slice and serve.

NOTES

If you prefer, you can use your favorite seasoning instead of plain salt and pepper. Since tenderloin is so mild in flavor, I prefer to keep my rub simple to let the meat shine.

If your grill is small, you may need to rotate the tenderloin while on indirect heat so one side is not receiving significantly more radiant heat than the other.

ACKNOWLEDGEMENTS

I am fortunate to have an incredible network of people I can lean on for expert opinion, perspective, support and sometimes just soundboarding. I'm equally grateful for my amazing online community, whose persistent requests for another cookbook pushed me to make this one happen.

For their expertise and support while this book was coming together, my sincere thanks to: Justin Wolfers, Jane Morrow, Kirsten Jenkins, Rob Palmer, Kristy Allen, Virginia Birch, Gabriella Sterio, Hayden Walker, Davis Turner, Collette Kaster, Heidi Buske, Ben Tindall, Demi Lollback, Rick Higgins, Jesse Morris, Juan Rodriguez, Jamie Preuss, Max England, Dr Matt McDonagh, Clay Cowgill, Matt Serrano, Nick Hudek, Julien McCall, the H-E-B meat cutters, Rachel Hannaford, Ed Hall and Lone Star Meats, Dr Anna Dilger, Kaitlin Guthrie, Bryan Butler, Sharon KK Beals, Dr Carol Lorenzen, Dr Casey Owens, Dr Christine Alvarado, Kim Rice, Dr Elisabeth Huff-Lonergan, Dr Joe Sebranek, Dr Jeff Sindelar, Dr Matt Hughes, Adam Biderman, Aaron Haley, Evan LeRoy and Lindsey LeRoy.

And to Chris and the boys, for heroically taste-testing their way through endless rounds of recipes.

INDEX

C

D

E

F

G

H

I

J

K

L

M

N

O

P

Q

R

S

T

U

V

W

Y

Z

Published in 2026 by Murdoch Books, an imprint of Allen & Unwin

Murdoch Books Australia
Cammeraygal Country
83 Alexander Street
Crows Nest NSW 2065
Phone: +61 (0)2 8425 0100
murdochbooks.com.au
info@murdochbooks.com.au

Murdoch Books UK
Ormond House
26–27 Boswell Street
London WC1N 3JZ
Phone: +44 (0) 20 8785 5995
murdochbooks.co.uk
info@murdochbooks.co.uk

For corporate orders and custom publishing, contact our business development team at salesenquiries@murdochbooks.com.au

Publisher: Justin Wolfers
Editorial manager: Virginia Birch
Design manager: Kristy Allen
Designer and illustrator: mkanedesign
Editor: Gabriella Sterio
Photographer: Rob Palmer
Stylist: Kirsten Jenkins
Photoshoot sous chef: Davis Turner
Production manager: Natalie Crouch

Murdoch Books acknowledges the Traditional Owners of the Country on which we live and work. We pay our respects to all Aboriginal and Torres Strait Islander Elders, past and present.

ISBN 978 1 76150 128 9

NATIONAL LIBRARY OF AUSTRALIA A catalogue record for this book is available from the National Library of Australia

A catalogue record for this book is available from the British Library

Colour reproduction by Splitting Image Colour Studio Pty Ltd, Wantirna, Victoria
Printed in China by C&C Offset Printing Co., Ltd.

OVEN GUIDE: You may find cooking times vary depending on the oven and oven setting you are using. For fan-forced (convection) ovens, as a general rule, set the oven temperature to 20°C (25–50°F) lower than indicated in the recipe.

TABLESPOON MEASURES: We have used 15 ml (3 teaspoon) tablespoon measures. If you are using a 20 ml (4 teaspoon) tablespoon, use one less teaspoon of the ingredient for each tablespoon specified.

DISCLAIMER: Raw or undercooked meats can contain high doses of dangerous bacteria that can cause food poisoning. Correct cooking and commonsense handling are necessary to destroy these micro-organisms.

Those who might be at risk from the effects of salmonella poisoning (the elderly, pregnant women, young children and those suffering from immune deficiency diseases) should consult their doctor with any concerns about eating raw eggs.

While care is taken to ensure safety, food safety practices must be followed during preparation to avoid illness. It is essential to follow all instructions for the preparation of meat products with the utmost accuracy, and in clean and sanitary conditions. When using sodium nitrite or sodium nitrate, always be sure to strictly follow the manufacturer's instructions. While we try to keep all information up to date and correct, the author and publisher do not assume and hereby disclaim any liability for any loss, damage or disruption caused by errors or omissions, whether such errors or omissions result from negligence, accident or any other cause.

10 9 8 7 6 5 4 3 2 1

FSC www.fsc.org MIX Paper | Supporting responsible forestry FSC® C008047

JESS PRYLES is a cook, author, and television host recognized globally as a leading authority on meat and live-fire cooking. With a no-nonsense approach and deep technical expertise, she has built her reputation on mastering the craft of cooking with fire. Originally from Australia and now based in Austin, Texas, Jess has spent over a decade traveling the world to study meat from ranch to table, bridging the gap between the butcher shop and the backyard cook.

A certified meat scientist with a Graduate Certificate from Iowa State University, Jess is the founder of the global lifestyle brand Hardcore Carnivore® and the co-founder of the Australasian Barbecue Alliance, as well as being the author of bestselling cookbook *Hardcore Carnivore: Cook Meat Like You Mean It*. Her expertise is sought after by the industry's most prestigious institutions; she is a regular presenter at Texas A&M University's famed Camp Brisket and has been a featured speaker for the American Meat Science Association and SXSW.

Jess is a veteran of culinary media, known for her ability to break down complex 'meatducation' into approachable, high-stakes cooking. She hosts hit TV series Food Network's *Pitmasters*, *Hardcore Carnivore* and *Feast by Fire*, has co-hosted Hulu's *BBQuest* and is a regular fixture on major networks as a judge for *MasterChef*, *Beat Bobby Flay*, and *Kids BBQ Championship*. Her expertise has also been featured on *The Today Show*, *SEC Nation*, and *The Cook Up*.

Whether she is developing new seasoning profiles or teaching a masterclass, Jess's mission remains the same: to strip away the intimidation and give every cook the knowledge and confidence to cook meat like they mean it.